D1527973

Vygotsky's and A. A. Leontiev's Semiotics and Psycholinguistics

Tatiana Vasil'evna Akhutina and Alexei Alexeevitch Leontiev

Vygotsky's and A. A. Leontiev's Semiotics and Psycholinguistics

Applications for Education, Second Language Acquisition, and Theories of Language

DOROTHY ROBBINS

Contributions in Psychology, Number 44

Westport, Connecticut
London

Library of Congress Cataloging-in-Publication Data

Vygotsky's and A. A. Leontiev's semiotics and psycholinguistics :
applications for education, second language acquisition, and theories of
language / Dorothy Robbins.
    p. cm.—(Contributions in psychology, ISSN 0736–2714 ; no. 44)
  Includes bibliographical references and index.
  ISBN 0–313–32224–4 (alk. paper)
  1. Second language acquisition. 2. Language and languages—Study and
teaching. 3. Psycholinguistics. 4. Semiotics. 5. Vygotsky, L. S. (Lev Semenovich),
1896–1934—Contributions in linguistics. 6. Leontiev, A. A. (Alexi Alexeevitch),
b. 1936—Contributions in linguistics. I. Robbins, Dorothy, 1947–. II. Series.

P118.2 .V95   2003
418′.0071—dc21   2002029874

British Library Cataloguing in Publication Data is available.

Library of Congress Catalog Card Number: 2002029874
ISBN: 0–313–32224–4
ISSN: 0736–2714

First published in 2003

Praeger Publishers, 88 Post Road West, Westport, CT 06881
An imprint of Greenwood Publishing Group, Inc.
www.praeger.com

Printed in the United States of America

The paper used in this book complies with the
Permanent Paper Standard issued by the National
Information Standards Organization (Z39.48–1984).

10 9 8 7 6 5 4 3 2 1

Copyright Acknowledgments
The author and publisher gratefully acknowledge permission to quote from the
  following sources:
Noam Chomsky, Untitled chapter in *A Tribute to Roman Jakobson, 1896–1982*
  (New York: Mouton, 1983), pp. 81–83.
G. L. Vygodskaia and T. M. Lifanova, "Lev Semenovich Vygotsky (Part 2),"
  Journal of Russian & East European Psychology, 37, no. 3 (May–June 1999).
  English-language translation copyright © 2000 by M. E. Sharpe, Inc. Reprinted
  with permission.

This book is dedicated to my mentors, A. A. Leontiev and
T. V. Akhutina, who have continually supported me in understanding Russian psychology. A. A. Leontiev has remained loyal to
Vygotsky and his father, A. N. Leontiev. T. V. Akhutina has
remained loyal to Vygotsky and to A. R. Luria. It is no surprise that
they have been close friends since the 1960s, and I view them both
as two of the top psycholinguists in the world. My life has been
deeply enriched by their teachings, support, guidance, patience,
grace, and true friendship.

Alexei Alexeevitch Leontiev

L.S. Vygotsky (Photo courtesy of Janna Glozman)

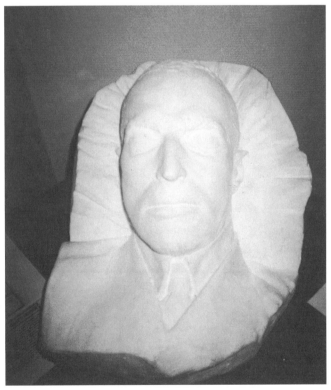

Death mask of L.S. Vygotsky (it is housed in the Vygotsky room of the Vygotsky Institute of Psychology, Russian State University for the Humanities, Moscow)

Contents

Series Foreword

The stated purpose of this book is to present some of the lesser-known theories of Vygotsky and his colleagues and demonstrate their relevance for consciousness-raising in teaching. Vygotsky's theory-building describes a uniquely valuable alternative to conventional psychology with regard to language and education and particularly with regard to the role of consciousness. While consciousness was the original focus in psychology as a newly developed field, psychology has largely, and prematurely, abandoned the topic of consciousness as a serious psychological construct.

The purpose of the Praeger series Contributions in Psychology has been to present new perspectives of psychology that have been overlooked or bypassed. The writings of Vygotsky are only now beginning to attract the attention they richly deserve. The cultural bias against "things Soviet" in the last century discouraged American psychologists from taking psychology in the USSR seriously. At that time, the leaders in psychological thinking the USSR were required to find their own way. The result was a series of refreshingly new and unique insights about human behavior that flies in the face of Western theories. Piaget, for example, is turned on his head by Vygotsky very convincingly, with regard to inner speech as a higher-level rather than a lower-level capability.

Vygotsky's genius was to move across disciplines in gathering his ideas about human behavior. For that reason the following chapters focus on language, education, second language learning, philosophy, semiotics, psychology, and many other disciplines. Vygotsky's perspective fits better with the newly popular perspectives of chaos theory and complexity theory than conventional psychological theories, demonstrating the linear self-regulating "living" dynamism of thoughts about human behavior.

While Vygotsky's ideas and thinking are not easy reading, and many paragraphs need to be read several times to understand what Vygotsky meant, understanding is well worth the effort. The reader just now discovering the ideas of Vygotsky has an exciting adventure ahead.

The other books in the Contributions in Psychology series have each filled knowledge gaps across the fields of psychology, broadly defined. The focus in this series is on underserved populations, undervalued theories, unfamiliar leaders, and untested methods of psychology, and this has resulted in an exciting collection of books for readers wanting to look beyond the obvious and standardized thinking about conventional psychology. This book on Vygotsky does an excellent job of continuing that task and challenging the reader to rethink the foundation ideas of psychology they have accepted unquestioningly in the past.

Paul B. Pedersen, Psychology Series Editor
University of Hawaii, Department of Psychology
June 4, 2002

Introduction

This book takes the perspective of mixing theory with practice regarding Vygotskian thought. The first chapter is an introduction to Vygotsky's cultural-historical theory, which differs from sociocultural theory in the United States. The purpose of this chapter is to introduce the reader to Vygotsky's Russian background, which is based on the thinking of von Humboldt, Spinoza, Marx, and German and Russian psychology and philosophy. This chapter offers a concept called educational semiotics, which bridges together aspects of Vygotsky's overall method. The second chapter, by Alexei Alexeevitch Leontiev, was written for the Vygotsky centennial celebration at the 1996 International Applied Linguistics conference in Jyväskylä, Finland. Professor Leontiev looks at Vygotsky from a Russian perspective, focusing on one core idea related to Vygotskian thought: personality development. Chapter 3 begins with an introduction to Vygotsky's educational approach that was called pedology, which was an interdisciplinary focus on how to improve schooling to enhance both the individual and society at large. A general history of pedology is offered as background information and sets the stage for better understanding the political climate of the time and place in which Vygotsky lived and worked. A discussion on learning and development follows, with a general summary of the concept of the zone of proximal development (ZPD). It should be understood that Vygotsky developed many of his practical ideas in education during the interfunctional and semiotic phases of his life (see Rieber, 1987, pp. 17–34), spanning from 1930 to 1934, which represents the last four years of his life. Chapter 4 reviews current, mostly Western, interpretations and adaptations of Vygotsky's educational theories. It includes a comparison with constructivism, which may be somewhat confusing in the sense that Vygotsky also used the term constructivism; however, there are major differences in educational constructivism as it is understood today in Western educational practice compared with Vygotsky's concept. Currently the focus within constructivism is on interaction, with attempts to go beyond a teacher-centered classroom. In moving beyond constructivism, a few guidelines are provided to demonstrate what a good learner is, along with what a good teacher should be. Describing the role of a good teacher would actually go against the grain of American political correctness. However, it appears that Vygotsky did have in mind what a good teacher should be, although this was not explicitly described in his writing. The discussion continues with an explanation of teacher-ability. It includes areas such as error correction within teacher-ability. Vygotsky's interest was directed at the whole personality of the learner and the teacher, and not their atomistic parts such as motivation, anxiety, empathy, tolerance to ambiguity, and risk taking. Chapter 5 returns to theory related to Russian psycholinguistics and the thoughts of A. A. Leontiev (son of A. N. Leontiev, founder of Russian activity theory, who was one of the closest collaborators of L. S. Vygotsky during the 1920s). This chapter outlines the tenets of Russian psycholinguistics, where theory and practice are not separated to the extent that they are in the West. It also includes a review of teacher-ability and learnability from the Russian perspective, with an overview of Vygotsky's pedology, ZPD, teacher-ability, and A. A. Leontiev's Russian psycholinguistic principles. Chapter 6 reviews some of the basic theories of second language acquisition (SLA) in the West from a Vygotskian-Leontievian point of view, with a focus on input-output, first language–second language transfer (L1 = L2), and markedness. Chapter 7 reviews the actual understanding of educational semiotics, focusing on the principles of code, representation, image (imagination), imitation, and mimesis. Chapter 8 returns to Vygotskian theories that are both theoretical and practical. It covers a discussion of code that was not dealt with by Vygotsky as such but was considered by a contemporary of Vygotsky, Roman Jakobson. Code represents a missing link in Vygotskian semiotics related to SLA. The discussion then turns to ideas on representation, images, imagination, imitation, and mimesis. This chapter then completes the circle by returning to general education, and it finally closes the circle related to pedology as it might be envisioned today within SLA. In other words, the book begins with a general overview of education in Russia during the 1930s, switching to Russian practice and theory, and slowly returns to the educational setting of the postmodern world today. For example, educators seldom talk about imagination and imitation complementing each other within the ZPD today.

It is demonstrated that Vygotskian cultural-historical theories are applicable to SLA, as well as to almost all areas of education. Chapter 8 returns to the area Vygotsky loved very much, aesthetics. Since a discussion of

Figure 1.
Vygotskian flow chart.

⇔ consciousness ⇔ social ⇔ motives ⇔ thought ⇔ internalization ⇔ inner speech ⇔ language ⇔ speech ⇔ tools,

psychological tools, signs ⇔ meaning ⇔ sense ⇔ concept formation ⇔ functional equivalents ⇔ word meanings ⇔

imagination ⇔ eidetic images ⇔ emotions ⇔ volition ⇔ will ⇔ motive ⇔ un(-sub)conscious ⇔ consciousness ⇔

aesthetics does not fit within the parameters of this book (see Robbins, 2001a), the closest analog is that of imagination and imitation. Chapter 8 also serves as a concluding summary of the book.

The purpose of offering these ideas is to demonstrate a parallel way to think about SLA, realizing that such alternative theories do not have to be anchored within empiricism and Cartesian scientific thinking, nor within the atomistic way theorists in the West traditionally divide up human personality. There is a call to restructure SLA according to some of the principles Vygotsky laid out in his semiotics, instead of fitting Vygotskian thought within Western structures. It is hoped that this book offers a fresh and exciting approach to both teaching and learning, as well as to research in education and SLA.

Just as Vygotsky's writings reflect his life and his beliefs, his life is also reflected in his writings; and together they represent a continuum of his psychology/philosophy that flows (dialectically, asymmetrically) along a functional trajectory. A metaphorical flow chart (figure 1) is offered, which is reversible so that the parts can be interchanged within the philosophical understanding of necessity. There is also an emphasis on the centripetal force—here, the direction of the social toward the individual—and the centrifugal force—here, the individual direction toward the social— viewed as one unit, called the zone of fusion.[1] Even though the flow chart starts at the level of consciousness, ending at the point of the unconscious, in reality it has no beginning or end point. The chart is heuristic and variant, cyclic and constantly moving. Within this flow chart, many thoughts regarding Vygotsky can be viewed, and the continuity of the flow chart is an underlying premise for all of the thoughts presented in this book.

NOTE

1. "Zone of fusion" is a term that relates to the author's thoughts. It represents the unity of both the individual and the social, while guarding the uniqueness of both. It was offered by Andy Blunden on the xmca listserve discussion group, October 12, 2000.

CHAPTER 1

Introduction to Vygotsky's Education Method and A. A. Leontiev's Psycholinguistics

A major distinction exists between Vygotskian sociocultural theory and Vygotskian cultural-historical theory, although in the past these terms have been used interchangeably. Differences also exist among Russian activity theory, European international activity theory related to cultural-historical theory, and sociocultural theory. Many people will wonder why it is important to point out these differences, especially related to education, second language acquisition (SLA), and applied linguistics. It is precisely that Vygotsky's overall intentions were based on understanding consciousness via thought and speech that results in the fact that Vygotsky's cultural-historical theories are indeed a philosophy of language and semiotics related to human activity.

The theory that Vygotsky was associated with is called cultural-historical, and at the beginning of the 1930s two things happened that have not yet been documented in full. Firstly, the political climate was deteriorating, and Russian scholars were forbidden to collaborate with Western scholars or to even quote them. One focus Vygotsky maintained was to use his method to help change education in Russia, within a utopian view of Marxism. His contributions to pedology (interdisciplinary education founded upon a mixture of utopian Marxism and Western thinking) were enormous (see chapter 3 for an overview), and it was Vygotsky's hope to establish a truly interdisciplinary focus within education via pedology. Scholars were starting to turn against one another as political repression became more evident, and Vygotsky did not remain exempt from harsh criticism. In 1936 (two years after his death), both pedology and Vygotsky's works were completely banned. Vygotsky could be read and discussed openly only from 1956 onward, and even then there was little access to his published works.

Vygotsky's *Collected Works* did not appear in Russian until 1982, and prior to that, most of the knowledge about Vygotsky and his work was gained through the lens of his students and collaborators, and not from original sources. Secondly, in the early 1930s, A.N. Leontiev moved to Kharkov (then the capital of the Ukraine) because of many difficulties. "In 1930, circumstances forced Aleksei Nikolaevich to leave both the Academy of Communist Education and the All-Union State Institute of Communism" (A.A. Leontiev, 1984, p. 14), and as well, he had to resign his position at the State Instiute of Cinematography in 1930 (Kozulin, 1986a, p. 269). A letter (Leontiev, 2003) from A.N. Leontiev to Vygotsky on February 5, 1932, explained the frustrations Leontiev was feeling and expressed his clear intentions of establishing his own path. Another example of his problems can be found in a letter from Vygotsky to Leontiev, written in August 1933:

I feel already and not for the first time that we stand before a very important conversation, as it were, for which we both, apparently, are not prepared, and the contents of which we can only vaguely imagine—your departure [for Kharkov]—is our serious, maybe irremediable, failure, resulting from our errors and real negligence of the cause that has been entrusted to us. Apparently, neither in your biography, nor in mine, nor in the history of our psychology, will what has happened be repeated. So be it. I am trying to understand all this in the Spinozist way—with sadness but accepting it as something inevitable. (cited in van der Veer & Valsiner, 1991, p. 290)

There is much documentation regarding the fact that A.N. Leontiev wanted to take an approach different from that of the Vygotskian method, and although his research took another direction, Leontiev never wrote anything that would dispute Vygotsky's authority, although he established his own theories that were very different from the core intentions of cultural-historical theory. Hence, one refers to the Kharkov School or to Russian activity theory when speaking of A.N. Leontiev.

It is important to remember that Russian psychology was intrinsically tied to German philosophy and psychology during the 1920s, including the theories of Hegel, Feuerbach, and Marx. During the 1930s, Western bourgeois psychology was banned, and it was extremely dangerous for Russian scholars to be connected with anything from the West. During these years psychology and philosophy were combined in one department in what is now Moscow State University, and it was not until 1966 that these departments were separated, with A.N. Leontiev becoming the head of the Institute of Psychology. At that point, any philosophy that deviated from Marxism was not officially tolerated. It should be understood that many of the older psychologists had been trained in both psychology and philosophy, and that this trend continued, to some degree, as did discussions on Vygotsky's theories, albeit in a more secretive climate for many years.

One person remained loyal to Vygotsky throughout his entire life, following in Vygotsky's footsteps of studying language and cognition, inter alia. History will later recognize the importance of A.R. Luria's work as representing the unique and loyal bridge built upon Vygotsky's cultural-historical theory. Luria also worked together with A.N. Leontiev, and there is no documentation to date of written statements in which Luria disagreed with Leontiev or the Kharkov School.

Historically, Russian activity theory was very innovative in the sense that theorists were able to walk a fine line between Pavlovian reflexology-behaviorism and other aspects of psychological determinism. During June and July of 1950 the "Pavlovization" of Russian psychology was established, in which attempts were made to actually dissolve the study of psychology altogether, and activity theory proved to be very effective in carving out a new niche within Marxist structures, which were inflexible and dangerous for free thinkers. Activity theory viewed individual activity as linked to the social, however, with a focus on the entire personality of an individual within a systems approach theory. Within Russian activity theory the focus is on development, goals, mastery, and culture. This position is very attractive to many people in the West because it represents a balance that cannot be found in much of Western psychology. In the West, the focus appears to be either on behaviorism (viewing only aspects that can be objectified) or on cognitivism (viewing aspects that are only innate). In the past few years, Russian activity theory has gained much attention around the world. There are, however, basic differences between cultural-historical theory and Russian activity theory. Within much of Russian activity theory, Vygotsky's overall philosophy (the crowning point of his method) was deleted, and therefore the anchor that grounded his approach was radically altered.

OVERVIEW OF VYGOTSKY'S CULTURAL-HISTORICAL METHOD

Vygotsky always placed his focus within a dual vision, but never dualism. Working within the traditional German-Russian mode of philosophy, Vygotsky took consciousness as his highest explanatory principle. Because no one can step outside of his or her consciousness, areas of internalization and externalization became very important from the start. We will never completely understand human consciousness simply because we will never be able to stand outside of ourselves to objectify this term. Therefore, consciousness was/is itself viewed within a metatheoretical-metaphorical level. However, Vygotsky did not want to return to the problems of introspectionism (nonobjectified understanding only), nor to the problems of empiricism-behaviorism (objectified understanding only). With his dual vision and understanding of psychology in the 1920s, Vygotsky established a method that was both abstract and concrete, one that would amplify and reflect upon consciousness related to the theories of European philosophers such as Spinoza, Marx, von Humboldt, and others. Therefore, he selected thinking and speech as his second explanatory principle that would be used as the instrument(s) reflecting consciousness. This process always included a dialectical approach of positioning varying structures within opposite poles, yet, within a holistic structure, in this case, consciousness. He viewed many trajectories of functional capacities that maintained opposite points of origin and would hold an explanatory power regarding thought/speech and growth from a historical perspective, which would always include change as a common dominator. It was the trajectory of development that interested Vygotsky, and growth could take place only within the development of thought and speech, or variations such as sign language or braille. For example, the origins of thinking include the disposition of a preintellectual structure, whereas the origins of speech maintain the disposition of a prelinguistic structure. It is through the dialectical process of engagements and separations of opposite poles of relational growth that development can occur. However, the maturity of concept formation is necessary for meaningful generalization to take place. In order to understand psychology-philosophy from the perspective of a dual-dialectical vision, Vygotsky needed to have a common denominator (both abstract and concrete) in order to measure thinking and speech that would then reflect and mediate consciousness. It was here that Vygotsky discovered the power of word meaning as the unit of analysis. To date, most researchers in the Cartesian tradition view any science from the inductive, bottom-up perspective, deriving truth(s) from individual, often isolated, experiments that strive for identical results even when carried out in different conditions. This is also true of much applied linguistic theory today. Vygotsky's focus was to view holistic units first, capturing their essence, to then proceed by analyzing the elements, always connected to the whole structure. In other words, Vygotsky viewed elements within a dialectical frame of reference (which was asymmetrical and nonlinear), as well as viewing the more absolute level of higher explanatory principles. Development is located within the emerging relationships when the individual is ready to absorb a new concept. For example, thinking is completed in the word, and the word is completed in thinking, when the conditions are right. For this to happen there needs to be a general understanding that the development of concepts and word meanings represents identical levels within a metaphorical framework. Word meanings are both concrete and abstract, just as grammar is both concrete and abstract. With Vygotsky's development of spontaneous (everyday) concepts and scientific/nonspontaneous (academic or scientific) concepts comes a misunderstanding in many Western interpretations of Vygotsky. One pole is not higher or better than the other, and both of these seemingly opposite poles must merge in an asymmetrical fashion to complement each other. Vygotsky viewed spontaneous concepts from the bottom up, while scientific/nonspontaneous concepts were viewed from the top down. However, this was a dual-dialectical vision without Cartesian dualism. Both directions of development are necessary in establishing a holistic unit, and both directions of individual development are related to a monistic completeness.

Since his youth, when his father first gave him a book by Spinoza, Vygotsky had viewed life from Spinoza's philosophical perspective. It is this exact point that differentiates cultural-historical theory from activity theory and sociocultural theory. Spinoza understood the world from a higher unified philosophical perspective, which he called the monad. At this point, the monad is not compared with Leibniz's monad.[1] Spinoza's understanding represented a simple metaphor of the absoluteness ascribed to nature or God, sometimes referred to as one substance. It was within this higher explanatory principle that Vygotsky positioned his method as a metatheory. In particular, it is important to understand that absolute and relative aspects stand in relation to each other, just as the monad and dialectics (or spontaneous and scientific/nonspontaneous concepts) complement each other. In an aside, it should be understood that Vygotsky did not accept all aspects of Spinoza's philosophy in explaining contemporary problems during his lifetime; for example, Spinoza did not deal with dialectics, a focus of philosophical inquiry that became popular long after his death. However, there was a realization that the whole is connected to the parts, just as the parts are connected to the whole, and it was this vision of completeness that governed Vygotsky's method throughout his entire life. Within the individual plane of consciousness, Vygotsky's philosophy of language and semiotics was directed at the potential free action of each person. This understanding of free action is not in line with the Western tenets of the pursuit of individual happiness. Vygotsky's dual-dialectical vision always tied the individual to the social, with the internal being connected to the external. However, it is precisely the value placed on the internal aspects of human life that distinguish Vygotsky's method. This position has been completely misunderstood in much American and international sociocultural theory, which prioritizes external action and speech over internal functions. However, the internal aspects are first influenced by the external, logically following the model of Vygotsky's dual-dialectical vision, which always focuses on a unified whole. In understanding the individual, internal side of existence, a short note on Spinoza is offered. Spinoza distinguished between two types of affections: actions, "which are explained by the nature of the affected individual, and which spring from the individual's essence" (Deleuze, 1981, p. 27), and passions, "which are explained by something else, and which originate outside the individual" (Deleuze, 1981, p. 27). Therefore,

he [Spinoza] believed that human freedom was not, as was commonly held, inde-terminacy of choice, but was self-determination, entirely by one's own nature, free from external compulsion. This, for him, was action proper, while determination by extraneous causes was passion, the subjection to which he called bondage. (Harris, 1992, p. 6)

Vygotsky went a step further in viewing the social-individual nature as a holistic unit that could be broken down into meaningful elements only once the whole is understood. It is for this reason that one does not speak of a completed Vygotskian theory. In fact, Vygotsky did not want to be prescriptive (apart from describing the stages of crisis in child develop-ment), and this is a reason that there is no single Vygotskian method. To go a step further, each educator needs to establish his or her own Vygotskian method that is different from anyone else's. The underlying premise is that no attempt is made to offer a simple approach, strategy, or method. What is offered is the ultimate level of consciousness-raising of each indi-vidual to establish his or her own working method/theory that can also be implemented in practice, particularly in the classroom. It is the higher level of metaphor that is first encouraged, viewing each student and fel-low traveler in life within a holistic perspective. The second principle is to always understand that we were not born into this world as free-thinking individuals, but instead born into a world of preestablished social norms and conventions. We can become individuals, in the true sense of the word, only by connecting to the outside, social world in a new fashion. Without this holistic unit we will not reach our potential of becoming self-actualized individuals. We must always incorporate the general genetic law of development into our own Vygotskian method: "[A]ny function in the child's cultural development appears twice or on two planes.... It appears first between people as an intermental category, and then within the child as an intramental category" (Vygotsky, 1987, p. 21). Another key component in establishing one's own Vygotskian method is to always keep the view of process and development in mind. Often in the class-room, we might view one bad test from a student as something that influ-ences our overall evaluation of that student. We then "fossilize" the capability of that student with the intentions we establish, which can be hurtful for the student, the class, and ultimately for the teacher as well. Vygotsky's psychology-philosophy is ascribed with attributes such as future-oriented, height (as opposed to depth), nonclassical psychology. It is the very act of viewing a student's "whole personality" within a zone of proximal development and change that leaves space for the student to actually grow in a way that is not completely prescribed by the curriculum or the teacher.

CONCLUSIONS

One of the problems within SLA and applied linguistics is that many scholars and practitioners are weary of the predominant Chomskyan approach that has claimed the ultimate status of being scientific. For this reason, various researchers and practitioners have slowly gravitated toward Vygotskian thought, but often this understanding is viewed only as the pole that is opposite to Chomskyan thought. This approach has resulted in an attempt to equate ethnographic studies with Vygotsky's cultural-historical method, and this should be avoided. There appears to be a tendency to view Vygotsky's work within the constructivist notions of interaction as well, and yet the core of Vygotsky's thoughts are related to the internal aspect of human nature. This internal—often unconscious aspect—is not dealt with in most Western interpretations of Vygotsky.

In order to understand Vygotsky's cultural-historical theory, or nonclassical psychology/philosophy, the following example is used, which is the philosophy of chaos theory as opposed to the thinking of R. Descartes. The fundamental principles of the Cartesian scientific method can be summed up in two words: control and product. There is a specific focus on control to replicate the same experiments in different places and at different times, with the same results—hence, the focus on product. Chaos theory is a very interesting principle in physics and philosophy, among other disciplines, and the underlying focus is on systematicity, not chaos. However, at the inner plane of existence (for individuals, as well as on the cosmic level), too many variables function together to be able to be controlled, replicated, or viewed as a final product. A sense of flow is continuous, maintaining its own rhythm, and this flow will never be fully understood within human three-dimensional existence. It is paradoxical to place so much faith in the Cartesian scientific method when ultimate answers of human existence will never be resolved that way. Fundamental questions have not been solved within this system, such as What is memory? Where does love come from? How does the brain actually remember? Where do thoughts originate? What are emotions? Two basic facts of life are that no single person created him- or herself, nor can any single person avert death. There is a certain power in relinquishing the need to have answers at every point in life—many answers that will never be forthcoming. At the same time, a certain power is gained from understanding Vygotsky's cultural-historical theory. It is a higher focus on an explanatory principle that cannot be totally understood through human mediation vis-à-vis consciousness. It is also clear that we will never have total understanding of the origins of thought and language and how they interact. Yet, it is empowering to start viewing life, education, other human beings, and research within a holistic frame of reference, albeit, one that constantly changes. Therefore, the focus within any Vygotskian method is on the flow of change and process, with a future orientation toward growth and

development. It is precisely these internal aspects that we cannot completely understand that can be connected to the holistic unit one designs
for him- or herself. In other words, there is a reconnection to the whole,
and a trust in the underlying chaos of the unconscious that can allow us to
reach a level of human freedom of action that is always related to the
social. Forming a model within this approach will be different for everyone because everyone is unique. Yet, at the same time, every person shares
qualities that are representative of all other humans on this earth. Vygotsky captured higher levels of human existence within his interests of
aesthetics, theater, film, poetry, and literature, as well as history, law, medicine, and the study of handicapped children, among other areas. Much of
Vygotsky's holism is captured in his own words:

The theory of the psychological materialism or dialectics of psychology is what I
call general psychology [p. 330].... Dialectical psychology proceeds first of all from
the unity of mental and physiological processes. Because for dialectical psychology mind is not, in the words of Spinoza [1677/1955, p. 128], something that is situated outside nature or as a kingdom within a kingdom, it is a part of nature itself,
directly linked to the functions of the higher organized matter of our brain....It
[dialectical psychology] does not mix up the mental and physiological processes.
It accepts the nonreducible qualitatively unique nature of the mind. But it does
claim that psychological processes are one....We must not study separate mental
and physiological processes outside their unity, because then they become completely unintelligible. We must study the integral process, which is characterized
by both a subjective and an objective side at the same time. (Vygotsky, 1997,
pp. 112–113)

    The title of this book—*Vygotsky's and A. A. Leontiev's Semiotics and Psy-
cholinguistics: Applications for Education, Second Language Acquisition, and
Theories of Language*—is very important in establishing the atmosphere to
better understand Vygotsky's method as a psychology and a philosophy.
The Greek word sēmeion means "sign," and it was Ferdinand de Saussure
who introduced the term sémilogie, used to bridge linguistics and social
psychology:

Saussure viewed language as a social phenomenon. His great contribution to its
study was the discovery that meaning does not reside in individual words but in
a complex system of relationships or structures. His motto was: "Il n'y a de sense
que dans la différence." He pointed out that language structures could be explored
by describing them in their current form (synchronically) or historically (diachronically). (Martin & Ringham, 2000, pp. 2–3)

From these beginnings different areas such as semiotics, structuralism,
and semiology arose. A caveat is given at this point related to the term
"holographic semiotics," a neologism that attempts to transcend the traditional understanding of structuralism and semiology. The American tradi-

tion of semiotics was developed by C.S. Peirce, who viewed the development of sign categories (i.e., icon, index, and symbol). The Paris School (Ecole de Paris) was founded by A. J. Greimas and was concerned with the relationships between signs and how they produce meaning in a certain text. One of the basic organizing principles of Vygotsky's method is the relationship of the part to the whole, and the whole to the part, in a moving and dialectical fashion. This trend of theorizing was found in various Russian disciplines, including that of V. Propp, who was instrumental in demonstrating the sequence of the parts of a fairy tale, "which together reflected the stages of all human action" (Martin & Ringham, 2000, p. 5). The contemporary understanding of a hologram is the best way to interpret the connection between the structure of whole-parts-whole within Vygotsky's method. The parts themselves maintain an imprint of the whole and are the vehicles for expressing the whole. In order to better understand Vygotsky's cultural-historical framework, the first explanation concerns a trajectory of action to thought, as opposed to thought to action, which is commonly understood by various followers of Vygotsky. Kozulin (1990) stated this clearly:

From action to thought. Rather than a simple extension of a natural process originating in human biology, the higher mental process is a function of socially meaningful activity. This emphasis on the generative aspect of activity is theoretically significant, because it distinguishes Vygotsky's position from that of the "substantialists" who envisaged the material substance of the brain or the spiritual substance of Mind as the true seat of mental function. Vygotsky's position was the opposite: higher mental function is created through activity, it is an objectivation of action. The traditional rationalist formula, from thought to action, is thus reversed and becomes, from action to thought. (pp. 113–114)

Within the holographic understanding that the whole is imprinted within the parts, it is also critical to understand that the whole cannot be broken down into its parts or elements, to then be reconstructed into the same whole. This type of process would lead only to reductionism. Therefore, the interrelations and functions of the whole vis-à-vis the parts are of ultimate importance within Vygotskian theory, all of which serve as an anchor for understanding Vygotsky's historical and genetic-developmental method. Understanding the whole means that one must enter the realm of the subconscious, something that Vygotsky accepted as the seat of creativity. In order to attempt any comprehension of the whole, one must start to think in terms of metaphor and metatheory. Within Vygotskian cultural-historical theory, the holistic focus on consciousness is used as an overarching philosophical principle, and the tools of analysis to understand consciousness are thought and speech, certainly connected with action. It is precisely the aspects of internalization and inner speech that best correspond to Vygotsky's holographic whole, with word meaning serving a mediating function between thought and speech, thought and action. Vološinov (1973) stated the following:

Closer analysis shows that the units of which inner speech is constituted are certain *whole entities* somewhat resembling a passage of monologic speech or whole utterances....These units of inner speech, these *total impressions of utterances,* are joined with one another and alternate with one another not according to the laws of grammar or logic but according to the laws of *evaluative* (emotive) *correspondence, dialogical deployment,* etc., in close dependence on the historical conditions of the social situation and the whole pragmatic run of life....Therefore, the semiotic material of the psyche is preeminently the word—*inner speech.* (p. 38, p. 29)

Semiotics—as a system—functions at both discursive and narrative levels. Some of the tools of semiotics as described by Martin and Ringham (2000, pp. 7–8) are as follows: (1) "Meaning is not inherent in objects, objects do not signify by themselves." (2) "Semiotics views the text...as an autonomous unity, that is, one that is internally coherent....Semiotic analysis becomes, then a discovery method." (3) "Semiotics posits that story structure or narrativity underlies all discourse, not just what is commonly known as a story. For instance, it underlies political, sociological, and legal discourse." (4) "Semiotics posits the notion of levels of meaning; it is, for instance, the deep abstract level that generates the surface levels. A text must, therefore, be studied at these different levels of depth and not just at the surface level as is the case with traditional linguistics." In relating the parts to the whole, and vice versa, Vygotsky always attempted to connect these levels through a dialectical semiotics. He also connected the semiotics of language to his innovative theories of education. It was a characteristic of the 1920s that European scholars in various fields were proficient in many disciplines beyond their own fields of expertise. For example, Sergei Eisenstein was a filmmaker and a semiotician. David Vygodsky (a cousin of L. S. Vygotsky) was a linguist and was very interested in art, aesthetics, theater, and film. Theories of language were combined with many other cultural disciplines, and Vygotsky built a direct bridge out of this renaissance mentality to include education, which was called pedology.

The second part of the title of this book relates to the Russian psycholinguistics of A. A. Leontiev. In the United States, psycholinguistics was born during the era of behaviorism and within it a different understanding is maintained in comparison to its Russian equivalent:

American psycholinguistics was born early in the fifties. Its foundations were in behavioristic psychology and thus it was almost synonymous with behavioristic learning theory. This mechanistic outlook...was unable to explain the richness of rational, conscious, integrative facts and context related to language and communication. Unfortunately, the assimilation of psycholinguistics into behaviorism generated its initial attack by non-behaviorists. Early adoption of psycholinguistic trends into applied linguistics was usually confined to the audio-lingual method of foreign language teaching, which involved repetition of pattern drills and memorizing dialogues, which lead to a mechanical acquisition that was fraught with problems. (Slama-Cazacu, 1983, p. 267)

Psycholinguistics in the Russian context includes semiotics and an attempt at understanding internal features of language. It also connects to the social sphere, with the single word being viewed as a generalization, united with other social components. In Western linguistics, the word is often analyzed as a separate feature, disconnected from the whole, and the focus is on associationism, rather than on deeper semiotic structures. One aspect of Vygotsky's genius was the fact that he developed a metatheory or metamethod, often writing in a metaphorical sense. When working on his understanding of concept formation (which was paralleled with word meaning in generalized terms), he wrote from a concrete point of view of child development; at the same time, he was writing from a metatheoretical point of view that can be applied to adult development. This approach has sometimes been misunderstood in the West as representing only cognitive development. However, Vygotsky also combined the emotional, creative, and playful development that goes hand in hand with cognitive development. Within semiotics is a special component that captures feelings and emotions, and these personal feelings (i.e., understood as "parts") are then correlated with various levels of a narrative program (i.e., here, understood as the "whole"). In semiotics this is called the thymic category.

Situated on the deep level of an utterance, the thymic category relates to the world of feeling and of emotions. It spans the notion made up by the two poles of euphoria versus dysphoria and forms the basis of positive/negative evaluation....To give an example: believing a statement to be true involves not only weighing what is being said for its accuracy but also evaluating it positively. (Martin & Ringham, 2000, p. 134)

Russian psycholinguistics incorporates the study of grammar, foreign languages (SLA and applied linguistics), semiotics, psychology, sociolinguistics, and various other disciplines.

The object of this book is reflected in its title, which aims at recreating a new theory of education and second language theory, via an expanded understanding of holographic semiotics (related to all human institutions) and Russian psycholinguistics. However, no approach, method, strategy, or even model is given to the reader. In fact, the focus is very different. Each reader is asked to develop his or her own approach, method, strategy, or model. The beauty of Vygotsky's work is that his method is not prescriptive, but offers each individual the possibility of taking the

responsibility of creating a personal psychology and philosophy. However, Vygotsky has given us some guidelines. It is the purpose of this book to attempt to view, through Vygotsky's prism, current issues of education and theories of language as parts of a whole structure (which represent the individual and the social simultaneously). Naturally, this view is filtered through the understanding and experiences of the author, who is responsible for any thoughts that might not be in line with Vygotsky's Russian cultural-historical method. The hope is to create a more expanded view of the social sciences through the perspective of education and SLA.

Each reader is asked to finish the book and sit down to actually develop a personalized and individual Vygotskian approach to education or SLA, teaching, and life.

Chapter 2 is by A. A. Leontiev, written in 1996. During that year there were many international centennial celebrations of the birth of Vygotsky. This chapter was given as a lecture at the International Association of Applied Linguistics Vygotsky symposium in Jyväskylä, Finland. It was also given as a lecture on the zone of proximal development at the Russian International Summer School in Zvenigorod, Russia, in June 2000. Professor Leontiev reviewed the Russian understanding of Vygotsky's work and placed Vygotsky's focus within the psychology of the whole personality.

For purposes of clarification throughout the book, A.N. Leontiev (1903–79) was one of the closest of L.S. Vygotsky's collaborators, at the beginning of their careers and started the Kharkov School, which metamorphased into Russian activity theory. At the beginning of the 1930s, A.N. Leontiev broke with many of Vygotsky's theories for personal and political reasons; however, Leontiev never disputed Vygotsky's authority. A.N. Leontiev's son, A.A. Leontiev (born in 1936) is a professor of psychology at Moscow State University. His son, D.A. Leontiev (born in 1960) is a professor of general psychology at Moscow State University, specializing in the theories of aesthetics, emotions, and meaning and sense. Both A.A. Leontiev and D.A. Leontiev have remained loyal to the teachings of A.N. Leontiev and the core intentions of L.S. Vygotsky. There are various transliterations of the spelling of Leontiev, such as Leont'ev, Leontyev, or Leont'yev.

NOTE

1. For more information on Leibniz's understanding of monads, refer to Jolley (1995, pp. 132–133):

[H]e [Leibniz] defines a monad as nothing but a simple substance that enters into composites—simple, that is, without parts.... Simplicity is demanded of monads, since without simples there would be no composites; composites, by their very nature, are nothing but collections, or aggregates.... However, in order to qualify as genuine simples, monads must be without parts, and hence without extension, shape, or divisibility. From this initial definition, Leibniz draws two important consequences. First, a monad is subject to neither generation nor corruption.... Second, there is no conceivable way in which one monad can be affected by another.

CHAPTER 2

Vygotsky's Theory: Yesterday, Today, and Tomorrow

A. A. Leontiev

For me L[ev] S[emyonovich] isn't history. *It is my today.*

—Daniel Elkonin

INTRODUCTION

To write something on Vygotsky is self-torture. Every thought of his is connected with hundreds of other thoughts and it is impossible to read him without finding and understanding these connections. And every idea of Vygotsky induces in your mind hundreds of your own ideas ... if, of course, you are able to generate them at all. (A. N. Leontiev, 1994, p. 65)

Everyone interprets Vygotsky according to the real depth of his own competence. The farther this competence is from Vygotsky's, the stranger the image drawn by the author. Kozulin's Vygotsky is a bit similar to Kozulin, Yaroshevsky's to Yaroshevsky, Puzyrey's to Puzyrey. In order to describe Vygotsky's ideas objectively one not only needs to be a psychologist, but also a historian. This does not imply an image of a historiographer who examines Vygotsky from the modern point of view, that is, how near Vygotsky's thoughts are to "mine" (seeing "my" ideas as a type of standard). A true historian understands his or her "hero" as a part of his or her epoch and one's own ideas—as a logical extension of those of one's predecessors and contemporaries. A true historian understands that if a researcher of Vygotsky's magnitude is not able to revert to his old position, he always advances. We need to see this point in order to comprehend the objective and subjective logic of one's inner development, and that every step in this scientific development is to be understood from within. I once had a similar experience working on the scientific heritage of the greatest linguist of the past century, Jan Baudouin de Courtenay. Therefore, we have to conceive of Vygotsky (or Baudouin) as a unique personality, to interpret his ideas as a part of his mental life in general, to know the circle of his friends and students, to question people who knew him personally about their impressions, and so forth. Here, I am in luck: I met practically all of Vygotsky's colleagues and students who were still alive during the 1950s, 1960s, and 1970s through my father, Alexei Nikolayevich Leontiev, including people such as Professors Alexander Luria, Leonid Zankov, Lidia Bozhovich, and Bluma Zeigarnik. All of my life I have breathed Vygotsky's air. That is why I undertook to review the problem of Vygotsky's school.

YESTERDAY

At this point, I discuss some widespread opinions of Vygotsky that in my opinion are totally incorrect. First, at the beginning of the twentieth century, Russian science simultaneously experienced many encyclopedic thinkers similar to giants of the Renaissance, including philosophers, psychologists, specialists in natural science, and cultural theorists. I refer to people such as Vladimir Vernadsky, Pavel Florenskii, Mikhail Bakhtin, Alexey Lossev, Yuri Lotman, and Roman Jakobson (and I knew the last three men personally). Lev Vygotsky was among this group. It would be senseless to seriously discuss the question of whether Vygotsky's scientific specialization was "narrow." Was he a psychologist? A linguist? A culturologist? An art theorist? Of course, all of these questions are to be answered in the affirmative. But Vygotsky was a great psychologist because he was a great linguist, philosopher, and culturologist. He cannot be pigeonholed into specific scientific fields. Second, I just called Vygotsky a great philosopher. His philosophical credo needs special analysis. It is usual in Russia to stigmatize Marx and Marxism as something unscientific. According to such a position, Vygotsky is eliminated from the list of Marxist philosophers. But it is an objective fact that Vygotsky was the leading theoretician of the Marxist-oriented psychology in Russia. I definitely reject the idea of the so-called unscientific character of Marxist philosophy. This area is a branch of classical German philosophical thought of the eighteenth and nineteenth centuries, particularly its Hegelian aspect. To be a Marxist in anthropological philosophy and gnosiology means to be both a consistent materialist and a Hegelian dialectician at the same time. We can accept or not accept such a position—that is another question; however, I see nothing unscientific in it. Some great scholars have accepted it, and it is hard to explain when viewing their adaptation to the concrete political situation only. There are highly honest persons, such as the great linguist Yevgeny Polivanov, Vygotsky, his older colleague Pavel Blonsky, and later, the philosophers Merab Mamardashvili and Evald Ilyenkov. In speaking honestly, the Marxist position is natural for professional psychology. However, very few scholars at that time were competent enough to share Marxist views, and not just parrot some pseudo-Marxist dogma. In psychology, these people were Vygotsky and Blonsky.

Second, there is a stigmatization related to Marxism that has its roots in the so-called Marxism-Leninism of all Russian scholars during the 1930s, 1940s, and 1950s. Once I analyzed whether there really was a real Marxism during that time, and I came to the conclusion that there was not. The leading ideology in a Communist state was not Marxism, since Stalin personally put together Abram Deborin's group regarding the so-called Menshevist idealism. Vygotsky stood very close to Deborin's group (see A. A. Leontiev, 1990).

Third, Vygotsky's Marxism was not dogmatic. In my essay "Ecce Homo" (1995) I tried to show that Vygotsky and Bakhtin developed their conceptions almost within the same direction; a detailed analysis of this problem (cf. Leontiev, 1995) is in the fourth part of this chapter.

The so-called Vygotskian school of thought consisted of A. N. Leontiev, Luria, Bozhovich, Galperin, Elkonin, P. Zinchenko, and some other scholars. Two similar opinions regarding this school exist, and both have nothing in common with the historical truth. First, Vygotsky's school had nothing to do with Vygotsky himself, rather, it was a group of psychologists having quite a different orientation. Second, part of the Kharkov group led by P. Zinchenko was the real Vygotsky School, but A. N. Leontiev—with his Muscovite colleagues—was not. In my book about Vygotsky, I tried to demonstrate the inner community and integrity of Vygotsky's school in its entirety, and the continuity of Vygotsky's ideas regarding the views of his school (A. A. Leontiev, 1990). This continuity is clearly seen in the recent book composed of Leontiev's manuscripts—mostly from the late 1930s (see A. N. Leontiev, 1994).

One unchangeable Vygotskian theory never existed, such as the "cultural-historical" theory. For most Vygotskians, Vygotsky moved from one topic to another inside the same circle of ideas. In reality, he went a long way from reflexology through cultural-historical theory and activity theory, to personality theory as the kernel of a completely new conception. The Vygotskian School is developing like Vygotsky himself, and the stages of this development are in basically the same order—from a cultural-historical conception (early 1930s) to activity theory and personality theory. It has faced the same problems Vygotsky himself faced.

TODAY

The Vygotskian centennial in 1996 (marking the 100th anniversary of his birth) was celebrated by different specialists in different countries, by trying to very clearly show the extreme popularity of his ideas, not only in contemporary psychology, but in all of the humanities today. The question arises: Is this only a transient scientific paradigm, or is Vygotsky's popularity within modern social science founded on some objective processes and tendencies? Before I answer this question, I will try to define two main categories of the history of every science: stage and school. The stage in the history of science is a totality of scientific views or scientific works characterized by the same or a similar methodological paradigm (in Kuhn's sense). For example, we can find the "young-grammatical" and "sociological" stages in the development of linguistic science. A school is a group of researchers acting within the same stage and is recognized by some factors: common theoretical positions based on the views of the leader(s), independent development of these views by every member of the school (that is, for example, why it is insufficient to require attendance at Saussure's lectures in order to be a linguist of the Saussurian school), and personal connections inside the school inter alia.

Usually we discuss the problem of the "Vygotskian school of thought" together with similar views. Yes, Leontiev, Luria, Gal'perin, and others have had common psychological views rooted in Vygotsky's own ideas. Yes, every one of them developed this theory in his own direction. Yes, they were personal friends and continually discussed different "Vygotskian" problems. Now, the second and third generations of the Vygotskian school of thought exist, without having seen Vygotsky personally; however, they have developed Vygotsky's ideas, not only the concrete ones, but his more general theoretical views as well.

It seems to me that the notion of "stage" is fully applicable to the history of psychology as a science. The inwardly determined evolution of psychological ideas in the United States and in Western Europe has reached the level where Vygotskian ideas nearly correspond to those in Russia. Let us review the development of psycholinguistics as a psychological discipline. The third generation of psycholinguists, according to G. Noizet, has independently evolved in a Vygotskian direction. There is no coincidence that not only is James Wertsch a leading American psycholinguist of this third generation, but at the same time he is the deepest interpreter and staunchest supporter of Vygotsky's theoretical views in general. Voluntarily or not, consciously or not, more and more psychologists are beginning to work inside the Vygotskian paradigm. And when they start reading Vygotsky himself, they comprehend his ideas as being very similar to their own. That is why Vygotsky is becoming the most popular psychologist nowadays, with one exception, Jean Piaget, and even some of his views stand close to Vygotsky's.

Until now, we have discussed Vygotsky's general theoretical positions, determining most of his more concrete views on different psychological (and psycholinguistic) problems. It is impossible to review all of these concrete points that are analyzed in the contemporary psychological literature. I mention only two of them connected with psycholinguistics: It was Vygotsky who first formulated the idea of the stage structure of the process of speech generation, along with some Russians after World War II who further elaborated on these ideas, such as Alexander Luria, Nikolay Zhinkin, and Russian psycholinguists Tatiana Ryabova-Akhutina and myself. The idea of psycholinguistics itself, related to the theory of speech activity, is rooted in Vygotsky's works. It was Vygotsky who interpreted the speech process as a sequence of classes of psychological operations, each having its own qualitative components (see A. A. Leontiev, 1996). The most important feature of Vygotsky's model is the synthesis of this stage structure with the heuristic principle as basic for activity theory in general (A. A. Leontiev, 1975). In short, the psycholinguistic theory traced back to Vygotsky allows the speaking person to choose the optimal model of speech generation. This is different from, even contradictory to, psycholinguistic models that can be experimentally confirmed. Second, until now, psycholinguistics has remained a theory of spontaneous (not controlled, unconscious) speech generation and speech perception. Only Vygotsky and his school (e.g., A. N. Leontiev) have analyzed different levels of consciousness in human activity, including speech activity. The basic idea of such levels was brought forward by the great Russian physiologist Nikolay Bernshteyn. It was Vygotsky who practically created the branch of psycholinguistics called reflexive (i.e., in the sense of reflexivity) psycholinguistics or the "psycholinguistics of psycholinguistics."

TOMORROW

In his commentary on the latest Russian edition of Vygotsky's works on pedagogy and pedagogical psychology (Vygotsky, 1996, p. 20), Yevgeny Yamburg, the well-known Muscovite teacher and head of one of the most popular experimental schools in Moscow, stated the following: "Vygotsky, as well as many of our other compatriots, demonstrated a type of *expansion of culture*." He was the predecessor of the new psychological paradigm, only some traits of which can be extrapolated from his ideas and from the ideas of other great scholars of the twentieth century. This fact alone, and not his popularity in today's psychology, is the most important and acute problem in the analysis of his scientific heritage.

This forecasting character of Vygotsky's ideas can even be found in the details of his works. For example, in "Concrete Human Psychology," Vygotsky's article first published in 1986 (written in 1929 and published in the English translation in 1989), we find the conception of social roles, officially attributed to George Mead in his works of the early 1930s (also attributed to Thomas Znaniecki). However, the idea of a dramatic nature of human personality that is contained in the same article seems much more important. Different roles are—according to Vygotsky—always struggling within the structure of the personality. The most general idea of this article is to prioritize the social determination of personality, not of consciousness or even activity. It seems especially interesting in comparison with most modern cognitive theories, where the process of socialization (internalization) is often reduced to cognitive processes. For example, in Cole and Scribner's famous book (1974), the role of culture in psychic development is understood only as the influence of culture on cognition. Even in Jerome Bruner's articles on Vygotsky we can find the notion that "the world is a symbolic world in the sense that it consists of conceptually organized, rule-bound belief systems about what exists, about how to attain goals, about what is to be valued" (Bruner, 1986, p. 32).

The world for Bruner and Cole is a symbolic world, only a conceptual construct and a theoretical world. Let us compare this position with some ideas belonging to A. N. Leontiev: "We are to return to building in a man's consciousness an image of an *external multi-dimensional world*, a world *as it really is*, in which we are living, acting, but where our abstractions don't 'live'" (A. N. Leontiev, 1983, p. 255).

Let us listen to Bakhtin (1986):

The world where an action in reality takes place—is a unique and integral world, experienced in a concrete way: the world which can be heard, seen, touched and is conceivable.... The integral unity of this world is guaranteed. (p. 511)

Otherwise, if we do not place ourselves into this concrete world—into the concrete situation and concrete time, under concrete emotional, motivational, and voluntary conditions—this world "would break down into abstractions and generalizations; this would only be possible within moments and relations that could be integrated into something similar, and this would only be possible in an abstract and general unity" (Bakhtin, 1986, p. 512). This is a world where our abstractions *live: we* live in *another* world, in the *real* world (A. A. Leontiev, 1992, p. 195). This is the psychological basis for the life of a person in a real world according to Bakhtin and A. N. Leontiev.

According to Vygotsky, our personality is of a dialogical nature, and there is a constant dialogue between the "larger" world and myself as a personality. Pavel Florenskii (1990) stated that "cognition is not the capturing of a dead object by a predatory gnosiological subject, but a living and ethical *communication* of personalities" (p. 73). A language in a broader sense is the understanding of this dialogue.

The Cartesian mode of scientific thinking presupposes a sharp distinction between my inner (mental) world and the World. We ask the question, how is the World reflected in men, in my mental world? But we cannot understand that "I" am a part of the World and *this* World exists only on the condition of *my* existence and *my* acting in it. I am the integral part of this World (A.N. Leontiev, 1994, p. 27). Otherwise, it is another World (A.A. Leontiev, 1992, pp. 200–201).

The psychology of tomorrow seems to be the psychology of personality as a dynamic system of relations of humans in the world, determining cognition, actions, and their relations in a single psychological structure. Today, "psychology has largely been transformed from a science of the infinitely evolving human being in an endlessly changing world, from a science about the *actions* of a free creative personality into a science of the *activity* of limited and rigid consciousness" (A.A. Leontiev, 1995, p. 45).

Vygotsky is the creator of this new view in psychology based on the priority of personality and on the idea of a constant dialogue between humans and the World, humans and culture, humans and other people, and humans and themselves.

CHAPTER 3

Semiotic Educational Perspectives

PEDOLOGY

Luria (1928, pp. 347–348) defined pedology as "the science of the growing organism and its symptomatic complexes (including the somatic, psychological, and social peculiarities of the child)." Vygotsky characterized pedology as the following, which is given in Russian transliteration, followed by an English translation:

Pedologija est' nauka o rebenke. Osnovnoj fakt, s kotorym my vstrecaemsja podchodja k rebenku, èto-rezvitie. Rebenok nachoditsja v postojannom processe izmenija I rosta, I poètomu prezde vsego sledeut vyjasnit' osnovnye momenty charakterizujuščie tot process, kotoryj my nazvaem processom detskogo razvitija. (Rissom, 1985, p. 39)

[Pedology is the science of the child. The basic fact that we need to face when we direct our attention to the child is development. The child finds him/herself in a constant process of change and growth; therefore, one must above all explain the fundamental moment that characterizes the process called child development.] (trans. D.R.)

Interest in pedology started around 1925 with a work written by P. Blonskij (1884–1941) of the same title, and it became very popular around 1928 with the First Russian Congress of Pedologists:

One of the characteristics of pedology was its insistence on the use of tests designed to determine the level of intelligence and ability of the child. The principal factors determining the psychological development of the child were considered to be heredity and environment, and psychologists were divided among themselves on which was the predominant factor. The "Biologists" (Blonskij, Arkin, Arjamov, etc.) held that inherited biological factors were the dominant element in development, the "Sociologists" (Basov, Vygotskij, Moložavij, etc.) emphasized the role of the social environment, while a third group, the "Biosociologists," attributed equal importance to both factors. (Payne, 1968, p. 48)

In contemporary terms, pedology would be called interdisciplinary educational psychology (Kozulin, 1994, p. xiv). Vygotsky was closely associated with pedology for the last seven years of his life, and his association with pedology caused the Soviet authorities to ban his works from 1936 to 1956. Even until the 1980s, the word "pedology" was carefully replaced by more neutral terms such as "school psychology," "child psychology," or simply "psychology."[1] Pedology was an attempt for Vygotsky to transcend parts of the narrow focus of pedagogy to include cultural and aesthetic areas he had studied during the 1920s, hoping to expand the field of education.

The history of pedology can be divided into three main periods: 1922–28, the emergence of pedology as a separate discipline; 1928–32, the development of pedology; and 1932–36, the period of decline (cf. van der Veer & Valsiner, 1991, p. 297). Luria (1928) stated that "it is the first time that pedology has been regarded not as child psychology and not as experimental pedagogy but as a genetic science of the growth of the child" (p. 350).

The 1920s represented a time when partial Marxist educational experiments took place in Russia, although at the same time ideas from the West were readily being adopted. Thus, Paul Natorp's social pedagogy, and Robert Seidel's labor school were popular models during the 1920s, contributing to the ideology of the labor school (trudovaja shkola) propagated by Pavel Blonsky. Ideas from Dewey were widely read, and the Dalton Plan, together with the Project Curriculum, were also read regarding the organization of children's lives (cf. van der Veer & Valsiner, 1991, pp. 296–297). The major difference between the models of the West and pedology was the attempt to place education within a socialist framework. One important point of discussion within pedology—and pedagogy in general—was the role that the environment plays on the individual. Even though Vygotsky stated that "paedology does not study the environment as such" (van der Veer & Valsiner, 1994, p. 338), the word "environment" appeared in many pedological texts: for example, "So, it is the *personally meaningful experience* that emerges in the child-environment relationship and guides the further process of development" (van der Veer & Valsiner, 1991, p. 327); " [B]y re-organizing the structure of the environment of the developing child, the educators can guide the child to the synthesis of qualitatively novel psychological functions" (van der Veer & Valsiner, 1991, p. 333); "I[I]t is the child's experiencing (perezhivanie) of the environment, organized by the use of meanings (the socially constructed 'stimulus-means') that constitutes the essence of the study of environment for Vygotsky's system of paedology" (van der Veer & Valsiner, 1991, p. 316).

Most of these statements were made during the early part of the century, when Pavlov was most influential. Certainly the main force behind pedology was Vladimir Bekhterev (famous for a Russian version of Pavlovian reflexology), who had expressed interest in the idea of pedology as early as 1903. Bekhterev was anti-Czarist, and it was therefore easy for him to establish the Psycho/Paedological Institute in 1907, having already been the head of the Psychoneurological Institute in Moscow. The first Pedological Institute was destroyed, only to be reestablished in 1918, including four sections: experimental pedagogics, anatomy and physiology, psychology of childhood (led by Professor Basov, who established his own version of activity theory), and a department on age and individual variability of constitutional types and behavior. The Institute was placed within a socialist framework where mothers were to leave their children while they went to work. As time went on, problems increased. In 1931, Professor Basov died, and Vygotsky took over his position, traveling regularly to the Herzen University in St. Petersburg to give lectures. The political climate was changing quickly, and pedology was becoming suspicious, in particular because so many of its proponents were familiar with Western traditions. In addition, many pedologists spoke various foreign languages, and many had studied abroad. Vygotsky was criticized so: "Sharply expressed eclecticism can be seen in the works of Vygotsky, who has united in his theory of cultural development behaviorism and reactology with Gestalt-psychology that is idealistic in its roots" (van der Veer & Valsiner, 1991, p. 304). The members of Vygotsky's group started experiencing trouble at the beginning of the 1930s.

In 1930, circumstances forced Alexei N. Leontiev to leave both the Academy of Communist Education and the Institute of Cinematography. Luria, although he was already a recognized psychologist, decided to return to medical school as a student, possibly in an attempt to shift to a less ideologically charged sphere of clinical neuropsychology (Kozulin, 1990, p. 243).

Even though there was a general focus on the socialization of the child, the clinical method Vygotsky used was that of case study within a longitudinal framework, focusing on the individual child. The case studies were then compared. In 1936, pedology was banned and for the most part has never been revived, although there is now a journal in Moscow called *Pedology*.

LEARNING AND DEVELOPMENT

Vygotsky was hoping to implement his ideas within the framework of pedology, but this attempt was not successful. However, Vygotsky's basic principles were applied within many institutional settings during the 1920s and 1930s. In Vygotsky's view, no single factor can be responsible for the development of psychological processes based on psychological capacities.

By developmental study of a problem I mean the disclosure of its genesis, its causal dynamic basis....It follows, then that we need to concentrate not on the product of development but on the very *process* by which higher forms are established. To do so the researcher is often forced to alter the automatic, mechanized, fossilized character of the higher form of behavior and to turn it back to its source through the experiment. This is the aim of dynamic analysis. (Vygotsky, 1978, pp. 62–64)

At this point in *Mind and Society,* Vygotsky (1978) introduced the concept of a historically based psychology. Many researchers and educators understand the word "history" to refer to the occurrence of a past event that precludes a better understanding of development. Vygotsky (1978) then extended this understanding by stating that *"to study something historically means to study it in the process of change;* that is the dialectical method's basic demand" (pp. 64–65). Vygotsky then viewed development as the gradual reorganization of consciousness. Wertsch (1985b) paraphrased Vygotsky when he stated that

the development of the child is a dialectical process in which the transition from one step to another is accomplished not by evolutionary, but by a revolutionary path, with Vygotsky stating that we need to concentrate not on the product of development, but on the very process by which higher forms are established. (pp. 71–72)

Development for Vygotsky took place in real time that was either cyclical or spiral in nature. This point is important in future discussions of the zone of proximal development (ZPD), where critics often state that Vygotsky's concept of development was linear. However,

Vygotsky emphasized the uneven nature of development: it proceeds cyclically or rhythmically and if one wanted to graphically depict it, the depiction could not be made with the help of an exponential straight line....All development takes the form of wave-like curves, both when we look at particular functions (e.g., weight, speech, intellectual development, memory, attention, etc.) and at development in general. (van der Veer & Valsiner, 1991, p. 309)

Perhaps the most important notion in this regard was the basic assumption made in psychology and education before Vygotsky that development precedes learning. For Vygotsky, learning precedes development (and commonsense logic requires both elements, not the exclusion of one or the other). Development is not the result of an accumulation of associations; rather, it presents qualitative leaps that then create new levels of reality and new levels of development:

Our concept of development implies a rejection of the frequently held view that cognitive development results from the gradual accumulation of separate changes. We believe that child development is a complex dialectical process characterized by periodicity, unevenness in the development of different functions, metamorphosis or qualitative transformation of one form into another, intertwining of external and internal factors, and adaptive processes which overcome impediments that the child encounters. (Vygotsky, 1978, p. 73)

Ultimately, development reflects the process of internalizing mediated sign systems with the realization of self-regulation. Although the controversy surrounding a comparison of Jean Piaget and Vygotsky has been intentionally omitted here, three points need to be made about their varying positions on learning and development: (1) Vygotsky felt that Piaget did not include any sense of functional relationships in his theories. (2) Vygotsky believed that Piaget did not emphasize the social context of the child (cf. Wertsch, 1981a, p. 165). (3) "In contrast to Piaget, we hypothesize that development does not proceed toward socialization, but toward the conversion of social relations into mental functions" (Vygotsky, 1981, p. 165).

Fodor (1972) and Sinha (1988) critiqued Vygotsky, generalizing points that for the most part Vygotsky addressed, albeit in works that have only been recently translated. A major problem concerns their criticism that the Vygotskian account did not really break with the behaviorist and empiricist paradigm.[2] Indeed Vygotsky used tenets of reflexology, behaviorism, and empiricism to establish his own understanding of the development of phylogeny (biological evolution) and ontogeny (human evolution). Vygotsky's overall method began with explaining the lower mental processes, embracing a foundation of initial reflex responses within the behavioristic-empiricist tradition. Then, he continued his line of thought with a detailed outline of the higher (including rudimentary) mental processes, subsumed under the understanding of what it means to be human:

For Vygotsky, becoming human implies the centralizing or cerebralization of mental processes—whether in development, in cultural history, or in phylogenesis. Emotion moves inward and escapes peripheral control. Speech starts externally and ends as inner speech. Imagination is play gone inward. (Minick, 1987, p. 11)

The role of development mainly focuses on the link between thought and speech during the period of development itself. Concept formation is discussed within that framework, which leads to the practical understanding of learning within the ZPD.

ZONE OF PROXIMAL DEVELOPMENT

One of the most important aspects of the ZPD is that it is used to describe the functions that are not yet visible. Vygotsky is given credit for coining this term, yet he himself gives credit to Meumann and to other Americans.[3]

The American researcher Dorothea McCarthy demonstrated that among children between the ages of three and five there are two groups of functions: those the children already possess, and those they can perform under guidance, in groups, and in collaboration with one another but which they have not mastered independently. (Vygotsky, 1978, p. 87)

To better explain the ZPD, it has been stated that

[f]irst, it [ZPD] entails a reference to a "zone"—essentially a field—theoretical concept in an era of psychology that has largely forgotten the gargantuan efforts by Kurt Lewin to adopt topology for purposes of psychological discourse. Second, the understanding of "development" has been highly varied in contemporary psychological discourse, ranging from loosely formulated ideas about age-group differences (or age effects) to narrowly definable structural transformation of organisms in irreversible time and within context....Finally—to complicate the matters even further—contemporary psychologists have to wrestle with the qualifier of "proximal" (or "potential," or "nearest"), as it is the connecting link between the field-theoretic "zone" and the concept of "development" in this complex term. (Cocking, 1993, p. 36)

The ZPD is defined as "the distance between the actual developmental level as determined by independent problem solving and the level of potential development as determined through problem solving under adult guidance or in collaboration with more capable peers" (Vygotsky, 1978, p. 86). In Russian, the ZPD is called *zona blizhaishego razvitia* (zone of closest or nearest development), and it has also been translated into English as the "zone of potential development" by Simon and Simon (cf. Valsiner & van der Veer, 1993, pp. 35–36).

The earliest documented mention of ZBR [ZPD] can be found in a lecture given in Moscow at Epshtein Institute of Experimental Defectology on March 17, 1933....In the first part of this text, Vygotsky emphasized the qualitative structural reorganizational (dialectical synthesis) nature of the developmental process....Six crisis periods in child development were outlined by Vygotsky: those of newborn age, 1st, 3rd, 7th, 13th, and 17th year. It is during these periods that the emergence of higher levels of psychological organization take place. Vygotsky was always ready to view developmental change as a process of dialectical synthesis...and the crisis periods in ontogeny guided him to look for relevant developmental phenomena. (Valsiner & van der Veer, 1993, pp. 40–41)

The ZPD is understood as being a descriptive rather than explanatory principle, and

the focus...is not on transferring skills, as such, from those who know more to those who know less but on the collaborative use of mediational means to create, obtain, and communicate meaning....The role of the adult is not necessarily to provide structured cues, but through exploratory talk and other social mediations such as importing everyday activities into the classrooms, to assist children in appropriating or taking control of their own learning (Moll, 1992, p. 13)

Here the scaffolding metaphor comes to play, and "at a certain point of development, adults will start to give them [children] cultural instruction....The child had [sic] now left the 'natural,' precultural stage and had become a fully fledged member of the society: a cultural being" (van der Veer & Valsiner, 1991, p. 226). In fact, Griffin and Cole (in Cocking, 1993) state that the scaffolding metaphor "leaves open questions of children's creativity" (p. 49).

It is important to know what the ZPD is not and to be aware of some of the traditional problems that have accompanied it; for example, the ZPD is not a method used to teach discrete, separable skills and subskills. According to Moll (1992) the ZPD, however, is used for

(1) establishing a level of difficulty. This level, assumed to be the proximal level, must be...challenging for the student but not too difficult; (2) providing assisted performance. The adult provides guided practice to the child with a clear sense of the goal or outcome of the child's performance; (3) evaluating independent performance. The most logical outcome of a zone of proximal development is the child performing independently. (p. 7)

The basic paradox of the ZPD is that it is used in measuring the child's potential age as compared with his or her actual age; however, at the core of the ZPD lies the potential that is neither past nor present, and hence difficult to measure. The method of dual or double stimulation focuses on techniques such as nonsense words, which do not allow the subject in experiments to use prior knowledge, with the goal of working their way through the experiment with guided help from the experimenter. The method developed by the subject in order to solve the problem at hand is observed.

At this point, a short review of the double method of stimulation is presented, since this is a core aspect of Vygotskian theory that can be adapted to education or second language teaching and research. During experiments, Vygotsky and Lev Sakharov presented two sets of stimuli; one set was used for the activity, while another set represented the signs involved in mediation of the activity. The difference in this type of experiment, compared with traditional ones, is that the subject is not placed within time constraints to learn how to answer the questions. Instead, with the help of the experimenter, the learner is guided in finding a procedure that works, and the subject's learning during this period is measured. The nonsense words used by Vygotsky and Sakharov—such as *mur, cev, lag*—were infused with certain properties that would prevent prior knowledge from distorting the experiment. Vygotsky stated that

> it is of principal importance that such an organization of the experiment arrange the pyramid of concepts "upside-down." The problem solving in our experiments follows the same path as it takes in real life, where the movement from the top of the pyramid to its bottom is no less important than the ascension from the concrete to the most abstract. (Vygotsky, 1994a, p. 105)

Certainly, the ZPD has not remained free of criticism. For example, the ZPD is considered to be a powerful rhetorical device, yet "it [the ZPD] pointed to the need to study processes of development on-line, but provided very little opportunity for an explicit theory of the developmental stages" (Valsiner & van der Veer, 1993, p. 47). However, this was not Vygotsky's intent. Another major criticism of the ZPD, which is still a persistent problem today, is that Vygotsky did not even mention how this concept is supposed to be dialectical, implying a unidirectional movement of development without a dynamic relationship between teacher and learner. For example, "when the child is with an incompetent adult, we can underestimate his developmental potential" (Valsiner & van der Veer, 1993, p. 56). Another problem is the relationship of the child to her social milieu. "The examples Vygotsky gave to demonstrate the use of the zone of proximal development suggest that he conceived of the environment as a static background to the dynamically developing child" (van der Veer & Valsiner, 1991, p. 343). The last problem raised in connection with the general discussion of the ZPD regards fossilization that is said to take place in classroom settings (not to be confused with the concept of fossilization in second language acquisition). Vygotsky addressed this problem by stating that

> these fossilized forms of behavior are most easily found in the so-called automated or mechanized psychological processes which, owing to their ancient origins, are being repeated for the millionth time and have become mechanized. They have lost their original appearance, and their outer appearance tells us nothing whatsoever about their internal nature. Their automatic character creates great difficulties for psychological analysis. (Vygotsky, 1978, pp. 63–64)

In relating Vygotsky's ZPD to second language learning (L2), the relationship of fossilization to the ZPD should be noted. Lantolf and Pavlenko (1995) reported that "Washburn, drawing on Vygotsky's account of *fossilization* in mental development, shows that not all expert/learner interactions result in L2 development and that learning is possible only if learners, in fact, have a ZPD" (p. 115). Vygotsky listed two ways to counteract fossilization in the general sense of the term, which can also be understood within the L2 construct: first, by using the genetic developmental as a guiding point of reference to counteract a phenotypic approach (i.e., description as opposed to explanation) (cf. Wertsch, 1992, p. 113); and second, disobjectivation, which is the "problem of grasping thought and life in their dynamic and open form before they are finished, before they become *things*. The disobjectivation procedure applied to human thought lies at the heart of Socratic *dialectic*" (Kozulin, 1990, p. 22). The understanding of disobjectivation as a basic premise in learning a foreign language, where the L2 learner must adapt to a foreign situation by the semiotic means of displacement, is discussed later.

Although there are many problems in applying the ZPD, this concept has become very popular around the world. Wertsch extended the ZPD to include a semiotic domain (with Bakhtinian concepts) and an activity-theoretical domain, basically Leontievian;[4] however, as Wertsch shifted the focus of Vygotsky's understanding of word meaning (i.e., rejecting this primary unit of analysis), the entire ZPD construct moved beyond Vygotsky's initial definition. No one can predict how Vygotsky would have altered and extended the ZPD if he had had more time to enrich it. It is often forgotten that the ZPD was discussed only during the last two years of his life, when he was very ill.

INTERNALIZATION AND THE ZPD

Vygotsky dealt with internalization within the higher mental functions, where the interpsychological (e.g., social) forms are transferred to the intrapsychological (e.g., personal) forms of meaning. Some have mistakenly viewed this as a transfer model; however, the key aspect of internalization is the rooting or the process of ingrowth that leads to personal transformation. Internalization is not understood as a reflection of the external, but rather a transformation of the external. No single view of the ZPD, consciousness, or internalization exists. For example, Berg (1970) stated that Vygotsky understood three types of internalization: structural-type internalization, stitch-type internalization, whole-type internalization:

To summarize the three forms of internalization, let us say that the structural-type internalization gives us the conscious use of internal signs and operations. It contrasts sharply…with stitch-type internalization, which gives us automatic, non-conscious operations, which are based directly on new neural structures, and with whole-type internalization, which gives us some sort of general concept. It would perhaps be foolish to view these as three independent processes that could each occur without any of the others. (p. 103)

In understanding internalization, there is a dialectic (which is also viewed metaphorically, not as a dualistic system) in place that ensues within a flow chart model of social ⇔ internal. In using tenets of semiotics (e.g., sign systems), concept formation (here, gesturing for others, object-regulation, other-regulation, and self-regulation), and the process of double stimulation, Vygotsky was able to deal with aspects of internalization that did not return to older introspectionist theories (e.g., Wilhelm Wundt), which were rejected by many in the late nineteenth century. According to Wertsch (1985a),

Vygotsky argues that there is an inherent relationship between external and internal activity, but it is a *genetic* relationship in which the major issue is how internal mental processes are *created* as a result of the child's exposure to what Vygotsky called "mature cultural forms of behavior." (p. 63)

In Russian activity theory, for the most part, internalization and externalization are viewed as the same phenomenon, with little focus on differentiating between the two; and North American and international sociocultural theory has, for the most part, eliminated the Vygotskian understanding of internalization, apart from a focus on communication and discourse. It is hypothesized that even within an international understanding of Vygotsky, there is often a polarized focus within the Cartesian framework, sometimes more so than a focus on the understanding of synthesis and unity that Vygotsky embraced. Various scholars of this polarized understanding then claim that Vygotsky was dualistic, which is not the case from a cultural-historical perspective.

Within the cultural-historical setting, these dichotomies are not viewed as being diametrically opposed to each other, just as the concept of "word" is not viewed as being isolated from its socialized context, unlike in Western linguistics. In attempting to correct the assumed problem of dualism, Wertsch offered two new terms for the concept of internalization, namely, "appropriation" and "mastery." However, Bakhtin used the term "appropriation" in so many contexts that this word is normally associated with his writings; and A.N. Leontiev applied the terms "appropriation" and "mastery" so often that one also thinks of Leontiev's application of this concept.[5] Since no new definitions of these terms have been offered, Wertsch has altered a holistic term within Vygotsky's context, namely, "internalization," and placed it within a dualistic structure, replicating the exact problem he was initially trying to solve. An example of the differences in internalization and appropriation/mastery might be a child who is Jewish needing to recite the Lord's Prayer in private school. It is clear that there are options in place: state the prayer, refuse to state it, or state it with different intentions. The fact is that most people are faced with similar problems on a regular basis, and there is a choice to appropriate or even master the response offered, all of which normally involves a conscious frame of mind. Internalization is different in the sense that it is an internal fusing of meaning, becoming sense, that can almost be felt at the "magic moment" when it is really experienced, sometimes within the sub-conscious, meaning that it "just happens." This moment has a force of its own beyond cognition, and it requires a moment of "catharsis." The spark of inner realignment jolts one to a new recognition. This is a moment of enlightenment we have all experienced, resulting in a new personal growth. The key element is that the potential ingrowth or rooting at the subconscious level may or may not take hold and grow, and if it does, it might not last. The main point in understanding internationalization is that there is always some type of personal transformation involved that is beyond the cognitive, and the result is not always positive. A historical example of this would be the moment when the soul of the German nation accepted Nazism as its predominant ideology, or the moment when real "rooting" took place collectively. This is an example of negative internal-ization where the intentions on the outer level meshed with the uncon-scious mythical Teutonic archetypes. Many Nazi soldiers were therefore willing to fight to their death to defend the fatherland based on the inter-nalized oath that they took to either win or die for Nazi Germany.

In returning to an understanding of mastery/appropriation there is another phenomenon that can be called "mixed mastery/appropriation." An example of this would be the fall of Communism in the Soviet Union. Marxism as a philosophy and economic theory was certainly mastered and appropriated (on a conscious level), but for the majority of Soviets these terms were not internalized (representing both conscious and un[sub]conscious levels). Therefore, the Communist State disintegrated before our eyes. At the same time, many people living in the Soviet Union, and others who were true Marxists, were not totally affected by the fall of Communism because their values were simply anchored at a deeper level, that is they were internalized. It is argued that the concepts of mastery and appropriation not only represent an unneeded dualism but can be reduc-tionistic in nature. For example, Yaroshevsky (1989) stated that

the elucidation by the Vygotsky school of the properly psychological laws of the development of the mind and other psychical functions involved the overcoming of two forms of reductionism—biological...and sociological (which reduced development to the "appropriation" by the child of society's gifts thrust on it by adults). (p. 277)

The understanding of internalization (including both conscious and un[sub]conscious factors), then, is a neutral term that underscores human freedom and will (as used for both good and evil). It is assumed that at the moment of transformation within internalization, neither appropriation nor mastery (which are attributes of the conscious state of being) need to always be in place, at least theoretically. The key elements regarding internalization are meaning (turned to sense) and intention. At the moment when a personal transformation is recognized (via catharsis and other aspects), a person is in a position to understand a key element of Vygotskian thought, namely, self-regulation. The goal of internalization is self-regulation, which represents human free will in the Spinozian sense. The purpose of stressing internalization is to enter the realms of individual self-regulation. Students cannot reach a sense of self-regulation by simply listening to the teacher or lecturer or by appropriating or even mastering the material without a concomitant internal adjustment. For example,

[f]irst, although Vygotsky used terms quite similar in meaning to self-regulation, he never employed the term other-regulation. Second, the use of this pair of terms is often grounded in certain assumptions, some of which may not be consistent with Vygotsky's intent. Specifically, their use implies a kind of direct parallelism between intermental and intramental functioning, something that Vygotsky... actually cautioned against in his comments on internalization. Finally, this parallelism implies a kind of modeling: The tutor models the appropriate forms of regulation to the tutee and the latter takes them over. (Wertsch & Bivens, 1993, p. 208)

The key element to understanding the semiotic nature of internalization is the general genetic law of development:

Any function in the child's cultural development appears twice, or on two planes. First it appears on the social plane, and then on the psychological plane. First it appears between people as an interpsychological [intermental] category, and then within the child as an intrapsychological [intramental] category....[I]t goes without saying that internalization transforms the process itself and changes its structure and functions. Social relations or relations among people genetically underlie all higher functions and their relationships. (Vygotsky, 1981, p. 163)

With all that has been stated, it is argued that the ZPD be viewed primarily as a metatheory. The ZPD, as a construct, deals with the fusion of the individual and the social setting. There is a positioning of the inverse, practical relationship of the general genetic law of development and the ZPD, with the realization that these terms cannot exist separately. This inverse, parallel positioning of internalization/externalization or individual/social, together with the ZPD, should be viewed within the Vygotskian framework of what can be called a "zone of fusion." In other words, the ZPD needs to be discovered as a space within the individual first, then within the social setting. It is, however, directed by the general genetic law of development, assuming the social setting is the first element of description, yet both aspects always work in tandem, never separately. Valsiner and van der Veer (1993) perceived the heart of this argument in the following way:

The ZPD is a concept pertaining to the realm of what kinds of further developmental accomplishments are possible for the given child at the given time in ontogeny, under condition of others' assistance. Therefore it is impossible to determine the empirical boundaries of ZPD in actuality. If the boundaries of ZPD are determined inductively, on the basis of empirical observations, the result of such study is the actualization of some subset of the ZPD, from which it is not possible to determine the full set of ZPD that was existing before the given subset was studied (and actualized by the study). (p. 57)

Life in Soviet Russia within a collective spirit was radically different from life in an individualistic culture. For example, the feeling of any metatheoretical ZPD (or any other similar concept) did not stop the minute school was over, as in the West. A general nurturing existed in the traditional Russian setting that was very different from what existed in an individualistic society. The ZPD was not viewed as being one zone, and the general feeling was that it (or similar constructs) extend outward, not to free speech, but to an internal individual freedom connected to the collective needs of the entire society. The differences of perception regarding the ZPD also represent the irony of life in a society, such as in Soviet Russia, that was traditionally viewed as being "closed," where there was very much of an "opening" in daily life. A closed society tends to have a collective spirit on a daily level, where people who are basically equals watch out for everyone (in both a positive and negative sense). The feeling was that most people were in the "same boat," and there was a lack of personal competition (as opposed to a capitalistic society). Life in all of the former Communist countries afforded a sense of security for children, with the conscious nurturing of children from many sectors of society. At the same time, within Communism it should be clearly stated that the Soviet Union in no way had a classless society. Yet in most Russian neighborhoods under Communism, people lived at a similar economic level. In an individualized "open" society, daily living is often more "closed" for children, with threats of violence coming from many directions. Therefore, some of the unspoken goals within child development of the ZPD in individualized societies regard freedoms such as movement, free speech, and general individual freedoms as not always connected with the needs of society as a whole. This is one reason why the constructivist system of Western education focuses on interaction within the school setting, including some aspects of Vygotskian thinking. Many American educational constructivists (working within a predominantly Piagetian, Cartesian mode of educational philosophy) often see Vygotsky's understanding of internalization as being dualistic. It is not that Vygotsky's concept of internalization is dualistic (although dialectical), but rather that constructivists tend to view it this way through their own lens of interpretation. Within the Soviet Union during Socialism and Communism, the overriding tenets of the ZPD (whether intentional or not) represented a construct to guide the child toward other freedoms, such as the high value placed on education, personal sacrifice for the good of the community, and guidance in learning to love high culture, as well as the freedom to evolve as a human being without having to think of material goods that have been equated with self-worth. To restate: The ZPD in Soviet Russia was not viewed as one zone; it extended beyond the classroom to time after school or with the family. Therefore, one must differentiate between the intentions of the ZPD in different cultures and within different educational settings. In Russia today, many of the psychologists within the Vygotskian tradition are interested in child developmental research that includes "periodization" (e.g., stages of development), within the ZPD. At the same time in the West, the constructivist trend represents a different focus. The aim is to transcend defined stages of child development, in particular the stages outlined by Piaget, by focusing on a wider, more fluid perspective; hence, the tremendous interest in the ZPD in education.

With this in mind, the method used to measure the ZPD is connected to the potential rather than the actual level of development of the child. Valsiner and van der Veer (1993) stated that

the ZBR/ZPD concept has been widely used as a metaphor, and its operationalization has been complicated when attempted. But of course not every theoretical concept in psychology needs operationalization and measurement, and arguments against turning ZPD into another measured characteristic have substance. (p. 57)

Before describing this paradigm, it is assumed that there is agreement with Vygotsky's belief that learning precedes development; however, this is not always the case, and in many areas the ZPD has been taken literally, which has been a source of controversy. Joachim Lompscher (personal communication, 2000) stated that

Vygotsky spoke about instruction or teaching (obuchenie) and development, and that education (including teaching) is a necessary condition for development. When he [Vygotsky] spoke about learning (uchenie), he stressed the difference (and interrelationship). Appropriation or acquisition is not identical with qualitative (and quantitative) mental development, and not the only cause of development. It is teaching (again, not only) that has to bring learning and development together.[6]

Newman and Holzman (1993) argue that "learning is not ahead of development. Learning is not temporally related to development at all. Rather the two form a unity—an active historical completeness" (p. 148).[7] Perhaps Vygotsky would not have totally disagreed with this statement mutatis mutandis, since his objective was to establish a philosophical construct ranging from aesthetics to defectology. "Defectology" refers to the study of human defects; by this term Vygotsky meant the study of brain-damaged

children and adults, as well as the mentally retarded. As a top-down ana-
lyst (who would today be referred to as a global thinker, although he was
also an analytical thinker), Vygotsky took the highest level of ontology he
could imagine as his starting point and measured the problem at hand in
view of the philosophical metastructure he had established. In the case of
the ZPD, a higher cultural-aesthetic consciousness was the unspoken highest level of positioning, assuming that the teacher was extremely competent, as was Vygotsky's own tutor of five years, Solomon Ashpiz. The
teacher/tutor would pass down cultural values to be internally transformed by the student and carried on by the next generation. While Vygotsky in no way endorsed pedantic teaching, or overexerted authority, the
authority he understood and accepted was derived from a competent
teacher, who could instill knowledge and motivate the student. It was the
student who bore the ultimate responsibility of learning, to then reach
autonomous behavior within societal constraints. The goal of such an education was to forge an understanding of internal personal freedom positioned within a higher order of social needs. Ashpiz consciously used the
Socratic method in discussions, which led him to offer a give-and-take
form of argumentation and clarification-modification of conclusions
made.

In using the ZPD within a testing mode, there are no prescribed guidelines for the initial learning situation, which influences the results of testing. Therefore, the entire undertaking becomes confusing from the very
beginning. However, it is precisely the potential for learning that is being
tested; therefore:

[T]o be able to predict the child's future cognitive development the investigator
should (1) establish the child's independently reached IQ score...the child of four
years reaches an independent score of 4.5 age years...; the child, therefore, is scor-
ing slightly above the average performance of his age group. The next step is (2) to
establish the child's score in joint performance, that is the child can make use of
various hints and prompts and is shown part of the solution, etc. Under this cir-
cumstance the child in our example is able to solve the tasks up to a mental age of
7 years' old. ...The child thus has a zone of proximal development of 2.5 mental
age years. We now can predict, according to Vygotsky, that in the next 2.5 years our
child's independent performance will become progressively better until it has
reached the level of the joint performance measured at the age of four. This level
will be reached after two and a half years have passed. (van der Veer & Valsiner,
1991, p. 342)

In viewing the literal results of such testing, to then extrapolate the results
on to the L2 adult learner, unusual results could be the norm. In fact, this
type of testing procedure within the ZPD has been criticized:

We would like to argue that testing the zone of proximal development as a means
of diagnosis requires a detailed task analysis of possible transfer probes. Without

this information it would be difficult to select either the series of graduated aids for the original learning task or suitable methods for assessing the speech and efficiency of transfer. In the Soviet diagnostic sessions, what is being measured is the efficiency of learning within any one-task domain. (Brown & Ferrara, 1985, p. 284)

And although Brown and Ferrara (1985) posited the fact that children may have a narrow ZPD in one domain and a broader zone within another part of the ZPD (p. 297), it is, in some respects, a typical reaction to Vygotsky's metaphor in general. Indeed, testing within the ZPD was an instrument that could be implemented, but it clearly involves a mixing of realities (i.e., the present, where approximated measuring devices can be used to infer knowledge, and the future, where outcome variables are not guaranteed, and where other variables cannot be mathematically secured). Vygotsky was obviously attempting to level the playing field of abstract, objectified measurements (i.e., IQ tests), which could easily determine the realistic expectation of a child's future development, including potential, future-oriented variables. Vygotsky's example of testing for potential development offers food for thought and can certainly be adapted to different testing situations.[8]

The preceding paragraphs regard the ZPD from a Western perspective. The Russian concept of the potential age of the child is very different and extremely important for understanding the overall context of the ZPD. Vygotsky's ideas on the potential age of the child were written in 1932 and were not published in Russia until 1983. G. V. Burmenskaia (1997) wrote:

Instead of separating processes and function as has been traditional in psychology (e.g., perception, attention, and thinking), researchers need to analyze holistic age periods. These periods have independent and structured dynamics, which determine "the role and weighted significance of every particular line of development" (Vygotsky, 1983[4], p. 256).... But what is a child's psychological age? Vygotsky described psychological age as "the new type of structures of personality and activity, those psychic and social changes that initially appeared at a given age stage and that determine the child's consciousness, his attitudes toward the environment, his inner and outer life, and all content of his development at a given period" (Vygotsky, 1983[4], p. 248).... Psychological age, therefore, is viewed as a triarchic formation with a complex structure and dynamics. (pp. 221–222)[9]

The most important point within the ZPD in the Russian understanding is the triadic component: (1) the age of crisis; (2) as a result of the crisis (also understood as the potential of development), the old situation of development is being destroyed; (3) an opening for new possibilities of development within another age stage (cf. Burmenskaia, 1997, pp. 221–222).

As Vygotsky (1998) claimed,

an ordered picture opens before us. Critical periods alternate with stable periods and are turning points in development, once again, confirming that the development of the child is a dialectical process in which a transition from one stage to another is accomplished not along an evolutionary, but along a revolutionary path. (p. 193)

The recognition of both stable versus critical periods of development—both forming a unity in personality formation, education, or the learning of a second language—present the opportunity of new research and new understanding.

EXAMPLES OF THE ZPD IN PRACTICE

It has often been noted that Vygotsky's major contribution to education was his concept of the ZPD. Scholars in various countries have written so many articles on the ZPD that it would be impossible to review all of them. Only a few selected examples are presented here, beginning with the research tradition in the former Yugoslavia, which has maintained a symbol-constructive nature regarding human development. Scholars within this tradition have viewed internalized experiences within a semiotic analysis of iconic systems (figural, nonverbal phenomena that occur in symbolic play and dreaming)[10] (cf. Valsiner & van der Veer, 1993, p. 55). This approach includes the following:

The main aim for this empirical elaboration is to retain the complementarity of the adult-child joint action in different contexts defined in respect to the child's process of development. The latter aim leads the researchers to view the ZPD in relation to other domains (or zones) of experience. Zone of Actual Development, Zone of Future Development, and Zone of Past Development (see Ignjatovic-Savic et al., 1988, p. 110). The developmental process proceeds by moving some aspects of joint activity from the Zone of Future Development to ZPD, and subsequently to Zone of Past Development. Phenomena from these different zones can be observed in microgenetic task settings intermittently—reminding otherwise all too enthusiastic Vygotskians that not every aspect of joint action is actually productive for further development. (Valsiner & van der Veer, 1993, p. 55)

Another approach has been established by Jaan Valsiner, based somewhat on the tradition of the ecocultural theory proposed by J. W. M. Whiting, elaborated by Charles Super and Sara Harkness (cited in Cole, 1996):

Jaan Valsiner (1987) distinguishes niches with respect to the role of adult involvement in a manner that complements the positions sketched out so far. The innermost level of the developmental niche is called the Zone of Free Movement (ZFM);

it structures the child's access to different parts of the environment, exposure to different objects and events, and ways of acting. Within the ZFM, adults promote children's actions in various ways, creating the Zone of Promoted Action (ZPA). According to this scheme, Vygotsky's idea of a Zone of Proximal Development (ZPD) is treated as a ZPA so matched to the child's present developmental state that it guides the child's further development. Each way of structuring interactions provides essential constraints enabling development. (Cole, 1996, p. 188)

Another example is Barbara Rogoff's fusion of person and culture, and although an interesting model, it does not include Vygotsky's understanding of internalization:

Starting from an interest in neo-Gibsonian ecological psychology on the one hand, and Leontiev's version of Vygotsky's perspective on the other…[Rogoff] moved to view the ZPD as a framework in which the stretching of the child's skill and understanding takes place.…The event (interactive setting) that is constructed jointly by the active (goal-oriented) child and the other person who is more knowledgeable about the cultural ways of acting than the child (but equally goal-oriented) becomes the unit of analysis of the guided participation process as the context for human development. (Valsiner & van der Veer, 1993, p. 54)

Another example was offered by Newman, Griffin, and Cole (1989) called the "construction zone," which is

a magic place where minds meet, where things are not the same to all who see them, where meanings are fluid, and where one person's construal may preempt another's.…Imagine, if you like, two people whose activities are linked together following relatively simple rhythms, routines, and prompts. The low-level cues sustain the activity, though the meanings and understandings possessed by each actor may be quite different. Through such shared activity a teacher may create (in Courtney Cazden's phrase) competence before performance or a zone of proximal development (ZPD). (pp. ix–xi)

Cole, a few years earlier, extended the ZPD to include collectively organized activity (cf. Valsiner & van der Veer, 1993, p. 52), with an emphasis on what Cole called mutual construction of culture and person:

In that joint activity, an individual person indeed develops from present to future on the basis of ideal models of the future, and of the past.…However, the emphasis on collective shared activities leads Cole into the theoretically central adoption of the Soviet focus on activity theory in general terms, and of the concept of leading activity in particular. This extension of Vygotsky's ideas to the domain of activity theory leads to the establishment of a hybrid theory.…Although an explicit emphasis here is made upon internal operations and internalization, the major focus remains on the different kinds of activities in which the child is embedded. (Valsiner & van der Veer, 1993, p. 53)

DOMINANT ACTIVITY WITHIN THE ZPD

Another area of importance relating to both development and the ZPD from the Russian perspective is the inclusion of the area of dominant activity. D. B. El'konin (Elkonin) completed much research and investigation in this area, claiming that every mental phenomenon occurring within a given period should be examined in the light of its dominant activity. There are two kinds of dominant activity for the child:

activity with things, during which the child assimilates socially elaborated means for coping with the real world about him; and activity with people, during which he learns the objectives and aims of the activity of adults and the social relations among them. (A. K. Marková, 1978, p. 189)

El'konin specified the ages and dominant activities as shown in figure 2 (cf. A. K. Marková, 1978, p. 201). The suggestion is that children move through dominant activities, which are sequentially specific:

Elkonin's schema of dominant activities has the following educational implications. First of all, it places a particular emphasis on the formation of learning activity in the primary school. If this activity is not formed in the primary school, it is twice as difficult to form later, because the focus of a child's interests shifts from learning to interpersonal relations. One may notice that his approach is at variance with educational practices in many Western countries, where primary-school curricula respond more to the needs of the child's socialization and general knowledge acquisition than to the acquisition of learning skills per se. (Kozulin & Presseisen, 1995, p. 73)

In comparing El'konin's stages of dominant activity to Vygotsky's overall psychology-philosophy, there are clearly major differences; as well, Vygotsky's understanding was more descriptive than prescriptive. "Child development is such a complex process that it cannot be determined at all

Figure 2.
El'konin's categories of dominant activities (cf. A. K. Marková, 1978, p. 201).

Age		Types of Social Interaction
0—1	infancy	social—emotional interaction
1—3	early preschool	operations with objects
3—7	preschool	play
7—10	early school	study
10—15	middle school	social interaction and communication
15—17	early adulthood	vocational study
17—60	later adulthood and maturity	vocational—social activity

completely according to one trait alone at any stage" (Vygotsky, 1998, p. 188). Even though Vygotsky specified ages of crises, periodization(s) (e.g., at ages 1, 3, 7, 13, and 17), he did not set out to offer descriptive stages of child development as did Piaget, and apparently El'konin's stages of dominant activity.

Vygotsky's theories of periodization of child development should be understood as a reflection of his entire theoretical structure. For example, within a macrophilosophical understanding of Vygotsky's complete system, the dialectic (e.g., asymmetrical, dynamic movement) fits within Spinoza's philosophical construct of monism. Put simply, the dynamic process of change is situated within a higher, more absolute understanding. However, this does not mean that monism is static. Within periodization, in other words, stages of child development, innate encoding levels of predetermined periods of crises (the word "crisis" can also be understood as "potential for development") are placed within the dynamic positioning of concept development. Together, this forms a living whole, extending beyond the limitations of existing psychological theories of Western child development. In other words, the absolute sense of predetermined periods of crises in child development is positioned within the dynamic flow of concept development. To state this graphically:

Overall Vygotskian Psychology-Philosophy
    dialectic (relative) ⇔ monism (absolute)   (1)

Periodization of Child Development: Changing Roles of
    Concept formation (relative) ⇔ innate (absolute)   (2)

Although Vygotsky spoke of periods of crises of development, he had a much higher vision in mind. This understanding included what could happen regarding the potential development at a certain age if the conditions were right, but not "demanding" that these changes take place at a precise moment. In other words, children have space and room to move within their own development. At the same time, "neither the presence nor the absence of some specific external conditions, but internal logic of the process of development itself is responsible for the critical, disruptive periods in the life of the child" (Vygotsky, 1998, p. 192). Vygotsky's psychology/philosophy maintained a focus on the synthesis of the individual-social or dialectic-monism, hence the "zone of fusion." There is also a synthesis of the age of crisis that promotes developmental change in the child, including a focus on external and internal factors.

An interesting paradox regards Vygotsky's views of child development as being so metatheoretical that apart from the crises of age development, it is suggested that his theories of concept formation can even be applied to adult learning, with discernment. This hypothesizing can take place only when we understand that the levels of child development can be viewed as a metapsychology. This all-encompassing philosophy of child development focuses on development as a continual process. Valsiner and van der Veer (2000) have stated that Vygotsky "was no child psychologist but a psychologist who became increasingly interested in the theoretical problem of development, which led him to study cultural diversity, brain pathology, and other disciplines" (p. 339).

In Western research there has been little discussion regarding Vygotsky's ages of crises in child development, as opposed to the Piagetian stages of development. At the same time, had Vygotsky not died so young, he would have surely revised his theories of periodization. It is difficult to accept his theories of periodization as being written in stone. For example, Vygotsky stopped writing about periods of age crisis after a young person reached the age of seventeen. Today, there are many questions: Are these ages of crisis consistent and universal across cultures? Do these ages of crises hold today as when they were proposed in the 1930s? Are the ages of crises the same for boys and girls? Are these ages of crises the same for children in developed and developing countries? Can these ages of crises be extended to include adult learning?[11] Many of these questions have not yet been raised in the West, and they offer a rich area of potential research to expand Vygotsky's psychology/philosophy.

In returning to the role of the ZPD, the discussion of periodization is important not only vis-à-vis the zone of fusion of individual and social development, but also in relation to the internal and external development of the child. For example, the "actual and potential levels of development correspond with intramental and intermental functioning, respectively.... It [ZPD] can be seen as having powerful implications for how one can change intermental, and hence intramental, function" (Wertsch & Tulviste, 1992, p. 550). In changing mental functioning, the role of inner speech and self-regulation once again resurfaces, with the important aspect here of mediation taking on a new and important meaning within the school setting. In the past, little has been written on the ZPD related to inner speech and self-regulation, or on the internal development of the child, as opposed to her development within an intersubjective level.

The next section bridges the ZPD and ages of crisis with a view to the flexible core of Vygotsky's model of scientific (here, academic) concepts and spontaneous (here, everyday life) concepts. The example of second language acquisition will used as the point of reference.

SCIENTIFIC AND SPONTANEOUS CONCEPTS RELATED TO A SECOND LANGUAGE

For Vygotsky, classical philosophical *necessity* accompanied his understanding of consciousness, and within the school setting the concept of *necessity* should be regarded together with mediation and internalization.

Just as scientific/academic concepts are learned in a typical school setting, they must also be mediated by spontaneous, everyday concepts in order to be meaningful. If the scientific concept represents the side that dominates throughout schooling, then the result will simply be verbalism.[12] For example, within the foreign language classroom, there is often a reversal of expectations that the students bring to the classroom, particularly at the university level. Students expect to learn the foreign language within a normal academic setting; however, they are often taught the second language (L2) within the setting of spontaneous concepts. Therefore, from the beginning, L2 students are sometimes confused when the L2 classroom is very playful, with motivating exercises, when in reality the student usually expects learning to take place within a typical college atmosphere of scientific (i.e., academic) concepts. Very often, the L2 textbook begins with attempts to introduce familiar, everyday concepts such as one would find in the real world, hence the simulation of spontaneous concepts. The learning strategies used are often based on the theories of innovative methods, which aim at motivating the learner and placing the learner in a situation of direct response. The basic problem is that many foreign language courses in high schools and universities simply mix up different approaches of spontaneous concepts, often using that approach for learning difficult linguistic structures, and then switch to the mode of scientific/nonspontaneous concepts when administrating traditional tests. This teaching approach results in confusion for many students and is one reason why it is often difficult to internalize the linguistic structures taught. As a result, many students in the West give up their learning of a foreign language because of the slowness and difficulty involved in the process, all of which might be explained by E. Claparéde's law of awareness (which Piaget supplemented with the law of shift or displacement):

To become conscious of a mental operation means to transfer it from the plane of action to that of language, i.e., to recreate it in the imagination so that it can be expressed in words. This change is neither quick nor smooth. The law states that mastering an operation on the higher plane of verbal thought presents the same difficulties as the earlier mastering of that operation on the plane of action. This accounts for the slow progress. (Vygotsky, 1994a, p. 164)

Vygotsky spoke humorously about the aspect of need: "[T]o say that awareness appears as a result of a child's need to become aware of something amounts to a claim that wings originate in a bird's need to fly" (Vygotsky, 1994a, p. 64). It is interesting that El'konin's understanding of the dominant activity for college-age students is vocational and social activity, which corresponds to a new approach in teaching foreign languages for specific needs, such as Spanish for nurses, German for physicians, French for tourism, and so on. The paradox is that there is a tremendous need to learn Spanish for specific purposes in the United

States; however, very few traditional Spanish courses, which normally focus on grammatical structures, can be entirely replaced by newer, less grammatical, approaches. Also, in learning to express oneself in a foreign language, a concept does not always exist behind the word; therefore, learners often speak empty words that are nonmotivated, and this is especially true in many traditional foreign language courses. In many presentations of L2 material within spontaneous, everyday life, the ideal goal behind the lesson plan is to present the family, or restaurant, or post office, as being similar to one's own familiar surroundings. Often there is an overexerted attempt to find the similarities between target cultures and the home culture. However, with children, Vygotsky discovered that the "child becomes aware of differences earlier than of likenesses, not because differences lead to malfunctioning, but because similarity requires a more advanced structure of generalization and conceptualization than awareness of dissimilarity" (Vygotsky, 1994a, p. 15). In the foreign language classroom, differences of the target culture are usually developed as stereotypes by the time the adolescent starts her first foreign language, and certainly by the college level; therefore, pointing out obvious cultural differences remains superficial and is not motivating. L2 students should have the opportunity to conceptualize even controversial cultural differences as well as similarities, and these areas should be presented in a framework of strategies that interest the L2 student. Later, after the student has developed the concept behind the foreign word, another step can be taken, called "displacement" or colloquially, "putting oneself in someone else's shoes." This process is also known as the phenomenological "bracketing principle" of suspending judgment, or "disobjectivation." This process may be artificial at the beginning stages, but mediated internalization can occur with more genuineness. Displacement (not equal to Freud's use of the term) means that the student can transport him or herself into a different realm of reality, for example, the target language and culture, and be able to cross-reference identity. This process implies the successful completion of the hermeneutic circle, which assumes that internal structuring (i.e., semantic, value-oriented, aesthetic aspects) will not only result in an internal change of understanding the world, but, above all, will invoke a better understanding of oneself. If meaningful dominant activities are in place,[13] assuming that they are derived from actual student interests and needs (and are not established a priori), then a tolerance for ambiguity will surely accompany development, as well as genuine interest in the subject matter.

For years, this author attempted to use the idea of El'konin's leading activity in beginning university-level Spanish classes. It was interesting to assume that the goal of any college-level Spanish course would be easy: learn how to communicate with native speakers for better job opportunities. However, the instructor established the goal, as in any other university course, predetermining the particular activity that was supposed to underlie the goal of being able to speak with a native speaker in Spanish. All students were required to have a thirty-minute taped interview in Spanish by the end of the semester.

Although many students had the same goal as the teacher (i.e., to speak Spanish for professional purposes), the means were different for each student. Some students resented being forced to have only one (teacher-dominated) path toward a common goal. Here is the approach used: In proceeding from the understanding of a dominant activity, as well as attempting to design course work based on the enhancement of each individual (within the construct of personality development), a simple format was used at the undergraduate university level.[14] The primary interest within the dominant activity of undergraduates is to instill an orientation toward future professional life and social interaction. The students were asked to form groups according to similar majors. These groups were further divided into minigroups, with conscious rules being implemented during the entire semester, all of which was designed to help students establish a classroom atmosphere with student empowerment. As a result, a collective teaching matrix was established. From the perspective of the teacher, there was a single goal for all of the groups, which was twofold: (1) to acquire enough Spanish vocabulary, grammar, and syntax, to be able to carry on an interview with a native speaker using only Spanish by the end of the semester; and (2) to use computers to research and find Spanish-language materials of interest relating to their future profession(s). In order to increase learner motivation and to foster language acquisition, this information would then be used to contact Spanish native speakers or to write for information that would help the students to make a personal and lasting connection and commitment to the Spanish language for later use.

In order to activate these principles, initial work was completed at the beginning of the semester, including establishing a positive image for the course work and making a commitment to work together during the entire semester. The linguistic goals established for the entire group were explained and broken down so that the textbook would be regularly used for one purpose only: to allow everyone in the class to be able to conduct an interview with a native speaker toward the end of the semester in the target language only. The operations listed were: (1) initial vocabulary work; (2) an introduction of oneself and family with pictures to the group; (3) interview questions prepared in class; (4) an oral mid-term with the professor only, using the list of questions already prepared by the entire group; (5) in-class interviews with students in other minigroups; (6) a capstone experience, with a Spanish native speaker (an international student) coming to class while the students asked their interview questions, speaking only Spanish for fifty minutes; (7) An interview with one of the Spanish professors at the university; and (8) the videotaped interview with the native speaker, in Spanish only. The purpose of this project was twofold: The first was to allow students to feel that continued hard work would indeed place them in a position to conduct the interview in Spanish by the end of the semester. Students who had gone through this process in previous semesters were asked to speak to the class to demonstrate that this goal could be accomplished if students used outside study time to focus on their goal. Second, by working in a minigroup—with students having the same major or similar professional interests—students were motivated to research different ways to use Spanish in their future professions. Students started to share what they learned with one another and discuss that information both in and outside of the classroom. At some point during the semester, some of the students started meeting socially to discuss topics or research on the Internet, and friendships were slowly formed. The results of this particular project were not compared with traditional classroom settings. However, in viewing and listening to the videotapes, the proficiency achieved was remarkable for first-semester students. In many cases, the most prized achievement was not their ability in spoken Spanish per se, but their ability to deal with the language itself as used by native speakers. In other words, on many of the interview videotapes, the native speakers started the conversation with extremely simplified Spanish, some of whom realized that the affective filter (i.e., personal barrier resistance to the target language) was lower than normal in many of the beginning students. At that point, the speed of the spoken Spanish rapidly increased; sometimes the native speakers were talking at the same rate as they would to other native speakers. Of course, the student interviewers could not understand all—or even most—of what was being said, but they simply were not intimidated and would either listen or ask for clarification in Spanish. Although this particular project was student oriented, the role of the teacher was very traditional; lectures on Spanish grammar, traditional tests, and language laboratory hours were all required. The normal power mechanisms were still very much in place regarding the role of the teacher. The approach of a leading activity was a step beyond the traditional focus of beginning foreign language studies. This approach, however, did not focus on the real interests and needs of the students, but rather on the presumed needs assumed by the instructor. Students were not allowed to be truly creative and to establish goals for themselves. This approach was then abandoned in favor of allowing more student input into the entire course, and more general creativity on the part of students in the classroom, with the inclusion of service learning. New Spanish courses were devised for which students were able to assess their own needs and interests and to help them become involved in Hispanic communities and volunteer with Latinos as a part of the Spanish course. Students could then construct their own goals and their own dominant activity and receive a certificate for the time they donated to working with the Latino community.

Within this model it was discovered that students need to have a teacher who is not just a coordinator of constructivist interaction in the classroom. The foreign language classroom of the twenty-first century will hopefully be an instrument for individual change and growth, and a means of passing down values that will be internalized and transformed by each single student for his or her personality development. It is for this reason that the role of the teacher will need to be reevaluated at many levels, from the level of the student to the higher levels of the administrators.

CONCLUSIONS REGARDING THE ZPD

In closing this chapter, the overall concept of the ZPD should be placed within the understanding of a metatheory, and there are as many understandings of the ZPD as there are scholars to contemplate it. For example, Vera John-Steiner has identified the ZPD as "the gift of dignity," while Gordon Wells spoke of the ZPD within "personal transformation," and Tim Murphey created the zone of approximal adjustments.[15] Instead of aiming at one definition of the ZPD, readers are encouraged to come up with their own working definition, one that will surely change and evolve over time. One must also be clear in establishing what the ZPD is not: for example, it is not a theory of learning, nor a method, nor a strategy. It does not involve the teaching of discrete, separable skills, and it is not always positive. The ZPD must have a regression factor involved for development to progress. There is not just one ZPD, but multiple zones operating simultaneously and changing at variable rates. Lois Holzman (1997) stated that the ZPD is not a zone; it is an activity and a life space. The ZPD is also a metaphor for total "consciousness expansion," and once teachers and learners grasp the expansive nature of personal empowerment, and what this implies for the classroom and for general living, methods and strategies will automatically evolve. The following list covers many of the areas of the ZPD as it is understood within Vygotskian theory:

1. The ZPD deals with the *potential* of the learner and teacher, focusing on the potentiality situated within a height psychology—as opposed to a depth psychology—where Freudian paradigms of the unconscious are understood within multiple personal problems. Height psychology, or Vygotskian psychology (sometimes referred to as nonclassical psychology),[16] incorporates the heights of potentiality of the individual, also including unconscious components; at the same time, the unconscious is viewed as the seat of creativity and problem solving.[17]

2. The ZPD relates to *functions that are not yet emergent.* Vygotsky used the term "functional" in reference to Horndike's "faculty psychology" (Lee, 1985,

p. 70).[18] Mike Cole referred to a concept developed by Rommetveit (1974) called "prolepsis." The example of adults reacting to a baby offers a good picture of prolepsis. Adults speak baby talk to very young infants, but they also speak an adult version of language as well. Adults do not expect the infant to respond in a proper fashion but assume that the infant will grow into the community and one day will be able to use social language. This example demonstrates that we often forget to use prolepsis within the educational setting. At this point, the focus should be on the potential versus the actual age of the learner. The goal is to view the learner within his or her highest potential age, not as he or she communicates today (cf. Cole, 1996, pp. 183–184).

3. The *personal transformation concept* represents the demonstrative aspect of the ZPD, which is necessary to internally comprehend if one has actually experienced the ZPD in a personal way. Personal transformation in no way implies a positive experience all of the time. In fact, regression must be accounted for if there is to be real growth and development.

4. The next two aspects form a unit that focuses on overcoming Cartesian dualisms. The first area Vygotsky called "dialectical unity." This process involves "a dialectical process in which the transition from one step to another is accomplished not by evolutionary, but by a revolutionary path—we need to concentrate not on the product of development, but on the very process by which higher forms are established" (Vygotsky, quoted in Lee, 1985, pp. 71–72). Within dialectical unity the underlying principle is the general genetic law of development that must set the boundaries of the ZPD.[19] The traditional definition of the ZPD is "the distance between the actual developmental level as determined by independent problem solving and the level of potential development as determined through problem solving under adult guidance or in collaboration with more capable peers" (Vygotsky, 1978, p. 86). The second area is called the "unity of development—overcoming dualisms." Within the ZPD there is no listing of stages of development, as found in Piaget's epistemological educational psychology. Vygotsky described critical stages of crises in child development (e.g., at years 1, 3, 7, 13, and 17); however, this labeling was descriptive rather than prescriptive. One should not fall victim to general dualisms, such as learning precedes development (where development is believed to precede learning in many traditional approaches of educational psychology). Both learning *and* development must go hand in hand with good teaching for growth to take place within the educational setting.

5. The Cartesian scientific method of focusing on product will not be an integral part of the ZPD; rather, the focus will be on *process.*

6. The basic paradox of the ZPD is contained within *assessment.* For the most part, the ZPD is placed within the traditional educational system around the world, without assessment being changed. For the ZPD to maintain a viable presence, classroom assessment will have to be completely restructured. One of the worst areas of adaptation of assessment within the ZPD to date is to simply create an atmosphere of "group work" or "team" testing, with the teacher serving the role as facilitator, to then assign a traditional grade. If this type of assessment is used, it is suggested that three elements be offered toward the final grade: student (personal) grade, teacher grade, and small group grade for

each student. In reality, when taking the ZPD seriously, the traditional mode of testing and grading will be completely questioned and revised.

7. *Internalization and personality.* A part of the ZPD that can be operationalized is concept development, which represents stages leading to rooting or ingrowth. These moments are accompanied by the experience of catharsis, or the magic moment where it all "clicks." The internal transformation that takes place affects the whole personality. This is not a call to implement a difficult study of semiotics related to personality, but to simply view the entire personality of each student as a whole. Within Cartesian science and much traditional educational practice, the psychology of personality is still viewed in atomistic parts, such as motivation, anxiety, personality types, styles of learning, and empathy. These traits are often viewed separately and not holistically. It is suggested that the ZPD contain an awareness of internalization related to the entire personality of both the participant and the teacher. For a good summary on this issue, see Gordon Wells (1999, pp. 315–319).

8. *Role of the expert versus the role of the competent peer.* Within the ZPD, the role of the expert will be reevaluated in terms of its needs. What is an expert? When is an expert truly needed? Should we develop the same trust toward competent peers? How has the role of expert changed over the past twenty years?

9. To learn in the ZPD does not require that there be a designated teacher. "Development does not have any predetermined end, or telos" (Wells, 1999, p. 333).

10. The ZPD is not just a cognitive zone. The ZPD should include some aspect of *play*. Lois Holzman (1997) stated that two of the most important tools for the ZPD are creative imitation and completion. Imitation was important for Vygotsky as it related to the ZPD, and he stated: "Speaking of imitation, we do not have in mind mechanical, automatic, thoughtless imitation but sensible imitation based on understanding the imitative carrying out of some intellectual operation. In this respect, on the one hand, we restrict the meaning of the term, using it only in the sphere of operations that are more or less directly connected with mental activity of the child" (Vygotsky, 1998, p. 202).

11. Within the ZPD, there should be a focus on pliability and reshaping the principles of learning in general. This new freedom of movement, thought, and action should be directed at *unfossilizing* older ways of thinking that have become rigid and do not allow for new learning. Carol Lerch (2001) has written about the philosophy of unfossilization when teaching math to adults: "I propose a process to unfossilize learning and develop new connections by using similar contexts, parallel concepts, or processes. New links to the fossilized end points are developed. Connections are made, and new categories are created. The old knowledge is reconnected, the new knowledge is added to the categories, and the students develop a broader understanding of the relationships involved. Unfossilization is not the same as relearning since relearning involves repeating the original process, retracing the same strands" (p. 81).

12. *Situation redefinition* is "something that involves giving up a previous situation definition in favor of a qualitatively new one" (Wertsch, 1984, p. 11).

13. *Contextualization of the ZPD.* Vygotsky's ZPD was outlined during the last two years of his life, and it was written in response to his work with handicapped

children. The ZPD was a concept dealing with the interrelatedness of the individual and society, and to a collective social undertaking within Marxism. In the West, the ZPD is often regarded as a model of constructivist interaction among students, as opposed to teacher-centered lecturing. However, within the Russian context, related to children, it is understood that the adult/teacher is in charge of creating the steps that will eventually allow the child to develop culturally and mentally. Even in the most innovative schools in Russia, classroom management is totally in the hands of the teacher and those in charge of the curriculum, who meet collectively on a regular basis. Every school day has activities that are completely planned, and the concept of spontaneity that accompanies the Western understanding of the ZPD is understood differently in Russia. In Russian education there is full participation among the students, often within a creative atmosphere. There is a basic focus on internalizing and reproducing deep-seated cultural values that are important in forming the personality of the Russian child; thus, Russian children acquire a multitude of capabilities allowing them to be creative on their own, with the least amount of processed materials. In the West, the ZPD is viewed as an open space (as opposed to the Piagetian lockstep approach), where inter/intramental development can take place between/within students via group projects, interaction, and a focus on finding innovative solutions within a student-centered (as opposed to a teacher-centered) approach. However, children in the West do not always leave school with the internal skills to be creative at home and with their friends. Western educators would benefit tremendously from a visit to innovative schools in Russia, or any collective society; and Russians would benefit from more exposure to Western schools. Interestingly, thousands of educators from the West and East have one word they both agree upon, the ZPD; yet, this concept is viewed from radically different perspectives.

14. *The ultimate paradox.* Russian psychology and education have less focus on the term ZPD than in the West. If anything, the ZPD is a natural metaphor in Russia, not only within the classroom but ultimately beyond the school setting, for purposes of internalization and personal growth of the individual. There is strict direction and leadership of the teachers, together with the collective or teaching laboratory (curriculum team) that updates and changes the curriculum. The Russian focus within Vygotsky's ZPD is on periodization (e.g., stages of development), referring to the ages of crises that translate into potential leaps of development. The process of mental development of the individual as connected to the needs of society is emphasized. In the United States, Jean Piaget's stages of development have been most influential in education, not only within the lockstep method, but also within national testing. Therefore, the ZPD is viewed as a more flexible approach to negotiated learning and to solving problems, often without a priori solutions given by teachers. Students and teachers are viewed as a team that interact and learn together. However, the overall focus of the ZPD in the West is not on process, but still on product, normally nationalized testing. Even though the ZPD is very popular at all levels of education in the United States, it is confined to the school setting (not to life after school), and it is still based upon the Cartesian understanding of dualism between the individual and society.

In closing, Newman and Holzman's (1996) new definition of the ZPD is offered:

A ZPD is a form of life in which people collectively and relationally create developmental learning that goes beyond what any individual in the group could learn on her or his own. Our effort is to create continuously overlapping ZPDs, a particular relational activity that simultaneously is and makes possible the transforming of rigified behavior (forms of life that have become alienated and fossilized) into new forms of life. (p. 71)

The next chapter discusses the similarities and dissimilarities of constructivism and constructionism related to Vygotsky, with a review of the ZPD. Vygotsky is often viewed as a contemporary constructivist in the field of education; however, this position should be viewed critically.

NOTES

1. See van der Veer and Valsiner (1991, p. 327).

2. See Sinha (1988, p. 103) for a critique of Vygotsky's idea of internalization and development in general. Also, see Jerry Fodor (1972, pp. 83–95).

3. "Vygotsky pointed out that Meumann and others had suggested that we should establish at least two levels of child development, namely, what the child can do already and what the child's potential is" (van der Veer & Valsiner, 1991, p. 329).

4. "By rejecting Vygotsky's strong emphasis on word meaning as a unit of analysis, and extending it toward text—semiotic mediation through Bakhtin's ideas...the ZPD concept is substantively enhanced" (Valsiner & van der Veer, 1993, p. 52). This statement is offered as information, not as an agreement.

5. "A key concept for explaining how cognitive change can happen is suggested by a distinction made by Vygotsky's colleague, Leont'ev (1981). While accepting the fundamental notion put forth by Piaget that children actively construct their knowledge through interaction with the environment, A. N. Leont'ev replaces Piaget's concept of assimilation with the concept of appropriation" (Newman, Griffin, & Cole, 1989, p. 62).

6. Personal e-mail correspondence, August 25, 2000.

7. Newman and Holzman (1993, p. 212) stated the following in a footnote: "It might strike readers as contradictory that we are saying learning is not ahead of development, given that Vygotsky says it is. Our point is that the language used connotes linearity or temporality, and, more generally, instrumentation."

8. The role of dynamic assessment has not been developed in this chapter. Refer to Carol Lidz, 2000.

9. Vygotsky's theories "on the problem of age" can be found in English in *The Collected Works of L. S. Vygotsky*, Vol. 5, Chapter 6 (1998, pp. 187–205). Burmenskaia was quoting from the Russian *The Collected Works of L. S. Vygotsky* ([Sobranie sochineny] El'konin, 1984).

10. See Ignjatovic-Savie, Kovac-Cerovic, Plut, & Pesikan, 1988.

11. Elena Kravtsova (Vygotsky's granddaughter), Gennadi Kravtsov, and Elena Berezhkovskaya use the stages of age crises (periodization) in their school

program in Russia, Golden Key. They understand the ages of crises as being descriptive and not totally prescriptive, and they have extended these points of crises (i.e., meaning the potential for personal growth) to ages twenty-two to twenty-four. Their view of child development within the ages of crises is placed within the ZPD, with an adult guiding the learning process. However, from ages twenty-two to twenty-four, they view the ZPD of the young adult within the construct of self-regulation and professional consciousness.

12. See Vygotsky (1994a, p. 149).

13. "Vygotsky's work on dominant reactions was not merely founded on an idea borrowed from literary analysis, for the study had become a 'hot topic' in the discourse of Russian psychologists, due to the publication by Ukhtomsky (1924; 1927) and other physiologists and psychologists who were also involved in related research....Ukhtomsky's idea of the dominant—the nervous center that at any given time coordinates the unity of an organism's behavior—was far more appealing to Vygotsky....Ukhtomsky's dominate was interesting for Vygotsky as a means of linking his own theories of emotional synthesis in art reception to the triggering of new holistic functional units in the human psyche as a whole" (van der Veer & Valsiner, 1991, p. 32–33).

14. Examples used by the author at Central Missouri State University from 1995 to 1998.

15. All of these associations were mentioned by Vera John-Steiner, Gordon Wells, and Tim Murphey at the American Association of Applied Linguistics conference, March 14, 2000 in Vancouver, British Columbia. The symposium was titled "Vygotsky's Zone of Proximal Development within L2 Pedagogy."

16. See D. Robbins (1999, pp. v–xii), prologue to *The Collected Works of L. S. Vygotsky*, Vol. 6.

17. "If superficial psychology (for example, behaviorism) passes appearance off as essence, and if depth psychology derives psychical existence from the sphere of the unconscious and the unconscious itself does not develop, that is, if depth psychology is in principle antisocial and antihistorical, then only our 'height psychology' is truly scientific, social, and historical psychology" (A. A. Leontyev, 1992, p. 42).

18. "Consciousness is not an attribute of any particular state or process such as attention or memory, but rather an attribute of the way in which such states are organized and functionally related both to behavior and each other" (Lee, 1985, p. 70).

19. This idea was derived from reading Lois Holzman (1997, pp. 58–59).

CHAPTER 4

Constructivism (Construction-ism) and Teacher-Ability

INTRODUCTION TO CONSTRUCTIVISM AND CONSTRUCTIONISM

Vygotsky has been labeled a constructivist and is often quoted within the current understanding of constructivism, yet a direct reference to Vygotsky as a modern-day constructivist is not entirely appropriate. Within this section the two terms "constructivism" and "constructionism" are not differentiated. However, constructionism foregrounds the social setting, whereas constructivism foregrounds the individual in the social setting.

Both constructionism and constructivism share in their critique of the empiricist paradigm of knowledge generation. In this sense, each is skeptical of the foundationalist warrants of logical empiricist philosophers. Rather, each challenges the traditional view of the individual mind as a device for reflecting the character and conditions of an independent world. (Gergen, 1995, p. 27)

One of the reasons Vygotsky is often cited as being a constructivist is that he used this terminology. For example, Vygotsky wrote that

a constructive method implies two things: (1) it studies constructions rather than natural structures; (2) it does not analyze, but construes a process (contra a method of grasping unexpectedly, analysis, tachistoscope; contra the systematic method of Würzburgians). But a cognitive construction in an experiment corresponds to a real construction of process itself. (Vygotsky, 1929/1989, p. 5)

Constructivism can be broken down into many categories, such as cognitive constructivism or social constructivism. For example, these terms are placed in opposition to rationalism when speaking of Chomskyan linguistics (cf. Botha, 1989, p. 45). Constructivism is sometimes referred to as interactionism and is actually attributed to Piaget's theory of knowledge, which included the knowledge of language. Piaget is the father of constructivism in the West. As Botha (1989) wrote,

Piaget...considers both empiricist and rationalist (or in his terminology, preformationist) theories of the genesis of knowledge to be devoid of concrete truth. As an alternative, only constructivism is acceptable to him. On Chomsky's...reading, Piagetian constructivism (also called vitalism by some) boils down to the claim that through interaction with the environment the child develops sensorimotor constructions which provide the basis for language, and as understanding and knowledge grow, new constructions are developed in some more or less uniform way. (p. 45)

It is paradoxical that Piaget is considered to be the founder of educational constructivism, since many writers place Vygotsky in the same school of thought, realizing that Vygotsky differed with Piaget on many issues. It is also interesting that constructivism does not include a holistic dialectic of interactions of the individual student with other students, as well as interactions with the teacher and society at large, to return back to a focus on the individual. Vygotsky's paradigm of constructivism is similar to current popular constructivist theories, yet there are differences;[1] therefore, discussions of Vygotsky as a contemporary constructivist and constructionist should be put into a historical perspective.

In certain respects, constructionism finds a close ally in Vygotskyian formulations. Both perspectives place community prior to the individual; both look at individual rationality largely as a by-product of the social sphere; and both hold cooperative or dialogic processes as central to the process of education. However, there is also an essential difference between the two orientations:

Social constructionism places the human relationship in the foreground, that is, the patterns of interdependent action at the microsocial level....Thus, the constructionist is centrally concerned with such matters as negotiation, cooperation, conflict, rhetoric, ritual, roles, social scenarios. In contrast, Vygotsky is centrally a psychologist. Although social process does play an important role in the theory, psychological process occupies the foreground. (Gergen, 1995, pp. 24–25)

Many other differences exist between the philosophies of constructionists/constructivists and Vygotsky, in particular regarding nonfoundationalism. One important distinction involves the constructivist rejection of apodictical, absolute certitude, to the point of pushing this understanding toward extreme relativism. "Constructivists have pushed nonfoundationalism so far that they are enmeshed in a completely unacceptable relativism—one that reduces knowledge to the level of merely belief, opinion, and/or taste" (Smith, 1990, p. 17). Smith adds that the core of constructivism maintains the regulative ideal of solidarity, not objectivity. Teachers who embrace this philosophy are coparticipants in constructing and negotiating reality with their students; and in fact, teachers view themselves as learners. Some of the tenets of constructivist teaching are that (1) teachers pose problems of emerging relevance; (2) learning occurs in context; (3) constructivist teachers look for and value students' points of view; and (4) constructivist teachers assess student learning authentically, within the context of teaching. For example, student exhibititions are encouraged, along with sharing ideas with classmates, and nonjudgmental responses (cf. Kaufman & Brooks, 1996, pp. 234–235).

The Vygotskian understanding of the teacher's role within the zone of proximal development (ZPD) takes a different stance, although it is similar in many respects. "Whereas they [constructivists] focus on the process of cooperation in the enhancement of capabilities, the Vygotskian centers on the zone of proximal development—essentially a mental space between actual and potential cognitive functioning" (Gergen, 1995, p. 25). Vygotsky believed in handing down cultural values to students via teacher modeling within dialectical discussions. In essence, this belief was a reflection of his own experience with a private tutor for five years—a tutor who was in authority by position of his knowledge and was simultaneously a coparticipant in discussions through the use of the Socratic method. Interestingly, as a teenager, Vygotsky and his friends established their own circles that resembled those of current constructivist methods. For example, they debated topics from the points of view of historical figures, wrote and acted their poetry, and discussed philosophical issues within a historical context. However, the idea of simply constructing knowledge on an ad hoc, dyadic, or interactional basis would have been totally foreign to Vygotsky if applied within a formalized school setting.

Vygotsky's focus was on the genetic-developmental method, which perhaps highlights the basic difference between the two philosophies. Constructivists view research results as the outcome of a process of negotiation: "The negotiations entered into by scientists deal with the conclusions, and the results, as claims not as evidence. That is why science as a process of negotiation is in principle a never-ending event, with no fixed Achimedean point" (Miedema, Gert, & Biersta, 1994, p. 79). Vygotsky did not share this relativist position, as his research methods were anchored in Humboldtian-Spinozist-Marxist theories that stand in opposition to Cartesian thinking.

To better comprehend the Western model of constructivism, a comparison of constructivists and postpositivists (based on a heuristic philosophy, which is similar to constructivism, but not the same) is reviewed here: (1) In gaining a theoretical superstructure of constructivism as compared to other fields, within the philosophical stance of ontology, the postpositivists are realists, and the constructivists are relativists. (2) In viewing epistemology, the postpositivists tend to be dualistic objectivists, with the constructivists being interactive subjectivists. (3) Regarding methodology, postpositivists are interventionist, while the constructivists relate to the aspects of the hermeneutic, dialectic tradition (cf. Lincoln, 1996, p. 78). The epistemological position of constructivism "dictates that the positivist subject-object dualism and objectivism be replaced by an interactive monism, that the interactivity between researcher and subject be recognized and utilized in the teaching and learning process between the two" (Lincoln, 1996, p. 78). By nature, constructivist research and teaching is qualitative rather than quantitative.

The convergence of a Vygotskian understanding and constructivism are now evident; however, differences still remain. Therefore, it is suggested that a "constrained constructivism" (cf. Hayles, 1993, p. 27) constitutes the meeting point for the future, arguing that constraints tell us something (though not everything) about reality, and it is how we chart a course through societal constraints that forms our own understanding of personal freedom. Constraints relate to constructivism by limiting the vastness of relativism and creating new discourses on representation(s) and language:

Constrained constructivism thus implies that all theories are metaphoric, just as all language is...and it has this double edge: while it implies relativism, it also indicates an active construction of a reality *that is meaningful to us* through the dynamic interplay between us and the world. Renouncing omniscience and coercive power, it gains connectedness and human meaning. (Hayles, pp. 39–42)

The focus within educational constructivism is on the learner, yet in Vygotskian thought there is a new focus on the role of the teacher. The next section takes a look at controversial ideas along these lines because in general, there are no prescribed guidelines as to what makes an excellent teacher. It is at this juncture that Vygotskian and constructivist theories can converge.

TEACHER-ABILITY: FOCUS ON THE SECOND LANGUAGE CLASSROOM

The following section argues that classroom foreign language teaching, or any classroom teaching for that matter, needs to switch its focus from separate domains such as communicative competence and proficiency, to a more integrated holistic structure of teaching and learning. It is hypothesized that theory must be placed within an extended understanding of teacher-ability, not to return the teacher to the center of attention within the classroom, but to establish a new relationship of the teacher as mediator between spontaneous (everyday) and scientific (academic) concepts. The teacher can be viewed as a competent peer in personality formation, using Vygotskian terminology; at the same time, the teacher can be viewed as a coparticipant, using constructivist terminology. A caveat is important: the teacher is viewed differently within the Vygotskian perspective, and the general genetic law of development is the guiding principle of the teacher. Dichotomies such as acquisition and learning are redefined within a more holistic understanding, which will relate to the needs of the twenty-first-century classroom. Related to the second language (L2) classroom, the term "L2 acquisition" (cf. R. Ellis, 1995, p. 87) is consciously used in referring to the L2 classroom as opposed to learning an L2 in a natural setting. The reason for using the term "L2 acquisition" within the classroom is to overcome the prejudice of the past few years in which acquisition was referred to only as natural acquisition.

It has become increasingly clear that a dichotomy between nativistic and behavioristic theories is too simplistic, and that integrated theories which relate linguistic structure and function to cognitive processes in general must be developed, for language is just one aspect of human cognition and cannot be properly understood apart from it. (Kennedy, 1973, p. 73)

Future research should examine the needs of learners and teachers within different developmental stages or phases of L2 classroom acquisition/ learning, using the different (sometimes invariant) ordering structures already established (be it syntax, morphology, tense use, etc.). It is time to transcend inflexible discussions on invariance, as they have been conducted in the past; surely there is some type of natural order, even if it is not universal. Another example of this new way of thinking comes from Snow (1986, p. 76), who argues that "the task of learning a language is quite different in different stages of acquisition" (Ellis, 1994, p. 268). To date, much SLA research remains within categorical lists, little of which have been translated into teaching materials, learner expectancies, or topics in teacher training courses. To some degree, this trend has resulted in theory for theory's sake. For example:

The intermarriage of theory exclusively with theory and not with practice, if repeated over generations of theories, results in at least two types of deformed offspring: one is inapplicable theory, and another is misapplied theory. The zealous exponents of the latter type of theory adopt terms from a jargon without understanding either the purpose of the mechanics of the theory, which spawned it. The former type of theory is the product of theoreticians who are content to theorize in a way that is quite unconcerned with the explanation, prediction, or understanding of the facts of language use or language learning. (Oller, 1973, p. 36)

The following summary is divided into two areas (L2 classroom acquisition and teacher-ability) based within a Vygotskian framework. When comparing L2 classroom learning with natural acquisition for adolescents and adults, there has traditionally been a conflation of terms. Various Chomskyan applied linguists have hypothesized that natural learning is better than classroom learning; however, the point of confusion has often revolved around Universal Grammar (UG) as the bridge to accuracy or fluency. Researchers disagree whether the adult L2 learner has accessibility to UG or not. In reality, there is an initial problem with this position. The disruptive factor within this approach is that conceptualized learning is fused with L1-UG in the first place, whereas this is not the case with adult L2 learning and acquisition. What follows is disagreement with statements such as the following, from Felix and Weigl (1991):

The good news is for linguistic theory. It seems to be true that without access to Universal Grammar language learning does not proceed beyond the more superficial properties of natural language. In other words, for true acquisition to take place UG is indispensable. The bad news is for language teachers and language pedagogy. Language teaching—at least in its conventional form—seems to systematically block access to UG and therefore tends to prevent rather than further the acquisitional process in domains that go beyond the more accidental and superficial properties of language. (p. 178)

Statements of this nature need to be analyzed and taken to task. First, current Chomskyan linguistic theory deals primarily with grammar, not with acquisition (unless acquisition means innatism, where the individual does not contribute to her own linguistic development via a conceptual, dialectical, or experiential base). Second, who would think that L1 acquisition would progress very far without UG, and why is this good news? Third, why would L1 UG be positioned within a comparative structure regarding L2 learning in the first place? Why is this bad news for language teaching? Fourth, since a hierarchical invariant structuring for the L1 acquisition is still in an early phase of being explained or even understood, how can this conjecture be imposed upon the L2 classroom, claiming that language teaching seems to systematically block access to UG? The truth is that Chomskyan-based L2 research to date has not been very successful in finding access to L2 UG on a large scale. At the same time, it claims that despite the lack of evidence, the best way to acquire an L2 is through applying various principles of Chomskyan linguistics. This debate takes on a circularity that ends in emotional positioning of theorists and heated rhetoric among applied scientists. In other words, in many respects it does not reflect a genuine scientific approach.

An important point to remember is that when analyzing L2 instructional/acquisitional theories, the traditional unidimensional, linear, symmetrical approaches of offering one theory at a time in order to define multiple categories will soon be outdated. Multidimensional L2 theories have already begun to influence certain areas of SLA, demonstrating that L2 instruction such as grammar and vocabulary learning are beneficial to

L2 learning/acquisition within classroom settings, whereas L2 acquisition in other areas, such as syntax and pronunciation do not benefit as much from classroom instruction.[2] There is no question that L2 learners and teachers should ultimately want to go abroad and experience the language within the target culture rather than just learn it in the classroom. Within the understanding of a dominant activity, trips abroad could be reorganized in order to avoid the ghettoized effect of taking groups of learners from one school or university and transplanting the same group with the same teacher or professor into a foreign culture. For example, majors in medicine or nursing or history, who are studying German, might go abroad with a group of students with the same interest and work in a nursing home or hospital in Germany, Switzerland, or Austria. Students would actually be learning the language from members of the nursing home, as well as gaining valuable input for personality formation, as well as historical information.

Various innovative programs of this nature are already in place, such as working in a Russian orphanage, once the learner has had approximately two years of Russian. Such an experience could completely change a young person's life, as well as the image of the target culture and language. It is assumed that the understanding of L2 classroom learning/acquisition must be ascribed a higher position, as a worthy subcomponent within SLA research. The current focus on communicative competence, proficiency, and culture must change in order to accommodate the development and formation of personality of the individual attempting to immerse her- or himself into a new reality. Most of all, the role of the teacher is entirely reversed. The teacher still directs the classroom, helping to guide the student in fulfilling personal goals that eventually fall outside of the realm of the classroom. Just as Vygotsky's focus is on synthesis, the new role of the teacher is the same; that is, to guide the learning and potential development of the student both inside and, hopefully, outside the classroom. The goal of this new approach is to teach within the understanding of the whole personality of the student, and not just within the partial aspects. The L2 is not viewed as an end or telos in itself, but instead as the means to allow for personal internal student transformation. By encouraging and allowing this transformation to take place inside the student, it is suggested that the teacher will also be transformed. For this to occur we need a revised understanding of Vygotskian concepts (the old), placed together with the interactionist perspectives of constructivism (the new).

TEACHER-ABILITY II

Returning to the concept of teacher-ability, one of the initial problems within SLA has traditionally been the high status of the researcher compared to the low status of the teacher. Action research has not bridged this gap, and it is puzzling why this problem has not been corrected within professional groups.

> Looking back over the history of language instruction in the last ninety years, one is filled with misgiving and a sense of malaise. We seem to have been marking time; perhaps we have even retrogressed. We are still plagued with a confusing array of methods; and experimental research on their relative merits is difficult because of the large number of variables involved, which are almost impossible to control. In most research schemes of this kind that have been undertaken in the United States, no very significant results have been obtained. (Christophersen, 1973, p. 20)

Although this quote is not new, it could have been stated yesterday. There is a logical conclusion to the hierarchical structuring within SLA, where the researcher is viewed as being positioned at a higher level than the teacher. The conclusion is ironic: within the classroom the same structuring often takes place, with the teacher usually assuming a higher level than the learner. Vygotskian theory, together with Russian activity theory and Russian psycholinguistics, offers some viable solutions to this problem.

One of the weakest parts within SLA theory is the lack a unified theory of teaching. Indeed, this plea could easily be misunderstood as a call for specific theories on how to teach. Or it could be interpreted in terms of the teachability hypothesis, which defines itself negatively. "So the teachability hypothesis negatively marks off the possible influence of instruction on the acquisition process. However, this negative definition does not imply that formal instruction has no influence on acquisition whatsoever" (Pienemann, 1984). Diane Larsen-Freeman (1990) counteracted with the following thoughts: "One of the basic starting points for enhancing holistic teacher-ability will be a discussion on theories of teaching, which should not be interpreted to mean discussions of methods, strategies, innovative methodologies, viewed atomistically" (p. 206). At this point, Larsen-Freeman (1990) offers ideas regarding suggestions for second language teaching, stating that

> a theory of SLT [second language teaching] would take into account an important agent in the process, namely the language teacher....First of all, it would need to be *grounded* in classroom data....A second quality of a SLT theory would be that it would be dynamic. It would allow for teacher growth....It must not ignore the fact that teachers' classroom experience transforms what they know....Finally, it would be a theory which would motivate research not only of what a teacher does, but also what a teacher thinks....In calling for a theory of second language teaching, I am submitting that the language teaching field need no longer look outside of itself for its theoretical needs to be satisfied....[T]rue interdependence of theory,

practice and research in second language teaching will be achieved only when SLT is illumined by a theory of its own making. (pp. 266–269)

Vygotskian theory can be introduced to the SLA classroom with the understanding that teachers will be asked to develop a new way of thinking within the mode of a metatheory. Vygotskian theory does not offer a cookbook method or a prescribed approach to teaching and learning foreign languages. Ultimately, within a Vygotskian understanding, the responsibility of an overall teaching philosophy is returned to the teacher. Hopefully, teachers, student teachers, and students in methodology courses will start to establish their own individualized theory of teaching that will automatically be theoretical and practical at the same time. When envisioning a Vygotskian approach to such an individualized theory, Vygotsky's ideas need to be reviewed, including the genetic-developmental continuum, dialectics, the lower and higher mental processes, concept formation, internalization, rooting or ingrowth, spontaneous and scientific concepts, ZPD, testing for the potential IQ, and dominant activities, among others. In addition, many of the theories of A. A. Leontiev can be used in order to further support and enhance Vygotsky's theories. Vygotsky's psychology-philosophy can be implemented when establishing such a research method: (1) Writing personal journals of practical activities in the form of an ongoing evaluation of the course. This type of student feedback could be valuable in better understanding the psychology of learning a foreign language. (2) Interviews with students on their reactions to various techniques used in class. (3) Specific research designs, perhaps using the method of double stimulation.[3] (4) Designing experiments that can be conducted in the classroom. (5) Testing by way of the potential growth factor. Tests may be given once, then given again with the help of qualified peers, with the same test being given a third time for the individual to monitor her growth and learning.[4] (6) The use of basic statistics should be a part of a methodology course; however, from the Vygotskian perspective, conclusions should also be drawn from hypotheses, notes, and memos in journals that are inferred from classroom experiments, and derived from negotiated discussions with other researchers or colleagues. (7) Formal discussions with students on the individual theory each teacher has developed, allowing students to comment and critique the daily practice, which should be rebuilt into further theory. (8) The inclusion of service learning into the L2 classroom by allowing high school or university students to use foreign languages in a variety of fun-filled atmospheres, such as with small children at schools; or to visit patients in a hospital to try and cheer them up in their target language; or to collectively solve certain problems. For example, one high school Spanish class discovered that many Latinos in their community could not read in Spanish; therefore, the students made videotapes on various health issues in Spanish for the new arrivals.[5]

Error Correction within Teacher-Ability

Research into mistake and error analysis should be revised according to teacher and learner needs. In particular, learner feedback should be evaluated as to the usefulness of error correction hypotheses, such as the Garden Path approach: "[T]he current results clearly indicate that leading students "down the garden path"—inducing them to make a grammatical error which is then immediately corrected—is an effective technique for teaching grammatical exception in the foreign language classroom" (Tomasello & Herron, 1988, p. 244). This approach is controversial and can lead to discussions regarding developmental stages of the L2 learner, different teaching philosophies of individual teachers, and feedback that can be gained from learner input. Analysts conducting research on error analysis must be aware that in normal circumstances, it is often not known what type of error is made with respect to a developmental continuum, and that even the same errors occuring in different situations do not account for the psychological force behind why they were made.[6] In the past, the analysis of errors has remained somewhat simplistic, with behavorist theories focusing on a negative transfer of L1 habit formations, and mentalist theories focusing on intralingual errors, such as those made in the first language of the speaker. Rod Ellis (1994) wrote: "It should be noted that...subsequently, researchers have come to recognize that the correlation between behaviourism and transfer errors on the one hand and mentalism and intralingual errors on the other is simplistic and misleading" (p. 60). A problem in the L2 classroom, as has already been stated, is that an L1—at the beginning stages—is often placed within the atmosphere of spontaneous concepts with much contextual cueing. Attempts to establish a spontaneous atmosphere in the L2 classroom should suggest that errors are not so important, and that learners will eventually develop beyond many of the mistakes made. On a practical level, it is often assumed that neither fluency, nor comprehensive understanding of L2 grammar, will result from the learning within the L2 classroom. Therefore, it follows that a certain amount of fossilization is inevitable as a result of foreign language classroom learning.

Paradoxically, many classroom teachers try to present everyday spontaneous L2 language while assuming that L2 students will not actually be proficient one day. It has already been suggested that the classroom (at the high school or university level) be established within the mode of a strict division of scientific and academic concepts. Grammar would be introduced and understood as a bridge between scientific and spontaneous concepts, with more imagery accompanying grammar exercises, and less imagery in communicative practice. In deciding which errors and mistakes to correct in the L2 setting, the aspect of group work and interaction should be discussed vis-à-vis learning and error correction in general.

A second issue concerns learners' attitudes towards error treatment. Cathcart and Olsen (1976) found that ESL learners appreciate being corrected by their teachers in a supportive atmosphere, and want more correction than they are usually provided with. Chenoweth, et al. (1983) found that learners liked to be corrected not only during form-focused activities, but also when they were conversing with native speakers. (R. Ellis, 1994, p. 584)

Vygotsky affirmed that the teacher needs to be a role model, and that the ZPD should establish direct lines of potential development between the student and teacher, or between the student and a competent peer. Traditionally, little emphasis has been placed on group work within formalized schooling, perhaps because during Vygotsky's youth, students had time to meet after school at various activities and interact with one another. Today, various perspectives are taken regarding L2 classroom interaction and group work, and not all researchers and teachers agree on the format of group work. Prahbu (1987) stated that

the project did not use group work in the classroom, in the sense of putting learners in small groups and asking or encouraging them to attempt tasks jointly. Learners were, however, given the right at the task stage to consult fellow-learners or the teacher if they wished to, either briefly or to an extent amounting to collaboration. (p. 81)

M. Long, on the other hand, supported modified interaction: "[T]hese interactive features consist of ways of negotiating comprehensibility and meaning. Long suggests, in fact, that interactive modifications are more important for acquisition than modifications of NS [native speaker] speech that only result in simplified TL [target language] syntax and morphology" (Chaudron, 1988, p. 9). In reality, there should be no attempt to universalize group work, yet varying discussions of this nature are an integral part of teacher education courses, and later, part of the teacher's repertoire.

Anxiety and Teacher-Ability

Regarding what has been previously stated about transfer and error correction, another important concept for teachers—when developing their theory or praxis—deals with student anxiety. One of the problems in L2 instruction is that students are often not able to use what has been learned—to transfer it to spontaneous speech. Anxiety plays a role in some transfer situations, and certainly the overall problem is epistemological in nature. Since there is often ambiguity between the teaching of scientific (academic) and spontaneous (everyday) concepts, it is confusing for an L2 student to switch between the two perspectives, knowing what the teacher actually wants, unless specific exercises have been a regular part of the curriculum. Another interesting problem is the way that natural speech is expected to occur (such as in everyday life), when in reality most of the speech patterns within the L2 classroom are based within an understanding of scientific concepts. Therefore, as A. A. Leontiev (Leont'ev, 1973) wrote:

[I]n principle we teach active speech. In methodological practice, however, we give preference to reactive speech, which assumes a place here that does not correspond to its real significance for the pupil. We do everything possible to encourage the student's habit of reactive speech and then are surprised that he [she] does not have an active command of speech. (p. 17)

A. A. Leontiev discusses the aspect of anxiety (although he prefers the word tension), using the analogy that tension can be positive, such as when settling into a situation and mastering it. He offers the example of a pilot landing a plane, or a surgeon before an operation. Indeed, one would hope that a pilot or surgeon would maintain a healthy sense of tension while working. In addition, we need further discussion regarding the correlation of anxiety and motivation, which are not always linked together in SLA. For example:

It may be, however, that the key factor is not motivation but anxiety, both state anxiety—the condition associated with performing a task—and trait anxiety—one's habitual response to stress. Furthermore, it may be important to distinguish two sorts of anxiety: debilitating and facilitating. (Crookes, 1993, p. 119)[7]

The question then arises as to the reason for state or situation anxiety, and Bailey claimed that it could be connected with the competitive nature of learners:

Bailey (1983) analyzed the diaries of 11 learners and found that they tended to become anxious when they compared themselves with other learners in the class and found themselves less proficient. She noted that as the learners perceived themselves becoming more proficient and therefore better able to compete, their anxiety decreased. Bailey also identified other sources of anxiety, including test and learners' perceived relationship with their teacher. (R. Ellis, 1994, p. 480)

Indeed, these specific traits relate to students learning a foreign language in the United States; however, this concept might not apply to other cultures. Certainly, it reflects the understanding of postmodern society where studying a foreign language may not always be regarded as a long-term commitment. One facet of mediating the problem of anxiety that ulti- mately results in many errors and transfer problems is the need for stu- dents to set realistic goals for themselves. It is suggested that the theories of goal-orientedness within Russian activity theory can be helpful for stu- dents and teachers in establishing a realistic target, with tangible rewards at the end of the journey. Interestingly, this is exactly what is expected to happen within the Russian understanding of goal-directedness, which can ultimately lead to self-regulation in the Vygotskian sense. However, in postmodernity images bombard the everyday world, and as a result, many people end up concentrating on two or three tasks and goals simul- taneously. This understanding can be reflected in aspects such as the new ability to watch television programs in a corner of a computer monitor while finishing a project on the computer.

Setting goals within the L2 classroom can perhaps help the learner to focus on one aspect of a dominant activity, to then complete that aspect before moving on to another task in order to reach the overall goal, that is, L2 learning. In the past, the eclectic method of establishing a syllabus for the foreign language classroom has resulted in the learner not always being viewed as a whole person within a changing, dialectical continuum. Much of the bricolage approach to teaching in some L2 classrooms can be changed if teachers learn to establish their own metatheories regarding teaching, while viewing L2 learners as developing personalities. In other words, as postmodernists have actually learned to do two or more things at once, teachers often view learners in the same split fashion. It appears necessary for all teachers, student teachers, advanced foreign language majors in methodology courses, and learners to establish personal criteria for a good learner and a good teacher, without becoming locked into an inflexible understanding of the definition. For example, Rubin (1975) many years ago listed the following characteristics for a good learner:

1. The good language learner is a willing and accurate guesser. . . . 2. The good lan- guage learner has a strong drive to communicate, or to learn from communica- tion. . . . 3. The good language learner is often not inhibited. . . . 4. In addition to focusing on communication, the good language learner is prepared to attend to form. . . . 5. The good language learner practices. . . . 6. The good language learner monitors his [her] own and the speech of others. . . . 7. The good language learner attends to meaning. (pp. 45–47)

Certainly, this list is offered as an example, within the framework of the predominant thinking during the 1970s; these points can be used with- out hesitation, criticized, or completely discarded to be replaced by new criteria.

Regarding specific strategies for good teaching, D. Brown (1993, p. 516) suggested that L2 teachers learn to lower inhibitions, encourage risk taking, build students' self-confidence, and help them to develop intrinsic motivation. L2 teachers should promote cooperative learning, encourage students to use right-brain processing, promote ambiguity tolerance, help them use their intuition, and get students to make their mistakes work for them. The last point is one of the most important: to motivate students to set their own goals. These criteria often go against the prevailing thinking within education in general, and where no specific goals of excellent teaching and learning are found in a codified form. Ironically, the current educational mind-set demands outcomes that are viewed in a lockstep fashion. It is argued that teachers and learners can return to a focus that implies doing one task at a time, within goal-directedness.

CONCLUSIONS REGARDING SLA AND TEACHER-ABILITY

Perhaps the first quest in developing a new SLA classroom theory would be to jettison the dichotomy between competence and performance, since there is no direct window of competence (cf. R. Ellis, 1994, p. 673). Oller (1973) stated that

if we assume with Chomsky (1965) that a model of competence need not account for the facts of performance, then a separate performance model does indeed seem to be called for. This seems undesirable, however, because it abolishes the original definition of competence—namely, the speaker's capacity to use his language. (p. 41)

At this stage, theorists have rejected the division of competence and performance in the Variable Competence Model, which is the first step toward real change in the L2 classroom. This model looks at developmental stages and demonstrates that "learners learn how to activate items and rules that are available initially only in planned discourse for use in unplanned discourse" (R. Ellis, 1994, p. 366). Within this understanding, it is implicitly accepted that variation per definition changes, whereas UG seemingly does not; however, in reality, UG theory itself as a description is constantly changing, which ultimately requires explanation. There has also been an attempt to position variability against systematicity, implying that one is changing and perhaps less scientific, with the other concept being more stable. For example:

[T]he relationship between variability and systematicity was formerly seen as one of opposition: only categorical phenomena would be considered systematic. More recently, the adoption of sociolinguistic models and the associated statistical analyses have resulted in the recognition that variability in IL can be systematic (Andersen, 1978; Borland, 1983; Hyltenstam, 1977)....The recognition that variability can be systematic does not rule out the concept of variability which is not systematic and some authors (e.g. Ellis 1985; Labov, 1970; Huebner, 1985) distinguish between systematic variability and unsystematic variability: The first is rule-governed, the second is random and unpredictable. (Pavesi, 1987, p. 73)[8]

One-dimensional and product-oriented expectations in SLA research often result in expectations of instant results for the L2 learner. The same conclusions apply to the L2 subject in research experiments. However, learning does not always correspond to development, and formal instruction often has a delayed effect (cf. R. Ellis, 1994, p. 621), while learning and development must be coupled with an understanding of variability. Although many agree with statements such as "variation... is not the duty of an acquisition theorist to explain" (Gregg, 1990, p. 379), it is clear that the basic problem lies within L2 acquisition theory, and not within the aspect of variation, which represents an inextricable aspect of human existence in real time.

Future discussions of SLA research in the L2 classroom might consider the following: (1) If a viable subdivision of SLA is to be set up for L2 classroom research within more extended parameters, the theory of teaching grammar will need to be reexamined. It appears that long after the L2 learning experience is over, students take with them sets of images, not a complete memory of grammar. For example, "a number of studies already referred to... indicate that the effects of grammar instruction may not last" (R. Ellis, 1994, p. 636); however, most grammar sequencing is given the least amount of imagery. If a viable subdivision of SLA is to be set up for L2 classroom research within more extended parameters, then new thought will need to be given to the theory of teaching grammar. (2) The inclusion of theories of variability requires a more comprehensive view of the individual L2 learner positioned within a social setting and influenced by factors such as postmodernism, power relations, and gender differences. Theorists interested in such variables are often not interested in sophisticated research. What research has been conducted with the inclusion of the aforementioned variables has focused on morphology and syntax, with little emphasis on lexicon (cf. Pavesi, 1987, p. 74).[9] (3) Although the question of IQ is certainly politically incorrect in the United States, it should be addressed within the context of potential foreign language parameters. Vygotsky maintained that in order to learn a second language, one must at least be competent with the grammar of one's first language. There are many conflicting views regarding this point, yet the question of intelligence is a factor that needs to be included in the debate. With a new focus on SLA classroom research, Vygotskian approaches to testing can aid in establishing an approximated IQ, which is future oriented, with a built-in potential growth factor. Presently, some evidence suggests that learners with high levels of intelligence benefit from a highly structured instructional method, whereas learners with lower levels benefit from a less systematic approach (see Carroll & Spearritt, 1967), although other studies cited in Skehan (1989) have suggested the opposite (for example, Maier & Jacob, 1966). At the moment, when looking beyond the evaluation of personal learning styles (R. Ellis, 1994, p. 648), results are inconclusive.

Certainly, the old approach that "product + results = IQ" needs to be completely reconsidered in order to enhance the learning process and empower, not intimidate, L2 learners. It is clear that foreign language learners process L2 material(s) at different rates, and different measures of potential growth should reflect this variation. Vygotskian theory speaks directly to all of the aforementioned points and can foster a better under- standing of L2 developmental learning/acquisition. A Vygotskian under- standing of concept formation is, in essence, the antithesis to much of the underlying associationistic trends, especially in mainstream developmen- tal or Chomskyan approaches to L2 learning (cf. Robbins, 2001). New test- ing and learning within a redefined ZPD—which restructures the role of the teacher—will add to the understanding within SLA research that there is indeed room for viable subcomponents such as Vygotskian classroom research. It should be noted that the idea of a subcomponent, such as cur- rent sociocultural theory, is not new. Certainly, the framework of class- room research yields to various subcomponents; however, it is suggested that all of these new aspects should be placed within the understanding of one continuum of applied linguistics/SLA, for example:

Some have suggested that we need a general theory to encompass a wider area than our theories to date (Spolsky, 1989). Others have suggested that we may have to accept that a theory of SLA will be modular, each module explaining different domains of language (Lightbown & White, 1987). Hatch, Shirai, and Fantuzzi (1990) have called for an integrated theory of acquisition. (Larsen-Freeman, 1991, p. 328)

What is important is that the various domains in applied linguistics/SLA will be somewhat interrelated and should be viewed as such. The differ- ence here is that no attempt is made to find a mutual consensus, but to strive for a higher level of synthesis. (1) Although an interdisciplinary approach is important, in order to gain the widest possible perspective it will be necessary to establish the "SLA classroom research component" as a separate unit that can function together with other recognized units modularly. (2) Indeed, new areas of significance will be identified, such as the ecology movement within SLA (e.g., van Lier, 1996), where cross- cultural comparisons of similar work in other countries can be arranged via conferences and the Internet. (3) Dialogue between theorists of various subcomponents will be encouraged in an interdisciplinary fashion to rec- ognize the existence of one continuum. (4) Regarding the current sociocultural trend within applied linguistics today, sociocultural theory has offered an alternative to the predominant Chomskyan influence over SLA but has become a means of using ethnographic studies to replace a genuine Vygotskian method, a trend that has resulted in confusion between Vygotskian thought and ethnographic research. The perspective taken here is different and relates to the Russian cultural-historical approach. (5) Furthermore, it is suggested that leading SLA research journals begin to go beyond "English only" as the language of written communication. It is paradoxical to have major journals within the field published primarily in English; in fact, one rarely sees quotes in foreign languages, and even when one sees quotes in French, German, or Spanish, they are almost always translated into English.

One of the virtues of Vygotskian-Leontievian thought related to teacher-ability is the simple fact that theorists and teachers alike are placed in the position of understanding and modifying Russian (not American) psycholinguistic theory, which forces one to think and strategize from an entirely different perspective. Sometimes, it is even forgotten that Vygotsky was actually Russian because of the fact that his ideas are so current in addressing the problems of Western culture. It is hoped that the results of such theorizing and practice in the classroom will lead to a new thrust of theory and practice within an energized approach to L2 classroom reforms.

The next section reviews the tenets of A. A. Leontiev, who is one of the most prominent Russians to bridge the school of Russian activity theory with the semiotics of Vygotsky. A. A. Leontiev incorporates foreign language acquisition and learning with the Russian understanding of psycholinguistics, which always views the individual within a social-societal setting.

NOTES

1. During Vygotsky's lifetime, "Russian constructivism" was a completely different field of study that had nothing to do with contemporary constructivism. For more information, see Lodder (1983).

2. "The question of whether L2 instruction has an *absolute* positive effect on acquisition will obviously depend on particular programs and circumstances, but in a synthesis of several studies which compared naturalistic with formal instruction, Long...argues that the outcomes favor instruction, *all other factors being equal.* In other words, instructional contexts appeared to contribute more positively to acquisition of the L2 than naturalistic exposure, when duration of exposure and other factors (e.g., age) were controlled.... That is, some classroom processes may aid the acquisition of certain structures (e.g., vocabulary) without influencing others (syntax)" (Chaudron, 1988, p. 4).

3. "By using this approach [method of double stimulation], we do not limit ourselves to the usual method of offering the subject simple stimuli to which we expect a direct response. Rather, we simultaneously offer a *second series of stimuli* that have a special function. In this way, we are able to study the *process of accomplishing a task by the aid of specific auxiliary means,* thus we are also able to discover the inner structure and development of the higher psychological processes" (Vygotsky, 1978, p. 74).

4. "The intention here is to use task analysis to break down complex instructional objectives within a curriculum area into component skill elements which can be programmed into manageable incremental steps. The model is essentially a test-teach-test mode. Once skill development strengths and weaknesses have been assessed, specific instructional objectives are written and particular strategies are used to teach the skill (Mercer & Ysseldylke, p. 1977)" (Lunt, 1993, p. 149).

5. The Hispanic project was initiated by Maria Lara at Warrensburg High School in Warrensburg, Missouri, in 1999.

6. See Chamot (1978).

7. For more information on anxiety, see MacIntyre and Gardner (1991, pp. 85–117) and R. Ellis (1994, pp. 480).

8. Andersen (1978), Borland (1983), Hyltenstam (1977), and Huebner (1985) are not listed in the references section, but in R. Ellis (1987).

9. "It must be noted, however, that research conducted on the influence of the language learning environment on the orders of acquisition (Pica, 1983; Lightbown, 1983 and on transitional structures; Felix, 1981; Weinert, 1985) has been restricted to morphology and syntax. Little is known of the impact of learning setting on variability and systematicity in the acquisition of the IL [interlanguage] lexicon" (Pavesi, 1987, p. 74).

CHAPTER 5

Introduction to Russian Activity Theory

> Just as the word penetrates the depths of the soul, so do we communicate to
> the world the contours of the word; and that is the principal research task
> before us. It is certain that neither linguistics, nor traditional psychology, nor
> logic, nor semiotics is capable of solving this problem separately.
> —"Recent Writings of A. A. Leont'ev"

G. V. Burmenskaia (1997) has stated that the traditional focus of Western
psychology has been dualistic, with two factors being analyzed: heredity
and environment. In fact, Russian psychologists have viewed Western
behaviorism as placing the individual within a passive rather than an
active state. "What Vygotsky himself sought and found in Marx and
Hegel was a social theory of human activity *(Tätigkeit)* set in opposition to
naturalism and the passive receptivity of the empiricist tradition"
(Kozulin, 1986b, p. 266). Within Russian activity theory, the activity of the
child/adult within its culture is analyzed, and the social experience is
then related to the mental development of the child/adult. Western psychological aspects such as habits, conditioning, and socialization do not
take center stage; instead the focus is on areas such as development, social
mechanisms, mastery, motives, operations, and goals. Although the word
"activity" *(deyatelnost* in Russian) is used, it should not be confused with
the American concept of behaviorism. The Russian understanding of
activity "is a coherent system of internal mental processes and external
behavior and motivation that are combined and directed to achieve conscious goals" (Bedny & Meister, 1997, p. 1). To understand activity theory,
it is important to grasp the importance of human needs and motives that

help generate activity, but these aspects must then be differentiated. For example,

[n]eeds may be transformed into motives only in those cases in which they acquire the capacity to induce an activity of a person to achieve a particular goal. Motives may derive not only from needs, but from desire, intention, aspiration, strivings, when these induce our behavior toward particular goal achievement. The more important the goal, the more motivated the worker will be to attain it, and the more she will expend physical and psychological energy toward achieving the goal. As can be seen, one goal may occasion different motives. (Bedny & Meister, 1997, p. 4)

One of the basic principles of Russian activity theory, as well as of Vygot-skian theory, is the system of self-regulation. Within such a system, goals and subgoals can be formed that will include cognitive, executive, evalu-ative, and emotional aspects of activity (cf. Bedny & Meister, 1997, p. 75). The integration of these aspects is combined with both external and inter-nal processes that can lead to self-mastery.

Russian activity theory from the 1930s through the 1950s remained an interesting paradox: It stood against the Pavlovian approach of stimulus-response, and yet it fit into the political constraints of Stalinism. Innatism, as characterized by the "unfolding" process of child development was rejected; therefore, this tenet would not challenge any theological differ-ences within the Soviet state regarding divinity or God. It was clear that during this period of time, activity theory was written both in favor of the new socialist personality, and against the individualism found in coun-tries in the West. For example, within Russian activity theory, cultural objects were viewed as being "fixed" with a cultural acceptance of right and wrong. This aspect is universally true regarding the development of babies and young children, but becomes problematic when dealing with teenagers and young adults. Another example is the predominant use of the phrase "socially developed." Here is an example of this type of lan-guage:

[N]ot every activity leads to development of the child's abilities and mastery of objects and socially accepted forms of activity. The child masters objects and phe-nomena and discovers their meanings only by behaving adequately with these objects in socially developed and accepted ways (A.N. Leont'ev, 1972). How do these adequate forms of activity develop?...[T]he activity itself should be directed and organized (Gal'perin, 1985) for maximum impact on development. The forms and organization of activity are not arbitrary, but are determined by certain condi-tions. (Burmenskaia, 1997, p. 217)

This last statement was made long after the fall of Communism and could have been written by anyone; however, there is a basic difference between focusing on a collective nature versus an individualistic nature of personality. This comment is not meant to be negative, but to elucidate the fact—often overlooked by current activity theorists around the world—that Russian activity theory was used to support the collective personality of the individual within a collective society. In other words, current international activity theory has been depoliticized and has been stripped of its intentions and social roots.

Interestingly, Vygotsky focused on a psychology that was indeed Marxist, yet its Spinozist roots transcended Russia. By transcending polarities, Vygotskian non-classical psychology moves on to a philosophical synthesis.

A. N. Leontiev's activity theory was an attempt to focus on real, concrete conditions, while placing Vygotskian theory on the side of the more abstract philosophy of German idealism. However, from the 1930s to the end of the 1950s, any type of Western philosophy was branded as being "bourgeois" and therefore not acceptable to the Russian political authorities. Activity theory in Russia can be divided into three phases up to the present: 1930s through 1950s, focusing on activity as such; 1960 through 1979 (the year of Leontiev's death), with a focus on consciousness; and 1980 to the present, with a focus on personality.[1]

A. A. LEONTIEV, RUSSIAN PSYCHOLINGUISTICS, AND THE SECOND LANGUAGE CLASSROOM

A. A. Leontiev's writings on psycholingistics and semiotics have direct applicability to the second language (L2) classroom. This section explores the relationship of A. A. Leontiev to Russian activity theory and to his father, A. N. Leontiev, who was its primary architect for fifty years. Because of the political ban placed on Vygotsky's works from 1936 to 1956, Russian activity theory changed direction. A. A. Leontiev is one of the foremost living psycholinguists in Russia, remaining true both to the teachings of Vygotsky and to his own father's theories, while forging new paths for foreign language learning, semiotics, psycholinguistics, and education. This section includes an overview of speech activity, inner speech, inner programming, language mastery, scientific/spontaneous concepts, functional grammar, goal-directedness, dominant activity, tension, imagery, and memory.

James Wertsch (1981a) stated that "A. A. Leont'ev [Leontiev] is the leading psycholinguist in the USSR today" (p. 241). A. A. Leontiev's semiotic theories and his thoughts on the psychology of foreign languages are the focus of this section. By the late 1950s, Vygotsky's psychology/philosophy was "rehabilitated" in Russia, and since then A. A. Leontiev and many others have based much of their thinking on Vygotsky's original teachings, expanding some of the relevant theories to other areas, such as foreign languages. Professor Leontiev has published over 800 articles and books from the 1950s to date. The majority of his works have not yet been translated into English.

Activity Theory Related to Foreign Languages

Perhaps the most important point regarding the difference in Russian psycholinguistics, Russian activity theory, and Western second language acquisition is the following:

Vygotsky's method is dialectical rather than dualistic. It is activity-based rather than cognition-based. Method is practiced, not applied. Whatever is to be discovered is not separate from the activity of *practicing method;* it is not "out there" awaiting the application of an already made tool, but is dialectically inseparable....*Practicing method* simultaneously creates the object of knowledge and the tool by which that knowledge might be known. (Newman & Holzman, 1997, p. 78)

Vygotsky often stated that thought is completed in word or speech, and this principle holds for any classroom learning. Learning results through meaningful activity, not just applied activity used for the sake of demonstrating theory. The basic goal of learning is not to apply theory that will automatically result in mastery. Vygotsky and Russian activity theory have taught us that it is precisely within activity that theory can become meaningful and internalized. Grounded theory then results within practical activity, fusing into a dialectic that forms a whole, and then becomes meaningful for learners. Just as development follows instruction/learning, meaningful theory follows from meaningful activity. This does not imply that theory is never used as a starting point in learning, but rather that theory is not viewed as a monolithic structure imposed on all learners—it is understood as a living, flexible tool that learners can shape for themselves. Theory can become an art form within this understanding.

The basic components of Russian activity theory are activity = act = operation. The corresponding conditions are need = motive = goal.[2] An interesting element of activity that A. N. Leontiev wrote about was called "afferentation." This term was understood within the metaphor of a circuit approach to activity:

All activity has a loop structure: afferentation-effector processes that make contact with the object-type environment correction and enrichment through feedback connections from the initial afferent image....The key point, however, is not the loop structure itself, but the fact that mental reflection of the object-type world is born not of direct external influences (including feedback influences). (A. N. Leont'ev, 1974–75, p. 12)[3]

Today the word "afferentation" might be replaced with the term "reflexivity,"[4] which captures the understanding of the observer viewing himself, where he becomes the actual instrument of the observation itself. A metaphorical example of this type of thinking is Heisenberg's uncertainty principle, which offers the philosophical understanding that any human observation of nature is affected by the act of observation itself.

Within activities, goal-directed actions are carried out, which are composed of mental and behavioral operations that vary with subjective and objective conditions. "Actions and operations are similarly non-contingent, since various operations are often available to meet the same goal, and the same operations may contribute to attainment of different goals" (Scribner, 1997, p. 231). As stated previously, the corresponding conditions of "activity = act = operation" are "need = motive = goal."[5] A.A. Leontiev (Leont'ev, 1973) gave a concrete example of this model:

Let us take an example of an elementary activity: a teacher interrupts the lesson to go and close the window. The motive here can vary: there may have been a cold draft; or the teacher may have seen that the pupils were getting cold; or perhaps a loud noise outside made it difficult to speak; and so on. The goal: closing the window. The acts: stepping down from the rostrum, going to the window, closing the window. The operations associated with these acts are determined by the height of the rostrum, the distance to the window, the construction of the window frame, and so on. (p. 23)

Here, A.N. Leont'ev [Leontiev] (1974–75) offered a starting point to understand this concept from a non-Western perspective:

Activity is a molar and nonadditive unit of a material subject's life. In a narrower and more psychological sense, activity is a unit of life mediated by mental reflection whose real function is to orient the subject to the world of objects. Activity is thus not a reaction or a totality of reactions, but rather a system possessing structure, inner transformations, conversions, and development. (p. 10)

This aspect represents the first feature of Russian activity theory, which Wertsch (1981b) called "activity analyzed at various levels" (p. 18). As Wertsch (1981b) pointed out, units of analysis used by activity theorists were defined "on the basis of functional criteria" (p.19). If the Russian understanding of activity theory were to be used in the West, then according to Wertsch, most Western psychologists would be concerned with operations rather than acts or activity. Similarly, the parameter of goal-directedness has not received much attention in the West.

In other words, an activity is usually realized by a certain set of actions that are subordinate to particular goals, which can be distinguished from the common goal. In this it is characteristic that for higher degrees of development, the role of a common goal is played by a conscious motive that is converted into a motive-goal precisely because it is consciousness....Another important aspect of the goal-formation process is the concrete specification of a goal, the discernment of conditions for its achievement. (A.N. Leont'ev, 1974–75, p. 24–25)

Wertsch then listed another feature of Russian activity theory as "activity [being] mediated." Within the Russian framework there is a focus on human consciousness, which is reflected in language, yet language is often viewed in a narrower framework than sign systems (cf. Wertsch, 1981b, pp. 24–26). Currently, the aspect of semiotics (i.e., sign systems) as influenced by Hegel and Marx, is now in place as a means of better understanding consciousness. As summarized here, the following quote is offered by A. A. Leontiev (Leont'ev, 1981):

As is well known, the ideal object (quasi-object) emerges in social activity as the converted form of actual connections and relations.... The apparent form of actual relations is substituted for the actual relations....Language is a system of such ideal objects—linguistic signs—in which an apparent form is substituted for real objects and phenomena, actualized in activity with these objects and phenomena...transformed into a new (linguistic) substance and filled with objectiveness and the qualities of language. (pp. 243–245)

The sign, according to A. A. Leontiev (Leont'ev, cited in Wertsch, 1981a), is then divided into three parts: (1) the sign as a thing, or *material, linguistic body;* (2) the sign *image* ("sign as the equivalent of the real sign in ordinary consciousness"); and (3) the *sign model* ("the product of scientific endeavors at understanding the structure and functions of the objective sign") (p. 245). One of the problems in working with this model, according to A. A. Leontiev, is that most investigators understand the sign image as if it were the sign model (p. 246).

Another aspect of Russian activity theory is the developmental or genetic explanation.

Calling his psychology developmental (*geneticheskii*—from genesis), Vygotsky meant much more than a mere analysis of the unfolding of behavior in ontogenesis. As a matter of fact, the very idea of development as unfolding and as maturation was alien to him. Vygotsky perceived psychological development as a dynamic process full of upheavals, sudden changes, and reversals. This process, however, ultimately leads to the formation of the cultural, higher mental functions. (Kozulin, 1986b, p. 266)

One of the basic premises of this concept is that human development "is oriented towards establishing increasing autonomy of the person relative to its environment" (Valsiner, 1996, p. 120).[6]

Another component of activity theory is social interaction, based on Vygotsky's thoughts:

To Vygotsky the notion of social interaction (*obščenie*)[7] means two things. There is immediate interaction, which we have with young children. This interaction manifests itself in cuddling and touching, that is, in affective reactions. This form of social interaction changes, however, to mediate(d) social interaction as soon as the child is able to use signs. (van der Veer & van IJzendoorn, 1985, p. 4)

The last element of activity theory Wertsch (1981a) listed is "internalization." He stated that "one of the major aspects of Vygotsky's theory is that activities are initially carried out by the child on the external plane, and then are internalized" (p. 31). On the internal plane there is assimilation and restructuring of the external plane via mediation. Wertsch (1998) then replaced the concept of internalization with the terms mastery and appropriation; however, it is argued that Vygotsky's concept of internalization does not need revision. This concept can be of vital importance to future second language acquisition (SLA) research. Vygotskian cultural-historical theory suggests that the principles of ingrowth or rooting can be further developed to enhance the SLA understanding of schemata, formatting, and chunking.[8] It should be clear that

it is not the social structures themselves that are internalized, but the meaning the individual learns to give to these structures in its interaction with others and in relation to what it has learned before. Internalization is an activity of meaning-giving and digestion, not a process of impression in which the individual stays passive. (Wardekker, 1996)

Speech Activity, Inner Speech, Inner Programming

Russian psycholinguistics has incorporated the primarily psychological theory of speech activity. For example, Průcha (1972) defined speech activity as reflected in "theories generalizing the linguistic characteristics of speech (text) and relating them to psychophysiological characteristics of the speech production and perception process" (p. 53). These processes are viewed within the understanding of a multistage approach, including a breakdown of speech acts ("only insofar as we are dealing with the characteristic features of activity that are independent of the conditions of the act and are determined exclusively by the structure of the activity as a whole"), and speech operations ("when...we refer to the characteristic features of activity that are determined by the conditions of the act and are not dependent on the structure of the activity") (A. A. Leont'ev [Leontiev], 1973, p. 31). The difficulty arises within the transition from speech acts to speech operations.[9] A. A. Leontiev's definition of speech acts within a psychological framework can be summarized as follows:

What, then, are the inherent, constituent parameters of the speech act? First of all, the structure of the speech act has certain general features in common with any voluntary act or activity as a whole—in particular, it consists of programming, carrying out the program, and comparing the program and the results....Second, the speech act is characterized by the gestures of the activity that are determined by the model of the past-present. These might be, for example, the presence or absence of the person or object spoken about within the visual field of the conversation partners, its place in the structure of the preceding act, and so on. Third, the structure of the speech act reflects the features of the activity that are associated with the place of the given act in the structure of the activity as a whole; for instance, we can construct a speech act in anticipation of a particular reaction by our neighbor, emphasizing or omitting various elements in the act accordingly. (A. A. Leont'ev, 1973, pp. 31–32)[10]

In order to understand speech activity as a whole, we need to review inner speech and inner programming. Vygotsky studied inner speech[11] within the relationship of thought to speech and the acquisition of speech by children.[12] Jan Průcha (1972) offered a general claim that

Inner speech (vnutrennaja rec) signifies a soundless verbalization process proceeding with various intensity and in dependence on many extra-individual conditions, when man [a person] is thinking about something, solving a problem, recalling memories, writing, reading for himself [herself]...also producing external speech. Inner speech is not solely subvocal soundless external speech as is sometimes assumed, but is a specific formation with entirely different properties and with a different function. (p. 67)

N. Sokolov, a Moscow psychologist, completed much work on inner speech, claiming that the components of inner speech can be actualized in both verbal-conceptual and visual thinking. Interestingly, Sokolov argued that inner speech contains the heard speech of others, which is produced by repetition, together with one's own speech, and that the relationship between external and internal speech maintains an evolutionary continuity and a functional dependence. Sokolov felt that inner speech has two main functions: as a means of thinking, and as a preparatory stage in external speech production (cf. Průcha, 1972, p. 69).

N. I. Zhinkin [Zinkin] analyzed another facet of inner speech by viewing the role of the object-representing code, although his understanding is somewhat contradictory.[13] Zhinkin's inner speech code consists of images, schemata, and intentions that represent a bridge from inner speech in children to inner speech in adults. Between external speech and inner speech, Leontiev and Akhutina posit "inner programming," which is a construction of a pattern or scheme based on the utterance to be produced, which may either evolve into external or inner speech. A. A. Leontiev also advocates an order of inner programming for nongrammatical languages, such as gesture for the deaf, or the early stages of child development.

In speaking of inner programming, we have in mind the programming of a verbal utterance, and by no means behavior (activity) in general, although the general physiological principles of programming can, in principle, be extended to the programming of speech....The difference between inner programming and inner speech is the difference between an intermediate stage in the process of production and a final stage, or result of this process. (A.A. Leont'yev [Leontiev], 1968–69, pp. 1–2)

The concept of inner programming is neither totally psychological, nor linguistic, but rather to some degree supralinguistic (A.A. Leont'ev, 1973, p. 33). Luria (1981) also contributed to inner programming called recoding, although it is not connected with Leontiev's concept.

The transformation of the initial thought into a sequentially organized speech utterance is not carried out in a single, instantaneous step. It involves a complex recoding of the initial, semantic graph into a syntagmatic speech schema. This is why Vygotsky argued that thought is not embodied in the word, but is *completed* in the word. It is in this process that inner speech plays a decisive role. (p. 153)

For A.A. Leontiev, the Vygotskian term "sense" (i.e., contextual, fluctuating understanding) serves as a semantic unit of inner speech, whereas "meaning" (i.e., the traditional, dictionary definition) serves as a semantic unit within a system of activity.[14] A.A. Leontiev's understanding of inner speech addresses the level of utterance, but not the entire message or text.[15] It is with this understanding in mind that A.A. Leontiev speaks about thinking in a foreign language, using the models of inner speech and inner programming, which are two of the most difficult aspects of reaching L2 fluency. A.A. Leontiev (1981) stated that

man does not memorize data imposed by language: he uses language to memorize that which he needs. Man does not think in a way determined by language: he mediates his thought through language to the extent to which language answers to the content and to the tasks of his thought. (p. 108)

Within the Leontievian model of inner language development, there is a codeterminancy of both semiotics and theories of the inner structure of language. A.A. Leontiev's focus is based on Vygotskian developmental theory-method, which views the potential of each individual student situated in the matrix of a social environment.

TEACHING FOREIGN LANGUAGES IN THE L2 CLASSROOM

A.A. Leontiev placed one of the core aspects of Vygotsky at the heart of his foreign language semiotics, namely, the personality formation of each individual learner. In referring to a statement given by his father, A.A. Leontiev (Leont'ev, 1998) noted:

As A.N. Leont'ev [Leontiev] said in one of his last writings, the study of the personality is "the study of *that for the sake of which* a person makes use of what is innate in him and what he has acquired, and *how* he uses these factors," and the psychological reality of the personality is "a special reality that *does not coincide* with the reality of psychological processes per se or with what a person can learn." ...In other words, "the human personality in no sense precedes a person's activity." (pp. 22–23)

With these thoughts we now focus on A. A. Leontiev's theories relating to the L2 classroom teaching-learning situation. It is remarkable how current many of A. A. Leontiev's ideas are when one considers the fact that most of the English translations are from the 1960s through the 1980s.

Under A. A. Leontiev's framework, students play an active role in language mastery. The term "language mastery" is used instead of "acquisition" or "learning." Often in traditional foreign language classrooms, students are hardly motivated to master the language being studied; if anything, the hidden motivation is one of failure. An example is given by A. A. Leontiev (Leont'ev, 1973) of a typical foreign language classroom session:

[T]his is a school. Inside the school is a classroom. Inside the classroom there are a professor and students. This is a wall. It is pointed out that most anything could be substituted for *wall*, and the student would hardly be motivated. Psychologically, it makes no difference to the student whether he says "this a wall or this is a dog." ...However, there is a general methodological principle, based on the specific psychological features of conscious human activity, that says that a person acquires first and retains longest the things that are specifically related to him, the things that are regularly associated with the characteristic features of his activity. (pp. 37–38)

Leontiev suggested that there be a reading of stories that place the student in the middle of the situation with a problem needing to be solved. For example, a teacher could use or alter detective stories,

and if we want the student to be interested in his activity, we must construct the fictitious circumstances in such a manner that he either actually finds himself in a situation where he has to act in a particular way or can readily effect a transformation—or, as psychologists say, transference—to the person acting in these circumstances. (A. A. Leont'ev, 1973, pp. 38–39)

In general, most of the foreign language textbooks used in American schools (whether focused on communicative competence, proficiency, or culture) maintain the atmosphere of a cold, objective world, asking the student to then produce interesting facts about herself. One of the problems in learning a foreign language at the college level is that the basic stance of schooling, or academic learning, requires in Vygotskian terminology the understanding of scientific concepts. This implies a focus on intellectual, formalized ideas. However, the mother tongue is acquired via spontaneous concepts, or everyday experientially based learning. For Vygotsky, successful education results from the convergence of the top-down approach (e.g., scientific concepts) with the bottom-up approach (e.g., spontaneous concepts), where constant dialectical cross-referencing occurs. At this juncture, grammar, in its extended meaning, serves, metaphorically speaking, as the contact point or bridge. Grammar is an area acquired via spontaneous concepts, yet must be enhanced via scientific concepts if intellectual maturity and mastery are to be reached. However, there must be a deeper, un[sub]conscious component to this understanding, which is internalization. The interrelatedness of both spontaneous and scientific concepts is then the key to concept formation, which lies at the heart of internalization and ultimately self-regulation. As already stated, one of the general problems regarding the psychological paradox in many foreign language programs across the United States is that students normally expect the mode of scientific, conceptually based learning in many courses, whereas beginning levels of foreign languages often attempt to approximate the ambiance of spontaneous, everyday, experiential learning.

Within Vygotskian theory or method, it is assumed that the degree of success a student of foreign languages has in the L2 classroom is contingent on the student's mastery of grammar in the mother tongue. Vygotsky (quoted in A. A. Leont'ev, 1973) stated that "the development of one's native language proceeds upward, whereas the development of a foreign language proceeds downward" (p. 19). The Leontievian position is the following: One of the major problems in using the L1 as the support grid (or transference model) for learning/acquiring an L2 is that neither the mother tongue, nor the L2 can be "reduced to the simple accumulation of certain skills, and even more, of certain ready-made elements" (cf. A. A. Leont'ev, 1973, p. 20). The Vygotskian and Leontievian approaches assume that both the L1 and L2 represent more than the sum of the total of their parts. However, the atomistic breakdown of analysis is appropriate within synthetic models, which Revzin attributed to the Chomskyan model.[16] At the same time, within an analytic model, a reconstruction of the individual parts will not recreate the whole, that is, sentences or utterances will not add up to the whole understanding of a language that an L2 student is learning (or even a child learning his or her mother tongue). What A. A. Leontiev suggested is to link together the various functional systems required in the production of speech (cf. A. A. Leontiev, 1973, p. 20), instead of reducing the material into incremental steps, attempting to replicate or create a "natural order" that is supposedly valid for each learner.

It is only toward the end of language mastery that functional grammar is introduced, which is "a model of the generation of verbal utterances based on a rule for moving from a given content to the various possible forms of its expression in a particular language" (A. A. Leont'ev, 1973, p. 22). The L2 learner must have an idea of content before expression takes place, or within Russian activity theory terminology, there must be a transition from the level of speech acts to the level of speech operations. Within the Western tradition of functional grammar, the rule system is viewed in functional terms, which enters the realm of pragmatics. At this stage four major functional-grammatical rules are offered, not taken from Leontiev, but rather from a Western understanding of functional grammar: predicate formation, term formation, assignment, and expression (cf. Siewierska, 1991, p. 12). This context dependency in functional grammar maintains a form/function correlation; however, it is not predicated on a one-to-one understanding. One structure, for example, may serve many functions (e.g., mulitfunctionality), and many functions may be served by one structure (e.g., redundancy) (cf. Siewierska, 1991, p. 4). Within the Leontievian perspective, the position of content of the foreign language resides within the concept of goal-directedness and the structure of activity. This direction includes the aspect of motivation, which influences the speech act itself.

The discussion so far has taken speech activity and inner speech as the starting point of an understanding of a Leontievian approach to foreign languages, including areas of inner programming, spontaneous/scientific concepts, functional grammar, and goal-directedness. While these facets do not fit into a systematic model of learning or teaching an L2, they are directed toward the ultimate mastery of a foreign language. Much of the problem regarding the mastery of a foreign language results from the fact that in the classroom reactive speech is often assumed, instead of active speech.

With this overall goal in place, students maintain a dominant activity or project they are sincerely interested in that does not necessarily have to correspond to the teacher's interests, but is nevertheless a long-range activity. A dominant activity is an ongoing project where many of the traditional structural exercises are learned to successfully complete the project. In referring to B. V. Belyayev's method, A. A. Leontiev (Leont'ev, 1981) stated that

the solution he [Belyayev] proposes amounts to the idea that one should link up the foreign language with various modes of the learner's activity, and construct teaching in such a way that language is not used only for communication purposes...but as a medium which will engage the thought, perception, and imagination of the learner. (p. 65)

The implementation of a dominant activity is an idea that complements the use of a textbook, traditional grammar exercises, and the like. There are many examples of introducing the dominant activity, including computer research where students look up specific information on the Internet and slowly integrate that information into the linguistic structures at hand. In a previous example, regarding a beginning level Spanish course, a dominant activity was used to prepare students during the entire semester for a taped interview with a native speaker of Spanish for at least thirty minutes. Students were encouraged to find native speakers of Spanish within their majors or anticipated future professions. The dominant activity was beyond the typical boundaries of a beginning level course, though it was discovered that there is not one single dominant activity common to all college students. It is wise to organize a foreign language classroom along lines of trust, by allowing students to find their own dominant activity.

The problem of student anxiety has been addressed at various levels within Leontiev's framework. In terms of theory, Leontiev has never referred to the word "anxiety," as we do in the West, but to the word "tension." Soviet psychologists distinguish between two different types of emotional tension. One is purely emotional, the other is operational:

Purely emotional tension arises when, in assessing a given stressful situation, one finds that there is a real or imagined incompatibility between one's motives, plans, possibilities, capacities, etc., and the demands of that situation, most frequently, when the aims and motives of the activity do not coincide....Operational tension is connected with the necessity of carrying out a particular activity: it allows a person to settle into that activity, and always leads to the best possible performance. A driver in the rush hour, a pilot at landing, a teacher in his classroom—they all experience a state of operational tension. (A. A. Leont'ev, 1981, p. 70)

The other aspect regards the image the student has of herself within the setting of the foreign language classroom, regarding the projected success of learning the L2 to any degree of fluency/accuracy. Different theorists have labeled this "the image of the result" (G. Miller, K. Pribram, E. Galanter), "the model of the future" (N. A. Bernshteyn), or the "imagined situation" (I. T. Bzhalava), and various Russian psychologists have labeled it "probability forecasting" (A. A. Leont'ev, 1973, pp. 25–26).[17] To better understand image, it is noteworthy that from the Russian perspective image is viewed as being not only individual, but also social in nature (cf. Yaroshevsky, 1989, p. 79).

Although contemporary theorists often believe that various aspects of the cognitive approach are superior to the behaviorist approach, in reality many L2 classrooms copy the old stimulus-response formula in the time allotted to L2 learning/acquisition. Within the Leontievian and contemporary ecological approaches, there is a direct connection to the Russian concept of environmental afferentiation (hence, reflexivity) by assuming that there will be a stimulus-regulation (as opposed to stimulus-response)[18] in place for beginning L2 learners. Students are then motivated to use the material learned to regulate their world view(s) via cultural-semiotic mediation, and not just in response to situations. This new and interesting element can be added to the understanding of consciousness, presenting activity within the metaphor of a circuit approach. Within an ecological perspective the terms "prospectivity" (i.e., the forward-looking character of agency), and "retrospectivity" (i.e., the rearward-looking character of behavior) are activated on a continual basis (cf. Reed, 1996, pp. 12–13). It is the role of both the teacher and learner to be proactive in establishing a sense of anticipation for success, because in many L2 classrooms, the unspoken truth is that failure is often programmed into the day-to-day learning experience. In addition, the understanding of potentiality and personality development should accompany the expected results of success. Prolepsis is a part of the image the student brings into the classroom setting, which is perhaps one of the most neglected aspects of SLA research and language acquisition that could be positioned within the zone of proximal development (ZPD), with the expected (future-oriented) possibility of a reasonably high level of fluency/accuracy being preestablished for each individual learner. In other words, students learn to anticipate their own success in the foreign language classroom, learning to create images of success. Michael Cole (1996, p. 184) used the example of a newborn baby immediately placed within the protection of its caregivers. From the very beginning, language is spoken to the baby with the anticipation that he or she will grow into the linguistic community and become efficient in language usage. In current L2 classroom learning, the ability to actually attain a valued level of proficiency in the foreign language is not often anticipated, and therefore not actualized.

In much of SLA, the overriding trends in research deal with mistakes, errors, fossilization, and general limitations, all of which have certainly had an indirect negative effect on L2 learning methods, and on classroom linguistic proficiency in general. Prolepsis—as a form of consciousness-raising—could easily be used in the L2 classroom setting as a type of student empowerment. Leo van Lier (1996) wrote about prolepesis from an L2 perspective by stating that

when Rommetveit (1974) proposed the notion of prolepsis, he was thinking of a speaker who gives the hearer clues for the enlargement of common ground without spelling out every detail. Proleptic discourse therefore is aware of gaps in understanding and invites the less competent into sharing with the more competent. Whereas ellipsis can be dismissive (or at best indifferent), prolepsis is always invitational and generous. (p. 182)

Another example of programming L2 learning for success is a new view of memory. The approach taken by A. A. Leontiev includes a tripartite model of immediate memory ("immediate memory involves the general psychophysiological capacities—abstracted from the tasks of activity—for imprinting and initially retaining material that has just been perceived"), and operative memory (that is "subordinate to the goals of the concrete activity. Its short-term nature is relative.... Though it is short-term in relation to long-term memory, operative memory may actually be long in relation to immediate memory").[19] Long-term or permanent memory is, of course, the overriding goal of any foreign language learning. Situation memory relates only to conditioning in the classical sense of the term. Leontiev also distinguished between arbitrary and nonarbitrary memory, with arbitrary memory being either direct or indirect. Indirect (mediated) arbitrary memory is the most complex and can be operationalized late in childhood (cf. A. A. Leontiev, 1981, p. 52). Clues were given in understanding memory when Leontiev (1981) stated that

verbal memory is, as a rule, voluntary and mediated; word memory is immediate and involuntary-obligatory.... The overall understanding of the functions of memory rely upon the organization of the dominant activity (of any meaningful activity of the learner) from a psychological point of view...rather than...on the assumption that a certain number of repetitions will of itself guarantee the imprinting of the necessary items in the memory. (p. 59)

CONCLUSIONS OF A. A. LEONTIEV'S PSYCHOLINGUISTICS

Although A. A. Leontiev did not speak directly about the importance of creating new spaces when learning a foreign language, he often referred to the restrictive nature of many classroom settings. Within his understanding of personality development, students should be given as much space as possible in order to increase their personal motivation. Although Leontiev did not write about this element specifically, Kris Gutierrez, Betsy Rymes, and Joanne Larson (1995) complemented the Leontievian spirit of L2 learning and teaching from a Western perspective. They stated that there are official and unofficial spaces, using the term "third space" "to describe how these spaces might intersect and, thus, create the potential for more authentic interaction and heteroglossia" (p. 446). Another way of looking at this idea has been described by Claire Kramsch (1993) as the "third place." She stated that

Growing into one's own is by essence recognizing the faultlines in the social fabric, admitting for example that even though we are of the same nationality and social class, "my" country might not be "your" country, and your understanding of our social class might not be the same as mine. It also means acknowledging differences within oneself and seeing oneself within the historic context of one's own biography. (p. 234)

The next idea along these lines is called "internal space" (Delacour, 1997), which can be a precursor to Vygotsky's terminology of internalization. One of the general problems of beginning to learn a foreign language in the classroom at the high school or university level reflects the nature of saturated images that most students carry with them. Within the L2 classroom there is often an overabundance of images in the form of interactive videos, foreign language films, classroom visual material, the use of overhead projectors, or even bringing in authentic music and realia. Students are often so saturated with images from the everyday world of TV that they are literally incapable of making space for new images, which must then be internalized before mature concept formation can take place in the target language/culture. Jean Delacour (1997) stated that

according to other metaphors, unification and integration are made possible by, and are the emergent properties of, an internal space... where processes which are independent in unconscious states interact, communicate.... A possible solution is that cognitive subsystems do not only generate first-order representations of external objects but also produce higher order representations of their own internal current state and that it is this recurrent representational activity that leads to or causes states of consciousness. (pp. 259–260)

Allowing external and internal spaces to simultaneously occur can enliven teaching methods and expand the open-ended potential of the teaching experience. By learning to form the imagery of the student's own potential, success in the L2 can result, as opposed to constantly focusing on the correction of mistakes and errors. Such an approach supports one of the basic motives behind the theories of both Vygotsky and Leontiev, namely the enhancement of the growth of the individual personality. In addition to the third space, the third place, and the internal space, one may speak of the "third meaning," a term coined by Roland Barthes. The Russian film *Ivan the Terrible*, produced by Sergei Eisenstein (Vygotsky's good friend), includes aspects of what Barthes calls the "first meaning," or the informational level, and the "second meaning," or the symbolic level. Barthes (1985) referred to the third meaning as the obtuse meaning:

[A]n obtuse angle is greater than a right angle: *an obtuse angle of 100°*, says the dictionary; the third meaning, too, seems to me greater than the pure perpendicular, the trenchant, legal upright of the narrative. It seems to me to open the field of meaning totally, i.e., infinitely. I even accept, for this obtuse meaning, the word's pejorative connotation: the obtuse meaning seems to extend beyond culture, knowledge, [and] information. Analytically, there is something ridiculous about it; because it opens onto the infinity of language, it can seem limited in the eyes of analytic reason. It belongs to the family of puns, jokes, useless exertions; indifferent to moral or aesthetic categories (the trivial, the futile, the artificial...), it sides with the carnival aspect of things.... The obtuse meaning is clearly the epitome of counter-narrative; disseminated, reversible, trapped in its own temporality, it can establish (if followed) only an altogether different script...an unheard of script, counter-logical and yet true. (pp. 44–57)

A. A. Leontiev takes the whole person in real time as the starting point of his theories within psycholinguistics vis-à-vis foreign language learning; and with the understanding of the individual being situated within a societal context, he maintains the goal of personality development of the whole person, which is an activation of the hermeneutic circle. What is important, within the concept of personality, is the creation of new realities, new spaces, and new relationships. L. I. Bozhovich (1977) offered a new understanding, now called the "third level":

In comparing individuals, it is not the primary or even the secondary relationships within the integral system of consciousness that are important, but rather the relationships that exist on some third level and the way the individual himself makes use of his own capacities, i.e., the place they occupy in his personality and activity. (p. 14)

In taking this journey we have entered into a new and hopefully refreshing approach to the L2 classroom, returning the responsibility of success back to the teacher and learner, while still anchoring the new approach in well-grounded theory. There is a focus on allowing learners and teachers more space, while placing L2 learning within the psychological understanding of personality development.

SUMMARY OF VYGOTSKIAN AND LEONTIEVIAN THOUGHTS REGARDING SLA

Within Vygotskian and Leontievian psychology/philosophy, a cultural dominance (i.e., some higher set of cultural values) stands as an ideal to strive for within traditional educational settings. The process described— via the L2 classroom setting—includes a teacher with an infused sense of energy serving as a role model, while viewing the student within the potentiality offered by the ZPD. Bearing in mind that conceptual processing takes place on the social plane first (i.e., intermental), before being internalized (i.e., intramental), techniques of assimilation are necessary. The successful process of internalization of an L2 is long and arduous and is ultimately a result of what Vygotskian terminology refers to as catharsis. In other words, the road to proficiency and fluency is filled with tension and anxiety at levels beyond the beginning stage, rather than focusing on fun and spontaneous conceptualization. Students will be aware of the fact that at some point the cathartic experience or the so-called magic moment, is experienced within an atmosphere where the tension level is simply transcended (i.e., the cathartic moment), and the learner can deal with the ambiguity needed in becoming proficient in the L2. The entire approach leading to the point of catharsis might be labeled the "principle of maximal frustration." This principle is the antithesis of many methods in practice today, where the lessening of frustration is the goal, with the concomitant result that learners often do not continue their studies of the foreign language for the long term. The process leading to the cathartic moment is variant and might assume a trajectory similar to that represented here: Teachers encourage students to engage in dialogue through established dominant activities, while reading, writing, and grammar serve as guidelines in developing inner speech. Many foreign language classrooms try to focus on the similarities of different cultures, yet Vygotsky was aware of the fact that children objectively process differences before similarities, and within semiotics it is hypothesized that there is no meaning without the recognition of differences. It is proposed that in learning to be bilingual and bicultural, we must past through the path of our differences to be able to come to a real acceptance of our similarities, and this path is filled with frustrations. It is precisely our inner speech/monologue and socialized dialogue that can direct us toward self-regulation and inner freedom of action, within meanings (and sense) we create for ourselves.

Inner speech, understood as a dynamic process, will then be connected to the Vygotskian concepts of word meaning and word. Through "engagements" and "separations," word meaning will be enhanced by established, conventional meanings, and a dynamic feel of *sense* will slowly allow the L2 student to create individual meanings for one's own personality. Through tools, psychological tools, and signs there will be an understanding and implementation of not only learning a new language, but of actual empowerment to mediate one's personal and social environment, with the ultimate goal of mediating one's own actions, using the process of object-regulation, other-regulation, and ultimately self-regulation. All of these types of regulation can be (and are) activated in adult behavior at will. Self-regulation will be based within a mature monologue-based dialogic framework. Concept formation is then viewed as a process, and it is understood that foreign words will be learned once a concept is in place to process the word. Activities incorporating disobjectification will be included, starting with the initial phases of the L2. A focus on dissimilarities and differences will be as important as a fun-oriented approach to activities that focus on holidays or varying cultural traditions. At the same time, cultural information will need to be offered, perhaps with students completing smaller research projects and sharing the information with other students. Much of classroom speech will take place within pseudoconcepts or functional equivalents, which will serve as a bridge of future understanding within a flexible nature. The road to genuine concepts will be long and will demand a partnership between teacher and student, and student and student, as well as student and teacher, and student and native speaker with the culture-environment. Participants will learn to incorporate a new understanding of images, imagination, imitation, and mimesis, and above all, the entire goal of the L2 process will be to develop the learner's whole personality. This process will take place within the mode of consciousness-raising of the learner within the highest planes of mental functions. As Vygotsky (1994a) once stated,

If language is as old as consciousness itself, and if language is a practical consciousness-for-others and, consequently, consciousness-for-myself, then not only one particular thought but all consciousness is connected with the development of the word....The word is a direct expression of the historical nature of human consciousness. Consciousness is reflected in a word as the sun in a drop of water. A word relates to consciousness as a living cell relates to a whole organism, as an atom relates to the universe. A [meaningful] word is a microcosm of human consciousness. (p. 256)

Often in the West there is interest in depth psychology, psychoanalysis, and Freud. A. A. Leontiev, on the other hand, is interested in fostering the Vygotskian understanding of height psychology. Vygotsky stated, "[O]ur psychology is height psychology (it defines not the depths but the heights of personality)."[20]

NOTES

1. These phases were given during a private discussion with Dmitry Leontiev in Moscow during July 2000.

2. See V. V. Davydov, Zinchenko, and Talyzina (1983, pp. 31–42).

3. "This means that the afferent which controls activity processes is primarily the object itself and only secondarily its image as a subjective product of activity that fixes, stabilizes, and assimilates its object—type content. In other words, we have the transitions of object ⇒ process of activity and activity ⇒ its subjective product" (A. N. Leont'ev, 1974–75, p. 12).

4. "The terms reflexive, reflexivity, and reflexiveness have been used in a variety of disciplines to describe the capacity of language and thought—of any system of signification—to turn or bend back upon itself, to become an object to itself, and to refer to itself. Whether we are discussing things grammatical or cognitive, what is meant is a reflex action or process linking self and other, subject and object" (Babcock, 1980, p. 2).

5. See V. V. Davydov, Zinchenko, and Talyzina (1983, pp. 31–42).

6. For other articles regarding the Vygotskian understanding of development, see El'konin (1967, pp. 33–41), A. K. Marková (1978, pp. 188–205), Wertsch and Tulviste (1992, pp. 548–557) and Wertsch (1988, pp. 81–89).

7. Here is an explanation of *obščenie* in German:

Für den deutschen Leser interessant ist, daß in diesem Zusammenhang von "obščenie: die Übersetzung "Verkehr," "Umgang," "Verbindung," in Übersetzungen von Texten Vygotskijs steht für "obščenie" auch häufig "Kommunikation." Das russische Wort "obščenie" ist verwandt mit "obščij," das man sowohl mit "allgemein," mit "gemeinsam" als auch mit "gesamt" übersetzen kann. "Obščij" bezeichnet das den zu einem Ganzen zusammenfaßbaren Glidern Gemeinsame. Weitere verwandte Worte sind u.a. "obščnost" (Gemeinsamkeit) and "obščestvo" (Gesellschaft). "Obščenie" hat einen inhaltlichen Umfang, der von keiner der deutschen Übersetzungsmöglichkeiten voll wiedergegeben wird. Es beinhaltet zugleich gemeisames Sein, sich als Mitglieder einer Sozietät zueinander zu verhalten und sich miteinander zu verständigen. (Rissom, 1985, pp. 135–136)

[For the German reader it is interesting that in this connection "obščenie" translates as "social intercourse," "social contact," "social connections," words which are used for "obščenie" in Vygotsky's texts, as well as the frequent translation of "communication." The Russian word "obščenie" relates to "obščig," which can be translated as "general" or "together," as well as "total or whole." "Obščig" characterizes a total, all encompasing link of togetherness. Other related words, among others, are "obščnost" (togetherness) and "obščestvo" (society). "Obščenie" maintains a wide range of content, which can never be completely translated into German. It simultaneously contains a "common being," such as a member of society remaining loyal, while making oneself understood.] [Trans. D.R.]

8. MacWhinney (1978, p. 100) detailed two stages of acquisition of morphophonology: "1. 'rote memorization,' where inflections are not yet recognized as separate elements and mistakes of construction do not occur; and 2. the early stages of synthesis." MacWhinney divides these stages into analogical formation and productive combination, which are characterized by errors of overgeneralization.

9. A key component to this transition lies within the concept of a speech situation, which includes three areas of the learning process:

First of all, it is the structural unit of any textbook, i.e., the element around which each lesson is built in the typical case (the term 'lesson' refers here to a part of a textbook rather than a segment of the learning process). Second, it is a kind of inner spring of the learning process, a way of presenting the students with the linguistic material in a lesson. And, third, it is a way of organizing the exercises so as to consolidate the knowledge the student has acquired. (A. A. Leont'ev, 1973, p. 35)

10. For information on A. A. Leont'ev's understanding of speech acts, see A. A. Leont'ev (1981, pp. 26–28).

11. For a discussion on Vygotsky's understanding of inner speech see Wertsch (1985a, p. 124), Vygotsky (1994, p. 182), and A. A. Leont'yev (1968–69).

12. Not all Soviet scholars agree with Vygotsky on his understanding of inner speech, for example, Blonskij. See Průcha (1972, pp. 67–68).

13. "Zinkin's hypothesis, however, concerning absolute material independence of the inner speech code on a particular natural language is contradictory to his concept of inner speech origin" (Průcha, 1972, p. 77).

14. See A. A. Leont'ev (1998, pp. 28–47) and Průcha (1972, p. 75).

15. "Internal programming *(vnutrenee programmirovanie)* is unconscious construction of a certain scheme on the basis of which utterance is then pro-

duced....Internal programming can then evolve either into external speech or inner speech....In this model, inner speech is not thus an inter-stage in external speech generation while in Leont'ev's concept it is only a consequence of the functional distinction between inner speech and external speech" (Průcha, 1972, p. 74).

16. See A. A. Leont'ev (1973, p. 68).

17. These authors are listed in A. A. Leont'ev (1973, pp. 25–26); however, they are not listed in the reference section.

18. See Reed (1996, pp. 9–19).

19. A. A. Leontiev (1981, pp. 85–86).

20. A. A. Leontyev (1992, p. 41).

CHAPTER 6

Second Language Acquisition

INPUT-OUTPUT

Within this section there is less focus on the practical aspect of teaching foreign languages, and more focus on applied linguistic theory, related to the tenets of Vygotsky and Leontiev. After discussing input-output, first language–second language (L1 = L2) transfer, and markedness, the discussion enters areas seldom discussed within second language acquisition (SLA). It is hoped that the areas that follow offer new insights into the possibilities of combining semiotics with L2 theory, research, and the foreign language classroom.

In beginning this analysis, the core of the problem appears to revolve around the concept of process and what that actually means, as well as the connection between input and accuracy. One major problem within SLA regarding input-output has centered around the attempt to place a scientific method as a type of grid over the basic understanding of this concept, which ultimately must include the unconscious. Vygotsky (1926/1971) stated that

the unconscious, it is said, is by definition something we do not recognize; it is something unknown to us, and therefore it cannot become the subject of scientific investigation. This reasoning proceeds from the false assumption that we can study only what is directly recognizable. This is obviously a superficial approach, since we do study many things of which we have knowledge only from analogies, hypotheses, surmises, etc. (p. 23)

The unconscious simply cannot be extracted from most clinical experiments and statistically verified. However, this does not stop historians from studying history, or archaeologists from studying archaeology. The same analogy can be applied to the problems of linguistic input-output, where there seems to be no conclusive evidence for or against the positions made, with statements such as,

[W]hereas Larsen-Freeman (1976a, and 1976b), Lightbown (1980), Hamayan and Tucker (1980), and Long (1981b) all found significant positive correlations between input frequency and accuracy, Snow and Hoefnagel-Höhle (1982), Long and Sato ([1984]), and Lightbown (1983) did not find any direction relationship. (R. Ellis, 1994, p. 270)

One of the problems within the input-output theories is the lack of differentiation between the surface and deep structure, which was detected in the 1960s:

J. Katz has attempted to spell out the doctrine of linguistic rationalism. He defines the observable grammatical features (input data) of a sentence in terms of what is directly predictable from final derived phrase markers (surface structures), whereas unobservable grammatical features are defined in terms of what can be predicted from its underlying phrase markers (underlying structures). Thus input data are restricted to surface structures, whereas output data contain allegedly innate elements found in the underlying structures, not in the surface structures. (Zimmerman, 1969, p. 202)

"Input," as a term, can be misleading because of the problems listed above; as well, forced or pushed output (i.e., speech production) in the L2 classroom does not always reflect the internal side of input. R. Ellis (1994) stated that it is not the case that pushed output will indeed "result in the acquisition of new linguistic features" (p. 286). Michael Sharwood-Smith (1994) added that

input, taken literally, is a misleading term. Since we cannot know from observation alone exactly what is processed by the learner at a given moment in time, many utterances to which the learner is exposed may contain elements which the learner does not register at all. In other words, the input data may be registered on the researcher's tape recorder as having been *available* to the learner at a given time....However, whether they have been registered consciously or subconsciously by the *learner* is another matter. (p. 8)

This line of thought automatically raises the issue of intake (Corder, 1981), which then opens up the discussion regarding the internal processing of the L2 learner. Yet as Ellis (1994) has argued: "it cannot be said to demonstrate that comprehensible input *causes* acquisition" (p. 278), which is also true for comprehended input (Gass, 1988). The entire input-output problem cannot be solved with inductive, quasi-scientific statements, because it will always remain a mystery as to how the conversion actually takes place. There are two basic problems with the input-output theory today. First, as Pienemann (1984) wrote: "Not only may the gap between comprehension and production be more than one acquisitional stage, but there is strong evidence that the interaction between the two sides of language processing does not necessarily have to be such that comprehension precedes production" (p. 208). For example, the fact that we as human beings can acquire language only by way of understanding messages or comprehensible input is not always the case, as paradoxical as that might sound. There is the example of dilingual discourse, which is defined as "[t]he use of two mutually unintelligible languages by interactants who do not comprehend one another" (Saville-Troike, 1988, p. 574). In dilingual discourse, speakers can communicate in a limited but meaningful way without being able to speak each other's language, and without exposure to comprehensible input. In the L2 classroom, the learner is required to produce various sentences in the foreign language, which are automatically judged according to form, correctness, and proficiency, rather than function, meaning, and attempts at conversation. Second, the distinction between high-input and low-input generators (Seliger, 1977) is also a result of product-oriented thinking, which appears to be biased toward extrovert students, who are able to make contact easily and search out such contact. This hypothesis cannot be proven and adds to the assumption that input-output research is of a static nature, as mentioned before, with little attempt to employ the genetic-developmental aspect. It often views L2 learners as atomized individuals, not living in a social and power dominated setting, with L2 learners sometimes being portrayed as having no varying internal processing mechanisms.

Without restating the problem within the SLA construct, it is hypothesized via a Vygotskian perspective that the input-out model traditionally places the L2 learner in a static environment, often eliminating the precise variables that could address a better understanding of the issue, determining whether input enhances output. Instead there seems to be a microoriented conflation of terms. Claire Kramsch (1995) stated that:

[O]nce the language to be learned had been identified as *input*, the notion of input itself became an object of research in need of further refinement through words....First, by metonymic reduction, it moved from an abstract entity called language or information flow to a tangible, concrete reality called input, which it could then endowed with causal attributes....In this discourse movement from the part to the whole, from the particular to the general, input came to be viewed as anything in the teaching and learning environment that might affect the acquisition of a foreign language....Thus, for example, the acquisition of cultural competence or of foreign discourse competence never did fit into an input-output model of language acquisition. (pp. 53–54)

Another view comes from the call to replace the concept of input with that of affordance, offered by van Lier (1996):

[T]he language of input and output permeates our discourses of language learning and teaching, and I suggest, not even the powerful ideas of Vygotsky...and Bakhtin...can change this, unless we make an effort to establish a new metaphor; not one that banishes input and output notions, but that incorporates them into a new, reconfigured universe of discourse. Indeed, I suggest that Vygotskyan learning theory will be severely hamstrung and will fail to fulfill its transformative potential, unless we dig up the doxa and reset the boundaries of the field. Failing to do so will result in all novel ideas and influences being interpreted within the parameters set by the universe of discourse. (pp. 1–2)

In order to unravel this problem, aspects of input-output are placed within a higher ordering system of comprehension-production, used to detach input-output from behavoristic connotations. It has been hypothesized that comprehension and production have different genetic roots, such as thought and speech: "First of all, comprehension and production must be viewed as separate processes. Encoding and decoding processes, in particular, cannot be viewed simply as mirror images depending on whether we are discussing input or output" (Ruder & Finch, 1987, p. 134). If this understanding were to be implemented in research, then the Vygotskian aspect of input-output research would focus on a developmental continuum, attempting to establish the point of convergence of the two processes, incorporating the maximal meaningfulness for the learner. The hypothesis here is that "a model of language production acknowledges the potential for and existence of different cognitive structures underlying comprehension and production" (Ruder & Finch, 1987, p. 134). It has often been stated that no matter what type of L2 method is in vogue, no matter what type of L2 research is discovered for the classroom situation, students still learn an L2 as they always have, via comprehension and production. One example of this attitude is this statement:

In over 30 years of teaching English as a foreign language to students of many different nationalities from many widely varying language and cultural backgrounds I have noticed no improvement at all in the mastery of English. Naturally, as English has more and more become the world language, more and more people are taught it and use it. But they do not speak it or write it or understand it *better* than people did before. (Gethin, 1990, p. 62)

If there were to be conclusive evidence that input—regardless of comprehensibility—is indeed the decisive factor for determining accuracy and fluency, then more than an interaction theory would be needed to supply an understanding of the correlation between input and accuracy/fluency. Currently, it appears that thought can simply be refracted through production mechanisms, such as input-intake-uptake-output, without approximating the internal processes that take place. There appears to be a one-to-one correspondence of input-output, which then automatically assumes a linear approach. However, in reality "linear modelling of second language processing is limited in its explanatory power since language processing is, in actuality non-linear."[1] In Vygotskian terminology, much of L2 output theory is a reflection of entification (from entities), which means that it measures static output. "From the emphasis on conditional-genetic study follows the impossibility of studying development via its static outcomes" (van der Veer & Valsiner, 1991, pp. 170–171). It might be meaningful to implement Vygotsky's understanding of rooting or ingrowth within the aspect of internalization, which could elucidate the transformation of input-intake-output. Vygotsky stated (van der Veer & Valsiner, 1994) that

such complete ingrowing is based on the fact that inner stimuli are substituted for the external ones. The first may be termed seam-like ingrowing. The seam connecting two parts of organic texture very rapidly leads to the formation of the connecting texture, so that the seam itself becomes unnecessary. (pp. 66–67)

Other stages are reached until there is complete ingrowing. With such a focus on input-output, research would automatically infuse aspects of semiotics into the overall picture. Research of this nature would demand the inclusion of variables that are hardly statistically verifiable, such as emotion, volition, motivation, and the general images of the learner-participant. In closing, it can be stated that "input hinges not so much on richness of input, but crucially on the choices made by individuals as responsible agents with dispositions to think and act in certain ways rooted in their discursive histories" (Lantolf & Pavlenko, 1995, p. 116).

L1 = L2 AND TRANSFER

Is the process of learning a second language similar to or even the same process as learning a first language? In discussing this question, people become dogmatic on what is for the most part anecdotal evidence. The apparent insolubility of the controversy can, to some extent, be traced to the differing levels of generality at which the various disputants are developing their arguments. (Rivers, 1983, p. 157)

The inherent problem of L1 = L2 often takes a polarized, somewhat politicized understanding, as everyone is aware that an adult is not a child, therefore the answer is no, L1 is not L2. However, the final linguistic product will proceed through certain stages, which will ultimately result in a shared, common understanding of language (often through the bridge of pseudoconcepts). Therefore, in some respects the answer is yes, L1 somehow allows for L2. In reality, this problem is psycholinguistic in nature and cannot be answered in full without knowing how languages are stored (inside and perhaps outside) the brain. A beginning step in applying Vygotskian theory to the L1-L2 problem is the understanding that internal processing results within concept formation. In general, many of the accompanying theories of L1 = L2, such as transfer, are directly or indirectly observed in an approach of quasi-associationism. As stated previously, Vygotsky (Kozulin, 1994) was of the opinion that

concept formation does not follow the model of an associative chain in which one link calls forth the next; it is an aim-directed process, a series of operations that serve as steps toward a final goal. Memorizing words and connecting them with objects does not in itself lead to concept formation; for the process to begin, a problem must arise that cannot be solved otherwise than through the formation of new concepts. (p. 100)

Vygotsky suggested that the brain has the capacity to support different cognitive systems, and Vivian Cook has made a similar statement, that "second languages may be learnt by many means rather than the single means found in L1 acquisition and consequently, may have a greater apparent hemispheric spread" (Cook, 1992, p. 572). To be even more specific, Sokolik (1990, p. 358) has given a good example of this new way of thinking by stating that "one possibility is that L2 learning may be associative in the connectionist sense, whereas L1 acquisition may be more rule driven in the generative sense." In other words, spaces are opening up for multilevel explanations, instead of singular and independent responses. Evelyn Hatch, Shirai, and Fantuzz (1990) called for the need of an integrated theory by stating that

as we think about our experiences as teachers and researchers and examine our beliefs about the learning process, it becomes clear that we have no all-encompassing theory of language acquisition that matches what we have learned from experience. Rather, we find a great deal of research on small parts of the total picture without an integrated theory to guide our work. (p. 697)

Whether one agrees or disagrees with the statement that L1 = L2, or rather L1 influences the acquisition of L2, it can be argued that L1 = L2 is a matter of degree, and that there remains a deceivingly persistent assumption that L1 and L2 are completely different systems, which are totally divided from each other. These systems parallel the unstated assumption that foreign language learners are atomized individuals without a social context. It remains unsettling that debates take place within an either-or stance, because common sense suggests that L1, L2, L3, L4 are linked, united in various ways, forming a whole. A Vygotskian approach focuses on concept formation, which—for children—is the initial starting point for internalizing mediated and arbitrary sign systems. For adults, there is some process of understanding how existing sign systems are slowly defossilized in order to expand beyond a conceptual basis of L2 learning. This view does not adopt the position that adult L2 learning is completely located within L1 structures. However, it argues that adults must find flexibility in initially placing themselves a position of a modified infantilization (in Lozanov's terminology, within Suggestopedia) in order to progress through the stages of L2.

In viewing children's L2 acquisition process, it is first necessary to correct an assumption in their L1 base, namely that meaning initially arrives at the moment when the child has names for nouns. As children activate object-regulation, moving on to other-regulation, somewhere between the two processes, the moment of gesturing establishes the first realization of what Vygotskian theory terms intentionality. It is perhaps at this moment that meaning arises, otherwise the child would not continue to develop from object-regulation to other-regulation in the first place. Susan Ervin-Tripp (1974, p. 126) suggested that in all L2 learning there is a process of overgeneralization and production simplification, which include aspects built upon the L1. At the same time, these aspects are separate (once again, assuming that all language learning is placed within a single continuum, with varying capacities). In other words, focus should be given to Vygotsky's complex concept formation[2] and its development, understood as a correlation between L1 and L2. When learning an L1, it is hypothesized—in Vygotskian terms—that meaning is created by the child long before naming nouns, and that when certain complexes have been formed in the L1, L2 arbitrary sign systems can then be learned in schemata, chunks, and gambits, not just in words. The bridge between L2 learning for children and adults is the understanding of a quasi-concept, which is asymmetrical, in flux at various stages, and often interpreted differently by everyone at different points in time, as well as being understood differently by adults, children, and L2 teachers and learners. The overall formula for using a Vygotskian method for adult L2 learning will remain relative and individual, implying not only the bridge of quasi-concepts, but the understanding of inner speech and self-regulation.

In returning to the general problem of L1 = L2, research conducted in Germany and in the United States is used here to demonstrate varying perspectives. In the past few years, many German researchers have approached this problem by viewing patterns and generalizations between the L1 and the L2,[3] yet in the United States there has traditionally been a trend against this approach. The main interest of SLA research has been the wish to gain more knowledge about the processing of American English as an L2, which correlates with English serving as the world's lingua franca, as well as serving as the baseline of Chomskyan linguistics. It is also interesting that fluency and accuracy in a foreign language are not even required of applied linguistic researchers in the United States.

The aspect of transfer is introduced at this point. Traditionally, this concept is often embedded in SLA research within the parameters of English as a dominant language in the world, with little research conducted in areas where two, three, or even four languages are spoken.

It would be salutary for SLA research if it started from countries such as Cameroon in which a person may use four or five languages in the course of a day, taken from the 2 official languages, the 4 *lingua francas,* or the 285 native languages. (Cook, 1992, p. 579)

Much of what results in transfer research is conjecture and is firmly based within a behavoristic paradigm, which does not theorize the internal processes of the individual. The concept of transfer has remained within the realm of linguistics, whereas a psycholinguistic theory is actually needed. Transfer analysis should also include L2 learners as individuals, not as an amorphic, abstract "whole." However, there are exceptions to the rule, and in this case, Kellerman (1995) reported that

a further study by Giacobbe...this time of lexical development, examines lexical acquisition by two political refugees in the early stages of learning French. Again the L1 is Spanish. This study shows that the extent to which the L1 influences L2 development can vary strongly from individual to individual. (p. 133)

Apart from the behavoristic trends in transfer research, there is another problem of the unidirectionality implied in much L2 research. Odlin (1989) stated that "transfer is the influence resulting from similarities and differences between the target language and any other language that has been previously (and perhaps imperfectly) acquired" (p. 37). In definitions such as this one, the understanding of transfer is used to explain the effects of the L1 on the L2, rather than the effects, if any, of the L2 on the L1; the influence is unidirectional rather than bidirectional. However, influences may flow in both directions (cf. Cook, 1992, p. 579). Cook went on to state that during the 1950s, Weinreich, for example, did allow for bidirectionality within his concept of interference (Cook, 1992, p. 580), leaving one to question why this is not the case today. Within the same framework, Cook believed that many definitions, such as that given by Odlin, are ambiguous regarding explicit terminology as to what is meant by transfer, whether it is transfer over time (hence, diachronic), or transfer that takes place at a single moment (hence, synchronic). Some areas of L2 transfer have been neglected in the research, such as the phenomena of accent transfer—which must be viewed psycholinguistically—and the role of imitation and mimesis in transfer. Huang and Hatch (1978) described a five-year-old boy, Paul, who was exposed to English abruptly and consequently learned enough English in 19 weeks that "at the end of the study it appeared that his language was indistinguishable from that of the American children with whom he played....Paul used two main strategies in learning his second language: imitation and rule formation" (p. 131).

Another interesting aspect of transfer is the revision of the contrastive hypothesis theory, which initially included a psychological and a linguistic component and was based on the need to find the best and most efficient way to teach foreign languages, which appeared to be comparisons of direct correspondence. One hypothesis states that "all L2 errors can be predicted by identifying the differences between the target language and the learner's first language....The weak hypothesis claims only to be diagnostic" (R. Ellis, 1985, pp. 23–24). From a Vygotskian point of view, the ensuing debate around contrastive analysis in the 1970s was not completely understandable, because the approach of a one-to-one correspondence between two languages boils down to a superficial attempt at analysis of surface structures. This approach disregards the individual positioned in the real world, with an attempt to draw conclusions from a product analysis of a static nature:

We have already seen that all errors could no longer be traced to L1 interference. Indeed, the contrastive analysis hypothesis, which stated that those areas of the TL [target language] which were most dissimilar to the learner's L1 would cause the most difficulty, was refuted by research that indicated that it was often the similarities between the two languages which cause confusion. In fact, Wode (1978) framed this observation as a principle: "Only if L1 and L2 have structures meeting a crucial similarity measure will there be interference, i.e. reliance on prior L1 knowledge...This principle is significant in two respects. First, it reflects the growing view that transfer could be seen as a cognitive strategy: Learners rely on what they know" (Taylor, 1975). Second, it foreshadowed specifying precisely when transfer would occur. (Larsen-Freeman, 1991, p. 319)

Contrastive analysts later viewed L2 learners as individuals, comparing aspects such as speech acts and politeness in projects such as the Cross-Cultural Speech Act Realization Project (CCSAPR) (cf. Blum-Kulka, House, & Kasper, 1989) and is certainly an important aspect when viewing L2 learning as a process of internal growth and development for the individual. As a result of contrastive analysis, there has been research in pragmatics and pragmatic transfer and in markedness. In 1983, Thomas defined pragmalinguistic transfer as inappropriate (negative) transfer, which Kasper (1992) expanded to include

transfer of politeness assignment as well as illocutionary force. Therefore, pragmalinguistic transfer shall designate the process whereby the illocutionary force or politeness value assigned to particular linguistic material in L1 influences learners' perception and production for form-function mappings in L2. (p. 209)

Less emphasis was placed on pragmatic error, as a result of suggestions from Rintell (1979) and others, in order to focus on pragmatic failure. Research was then conducted in cross-cultural politeness transfer and in issues regarding power and gender as parameters affecting L2 acquisition. These and other issues were used in interdisciplinary discourse analysis that included ethnomethodology and Goffman's concept of framing, later incorporating theories of motivation by expanding them to include investment (cf. Pierce, 1995). Research in markedness was also conducted with the goal of establishing a framework to address problems arising in the contrastive analysis hypothesis. The initial theory predicted that unmarked forms in the L1 would be easier to transfer to the L2 than marked forms. As discussed earlier,

> not all researchers take the view that learners will resist transferring marked L1 forms. White...argues forcefully that transfer is not confined to unmarked forms, that L2 learners may transfer marked forms from the L1 to the interlanguage, and that such transfer is compatible with the theory of markedness currently invoked in generative grammar. (R. Ellis, 1994, p. 321)

Of course, this position is still defended by some researchers and rejected by others. In touching upon some important research areas within SLA, such as transfer and subsets of this theory (e.g., contrastive analysis, pragmatic failure, politeness, and markedness), it is evident that much of the research is conducted in an independent fashion, often with little if any reference to other research in the same area. Greater coordination of the results of research would maximize the benefits that could be related to the classroom setting. Within a Vygotskian perspective, research regarding transfer is extremely valuable for the classroom experience and can be enhanced from the point of view of the higher mental processes; hence a better understanding of rooting and internalization develops.

MARKEDNESS USED AS AN EXAMPLE TO UNDERSTAND THE PROBLEMS IN RELATING CHOMSKYAN LINGUISTICS TO SLA

Before beginning this section, it is interesting to note that the discussion of markedness is situated squarely within structuralism, much of which is shared by Chomskyan linguistics and the Prague Circle of linguistics. However, little similarity exists between these two schools of thought. It is interesting to view functionalism from this perspective, with its core value having been established within the Prague Circle of structuralism. Chomskyan linguistics has paid only lip service to functionalism, and only within the minimalist approach. It is noteworthy that many of the theories of the founders of the Prague School, such as Roman Jakobson and Nikolai Trubezkoy, now stand on the margins of contemporary Western linguistics. One of the major differences between structuralism and functionalism within Chomskyan linguistics results in the fact that it does not base its understanding of higher, more complex structures as being derived from less complex structures. Yet the Prague School explains simpler structures in relation to more difficult structures, as does Vygotsky. Another difference between these philosophies of language is that within Chomskyan linguistics, the whole can be dissected into atomistic parts and then rebuilt for observation. Within the Prague School and the Vygotskian school of thought, the whole represents more than the sum of its parts. Members of the Prague School, as well as followers of Vygotsky, based their linguistic theories within a wide range of interests including literature, poetry, folklore, semiotics, film, art, history, neurology, and aphasia. And within the Prague School, the initial focus of study was not on the object or sign or linguistic structure itself:

To outline the approach of Prague structuralism to function we must first of all identify all of the components which participate in it. Not surprisingly they correspond to the three factors operative in the creation of structure—the object, social consciousness, the subject.... The most common error in attributing a function to an object according to Mukarovsky is to proceed from the object alone. This necessarily leads to an inaccurate stressing of one function over the others.... The fluctuation of functions is further facilitated by the fact that most manmade objects are essentially polyfunctional. (Steiner, cited in Matejka, 1980b, pp. 360–361)

Roman Jakobson (born in 1896, the same year as Vygotsky, in Russia), firmly believed in the relationship between things, often quoting the cubist painter Brage who stated: "I do not believe in things, I believe only in their relationship" (Waugh, 1976, p. 54). In 1921, Jakobson proposed the oppositional relation of markedness:

The terms marked/unmarked (originally *priznak* in Russian, and secondly *merkmal [Merkmal]* in German) were introduced and applied by Nikolai Trubetzkoy in his 1931 article on Die phonologische[n] Systeme.... However, Trubetzkoy's conception of markedness applied strictly to phonology. As early as 1927 Jakobson had already formulated certain notions, which were later to serve as the basis of his definition of morphological markedness. (Andrews, 1990, p. 13)

During those years, the marked or standard form was understood as the absence of the corresponding unmarked form. In developing the markedness concept, complexity was the guiding issue in determining the marked form; however, this was later changed with the extension of the concept of markedness. The general consensus is that the singular form is understood as unmarked, compared with the plural form, which is viewed as marked, regardless of the complexity involved. Binary oppositions were used in order to establish relationships, although from the very beginning, Jakobson and Trubetzkoy each maintained a different understanding of binarism.

Although Jakobson firmly adhered to the notion of asymmetrically defined binary opposition, where the unmarked term is not on a par with the marked term, the phonological distinctive features define the relationship marked/unmarked differently from the morphological conceptual features. (Andrews, 1990, pp. 13–14)

Therefore, distinctive features for Jakobson represent the minimal phonological unit, which are invariant oppositions understood paradigmatically, and which are necessary for speech perception and production. An explanation was offered by Andrews (1990):

Phonological features defined by syntagmatic properties (cf. tenseness and gravity in the Russian vowel system) are *distinct,* but not *distinctive* units. Distinctive units require the paradigmatic axis (the axis of replacement) in order to find positions of contrastive distribution.... Jakobsonian linguistic theory necessarily distinguishes paradigmatic, or invariant meaning, from syntagmatic, or contextual meaning. (pp. 16–17)

It is important to remember that there is no totally unmarked element in any linguistic system, and because of the asymmetrical and binary components, a hierarchical system can be established with the most unmarked element corresponding to a universal set. For Jakobson, the unmarked sign can have two distinct meanings:

The general meaning of the unmarked sign reveals nothing about the presence or absence of a particular property (P), but its specific meaning signals the absence of a property.... In comparison to the unmarked term, the marked term provides more information. For example, the statement "Michael is as big as John" is less informative than the statement "Michael is as small as John." Someone unfamiliar with the sizes of Michael and John knows a lot more about their dimensions from the second statement than from the first. "Small" is the marked term; "big" is the unmarked term. (Bradford, 1994, pp. 110–111)

Although it is debatable whether markedness as a theory can add information to "real time" development of language acquisition, there exists a general assumption that in real time, children usually (but not always) learn the unmarked term first and the marked term later. This does not mean that the marked term has a lower frequency than the unmarked term, as frequency and markedness are relatively autonomous (cf. Waugh, 1976, p. 89). Therefore, one of the problems in developing this logic has been the assumption that frequency can be equated with markedness; however, markedness is indeed a formal principle that cannot be easily reduced to statistical observation. In comparing the views of Jakobson with those of traditional mainstream linguistics, we begin with Ferdinand de Saussure. In order to analyze a stable component of linguistics, de Saussure selected synchrony over diachrony.

Jakobson was of the opinion that "synchrony contains many a diachronic element, and it is necessary to take this into account when using a synchronic approach" (Jakobson & Pomorska, 1983, p. 57). Jakobson went further in stating that "in other words, Saussure anticipated and announced a new, structural approach to linguistic synchrony but followed the old, atomizing, neogrammarian dogma in historical linguistics" (Waugh, 1976, p. 22). The initial notion of markedness, as envisioned by the Prague School, was to enhance and refine Saussure's concept of *valeur linguistique*. "Value" for Saussure (1959, p. 114), regarding language, implies the fact that "the value of each term results solely from the simultaneous presence of the others," using the example of a game of chess. Indeed it is exactly the opposition between synchrony and diachrony that is viewed as value.[4] Ferdinand de Saussure's inclusion of value in his system was to infuse cohesion into the linguistic structure. Without going further into a general discussion of markedness, the statements already mentioned are compared with Chomsky's views. The basic reason Jakobson could not become enthusiastic about the Generative School of Chomskyan linguistics was simply because he could not divide form from meaning:[5]

In particular, the Generative school redefined markedness relationships as properties derivable from a syntagmatic context in phonology, excluding any application of meaning. Noam Chomsky and Morris Halle, for example, redefined phonological markedness features for English based on distributional criteria in the form of general rules. The fundamental difference between Jakobson's work in phonology and that of Chomsky and Halle is the need, in Jakobson's theory, for a distinct phonemic level in phonology. Halle criticizes the phonemic level in *The Sound Patterns of Russian* on the grounds that this presence prevents the statement of certain linguistic generalizations on their simplest level.... Jakobson has carefully defined distinctive features as invariant oppositions which are paradigmatically given and are fundamental to both speech perception and production. (Andrews, 1990, p. 17)

During his years at Harvard, Jakobson was involved in a controversy between his philosophy and mainstream American linguistics, which was immersed in a rather formal and essentially mechanistic description of language during the 1940s and 1950s.[6] Jakobson's basic position has been described by Umberto Eco (1977):

Jakobson was semiotically biased from his early years: he could not focus on the laws of language without considering the whole of their behavorial background. Language and the whole culture are mutually implicated and it is difficult to isolate linguistics from cultural anthropology.[7] (p. 43)

The relationship between Jakobson and Chomsky should be highlighted as a testament of maintaining a division between personal relationships and scientific or academic convictions. Chomsky (1983) related a personal story regarding his relationship with Jakobson, which was one of mutual respect, although their opinions rarely converged:

I arrived at Harvard in 1951, after a couple of years of graduate work in linguistics, feeling quite confident that I knew my way about the field. One of the first things I did, naturally, was go to see Roman Jakobson, who was of course a legendary figure. Our first meeting was rather curious—we disagreed about everything imaginable, and became very good friends. I was at that time very much committed to a research program that had its roots in American descriptive linguistics, in relativistic anthropology, and in a kind of latter-day logical positivism. Roman's very different ideas posed a major intellectual challenge to this picture....For Roman, linguistics was a science that sought to discover something fundamental, something real and invariant in the real world—something analogous, let's say, to the laws of physics....In my own training, linguistics was a system of ingenious analytic techniques that could be used to yield a systematic organization of data, which in principle could be done in many different ways. For others, language was an adventitious habit structure mirroring the environment, and so on. As far as Roman was concerned, all of this was deeply wrong from the start....The enterprise was not one of data analysis, but rather of discovery, and it was therefore answerable to evidence of a very wide scope: from child language, aphasia, poetics, the study of the production and perception of speech, and many other areas. Linguistics had the task of discovering explanatory principles, and nothing having to do with language was alien to its concerns....I was never actually a student of Roman's technically speaking, but my own thinking was very much influenced by his work, and in other ways too, he had a significant influence on my personal life. In fact, it's very unlikely that I would have stayed in the field at all if it hadn't been for his interest and encouragement, which at the time was quite unusual among professional linguists. And this was all the more unusual, because he really didn't agree with what I was doing, and he thought it was probably not on the right track. But he nevertheless encouraged me to continue with it, even though I was somewhat reluctant to do so at the time, because of considerations that will not be foreign to students today: namely the uncertainty or apparent impossibility of employment, or ever, at that time, publication. (pp. 81–82)

Before closing this section on Jakobson's thoughts on markedness, it should be remembered that he established his own theories related to aphasia, which were influenced by the theories of A. R. Luria. Clearly, both of these theorists have influenced many linguists as to the internal understanding of speech production; however, not all theorists agree with Jakobson's clinical conclusions. One example is that of T. V. Ryabova (Akhutina 2003):

Thus, the combining of contiguous elements entails successive synthesis, and the retrieval of similar elements entails simultaneous synthesis. These two types of connections between linguistic elements identified by linguists correspond to the two types of synthesis performed by the human cerebral cortex, and, thus, the dichotomies of combining and selection, contiguity and similarity, succession and simultaneity correspond. Disruption of the first type of operation primarily induced impairments in expressive speech, and disruption of the second type is associated with impairments of both expressive speech and speech reception. Thus, for example, afferent motor aphasia, involving the impairment of expressive speech, is caused by a defect in the selection of a pattern of sound articulation. Therefore, the dichotomies listed above do not coincide with the dichotomy of impairment of expressive speech and speech reception. This conclusion contradicts the model of R. Jakobson, according to which the dichotomies of combination-selection, contiguity-similarity, coincide with the dichotomy of coding-decoding (expressive and receptive impairments of the speech function) but differ from the successive-simultaneous dichotomy. (p. 27)

Although not recorded, it is possible that Jakobson knew about the thoughts of Vygotsky early in his life or had even met him in Moscow, since they were both students at Moscow University around the same time. Lev Semonovich's cousin, David Vygodsky, became a noted linguist in Moscow circles, meeting with Jakobson and sharing ideas.[8]

Markedness and SLA

The history of markedness within linguistics and SLA has become blurred and confused with various divisions of the concept, such as core markedness, peripheral markedness, core-peripheral markedness, theory-exception markedness, in-core and out-core markedness, and unmarked markedness. Other examples of these definitions are syntagmatic and paradigmatic markedness, and synchronic and diachronic markedness. Marked terms can be over- or undermarked; and we have typological markedness, language-internal markedness, psycholinguistic markedness, and the projection model of markedness. One of the major flaws in the history of markedness has been the implementation of frequency distribution, with Rutherford (1982) stating that "the bulk of past research in markedness theory concerns itself with entities that are easily amenable to classification by means of the customary descriptive parameters for markedness decision, viz. frequency, neutralization, complexity, snycretization, etc." (p. 100). Until markedness is clearly explained, it cannot be viewed as an explanatory principle. According to Gair and O'Neil (1988), the many facets of markedness serve to complicate rather than simplify the study of Universal Grammar (UG) and acquisition. Detailed explanations of markedness have resulted in complicated ideas being made more complicated by the invention of new lists of markedness categories, without an understanding of the term in its completeness. If it can be assumed that language development represents a criterion for SLA research, then markedness and other such components should be defined precisely as to relational development, or it should be stated that there is no relationship or that one is not sure of the relationship. As a result of the ensuing confusion, Rod Ellis (1994, p. 49) hypothesized that "it is clearly premature to reach any conclusions as to whether markedness, as defined by the theory of UG, is a relevant factor in L2 acquisition." Ellis (1994, p. 443) even suggested that some of the major assumptions about marked-ness are not clear, such as the premise that learners acquire unmarked core features before marked peripheral features (he refers to the "case of dative alternation").

Irmengard Rauch (1980), offered a historical understanding of the historical lineage of Chomskyan linguistics:

[I]nterestingly, Saussurean tradition lives on in the classical generative concept of language in which "...a language associates sound and meaning in a particular way..." [Chomsky]. It is thus tempting to attribute to Saussure himself the under-standing of language as strictly verbal language and, as a result, the assignment of language to the aegis of linguistics. (p. 329)

If it is accepted that Chomskyan linguistics has followed the traditional line laid out by Saussure, then the following statement is critical to under-standing the philosophical underpinnings of the difference in beliefs between SLA theorists interested in the Russian tradition, and those with a proclivity toward Chomsky's point of view:

The classical case of a synchronic theory interpreted diachronically is generative transformational grammar. Like word order universals, it is a diachronic interpre-tation grafted onto a synchronic analysis...if markedness (or dispreferredness) is supposed to be sensitive to something that does not have psychological reality, but is a construct of descriptive synchronic linguistics, then how can it be an operative force in linguistic change? This points to the central difficulty of diachronic inter-pretations of originally synchronic concepts: the more purely descriptively syn-chronically orientated they are the less explanatory in terms of actual language behavior and the greater the problems in their diachronic interpretations. (Stein, 1989, p. 71)

At the same time there is little attempt within Chomskyan linguistics to equate the theory of markedness to real time; therefore, it is not expected to be a derivative of development. Within the Chomskyan understanding of acquisition, there is no developmental sequencing involved in the first place, with an instantaneous acquisition somehow being assumed. Within SLA, however, the premise is somewhat different. Barry McLaughlin (1988) argued that "it should be pointed out, as Cook...notes, that present Universal Grammar theory does not assume that markedness is directly reflected in development, even though this is usually assumed by second-language researchers" (p. 98).

Terry Santos (1987) discussed various aspects of markedness within SLA, including typological and internal markedness:

Typological markedness: which depends on cross-linguistic distribution and employs established linguistic procedures for assigning marked and unmarked status to pairs of related forms and structures, and has been used by Eckman...to predict and explain L1 = L2 transfer in phonology and syntax. (p. 207)

However, "Eckman (1981) showed that marked items in a language will be more difficult to acquire than unmarked items, and that degrees of markedness will correspond to degrees of difficulty" (D. Brown, 1993, p. 160). Are marked structures then more difficult to learn? Nina Hyams (1986) argued that

it seems reasonable to ask then whether it is legitimate to assign an initial parameter setting the status of unmarked value solely on the basis of its position in the developmental sequence and in the absence of any independent evidence (from linguistic theory or elsewhere) for its unmarked status. It is entirely possible, a priori, that a parameter is initially set at some value (or rule initially formulated) for reasons entirely independent of markedness. (p. 158)

One interesting example is that of pied-piping (which is traditionally considered to be unmarked, with examples such as "in which house did she live last year?") and preposition stranding (considered to be marked, such as "which house did she live in last year?"). Liceras (1986) looked at a study by Hirschbuhler and Rivero (1981) and concluded that "preposition stranding is not marked, a conclusion which goes against most of the analyses of preposition stranding that have been proposed" (p. 204). Many conclusions have been drawn regarding where children strand before they pied pipe. R. Ellis (1994) quoted Bardovi-Harlig's (1987) study, which indicates that "the markedness hypothesis is, in fact, not tenable for pied piping/preposition stranding" (p. 422).

Language-internal markedness is explained by Santos (1987) as "a perspective that...has proposed to explain the types of strategies L2 learners employ, the kind of order that learners naturally impose upon the data of their input" (p. 208). Klein (1990), however, pointed out that

in contrast to language-external criteria for markedness, syntactic markedness is language-internal....Indeed Chomsky's assumption of a clear relationship between syntactic markedness and real-time acquisition is arguable. First, it is possible for parameter settings to have no markedness values at all and therefore have no relationship to acquisition time. That is, if parameter settings don't determine languages in a subset relation, the values might be ranked for markedness or they might not be; there may be no logical argument from learnability for markedness ranking except for subset cases. (pp. 12–14)

Psycholinguistic Markedness

Psycholinguistic markedness "involves L2 learners' perceptions of similar structures in their L1 and L2, [and] has also been postulated to explain transfer tendencies and strategies" (Santos, 1987, pp. 207–208). Ellis (1994) stated that

indeed, not all researchers take the view that learners will resist transferring marked L1 forms. White...argues forcefully that transfer is not confined to unmarked forms, that L2 learners may transfer marked forms from the L1 to the interlanguage, and that such transfer is compatible with the theory of markedness currently involved in generative grammar. (p. 321)

In reviewing the ideas of Eckman and Kellerman regarding markedness within SLA, it should be clarified that although both men have different baseline philosophies regarding markedness, both share the view that L1 and L2 remain within the same continuum.

The last area to be discussed by Santos is the projection model of markedness,

as termed by Zobl (1983, 1984) who claims to provide greater predictive power of the L2 acquisition process by defining markedness in terms of attainability and taking into account both an external measure of markedness (i.e., input data) and a measure internal to the acquisition process (i.e. learners' hypotheses). (Santos, 1987, pp. 207–208)

In explaining Zobl's position, Rod Ellis (1994) commented that

Zobl (1983) advances a notion of markedness based on the learner's projection capacity....As in the Theory of UG, markedness is understood in relation to the amount of primary linguistic evidence needed to acquire a given property. Zobl's projection model considers property z unmarked in relation to v, w, x, and y, on the grounds that the acquisition device does not require any actual experience of z in order to acquire it....Instead, learners are able to infer the existence of z once they have discovered that certain other properties exist. Clusters of features—such as those associated with the pro-drop parameter—provide a basis for projection; evidence of one feature in a cluster may enable learners to acquire the other features associated with it, irrespective of whether they have experienced these features in the input. Markedness based on a project model is also a learner-internal phenomenon. (p. 449)

In using the example of markedness—that has for the most part been extrapolated from UG to SLA—we have only cursorily examined the following aspects: functional grammar; the genetic-developmental continuum; mechanisms in place for change, such as the dialectic; the social setting of the individual; and internal processes of the individual (although the projection model comes close to meeting this criteria by including some aspects—real time versus static time, among others). It is argued that some of the tenets of functional grammar from the West (e.g., Dik, Givón, Siewierska) and from Russia (e.g., A. A. Leontiev, Belyayev) could offer an enhanced view of some of the topics dealt within in SLA.

Markedness in general is understood to be context dependent, often with confusing results since one parameter can be viewed by some researchers as being marked, while others may view the same parameter as being unmarked. In SLA, McLaughlin (1988, p. 107) demonstrated this problem: "Ellis...cited the example of the pro-drop rule, which was viewed by White (1983) as a marked form, whereas Hyams (1983) regarded it as unmarked."

It is suggested that one of the main problems in viewing Chomskyan linguistics and mainstream SLA is not only the lack of a basic developmental stance, but the exclusion of the partial aspect of the developmental component, namely, real time. This problem should not be considered as trivial, because when Chomskyan linguists discuss time-related issues, there is a shared understanding that real time is not implied. This is not the case within mainstream SLA, where Chomskyan ideal time cannot be assimilated into the matrix of SLA, which must be located in real time. This problem is identical to the dichotomy between linguistic understanding of Saussure's and Jakobson's positions. For example,

Saussure's dichotomy relies on the rigid conception of time in classical physics. The present dwindles to an unextended thread. Jakobson's time conception, on the other hand, is inspired by cubist and futurist art and literature. He seeks to adapt their dynamic experience of time, which overflows the present moment, to linguistic findings....Saussure's scheme of time takes the form of crosshairs [sic], while that of the Prague structuralists is a prism in which the horizontal axis of the objective time sequence is projected onto the vertical axis of subjective simultaneity. What counts is not objective time but rather subjectively experienced time. (Holenstein, 1976, p. 31)

Some problems extend beyond time, such as directionality from the unmarked core grammar to the marked peripheral grammar. This particular line of argument touches upon the typological approach within the Accessibility Hierarchy, which automatically leads toward the Natural Order Hypothesis, which is at the heart of the L1 = L2 debate.

In the end, Jakobson's markedness theory takes a similar position in linguistics—related to Vygotskian semiotics—within a metaphorical parallel. The focus on structures is different, but there is an extension of grasping the relationship between the parts and the whole, and vice versa, that is important to the overall tenets of SLA and applied linguistics. It is suggested that within traditional SLA there is either a focus on parts of grammar, or on the whole of language analysis, all of which appear to be fragmented. Within North American linguistics, as well as applied linguistics and traditional mainstream SLA, categories are often emphasized, without a focus on function and connections via interrelationships that must be contextualized. Although markedness is a more obscure topic, its principles can be extrapolated onto a psychological-philosophical understanding, which helps to expand current theories in the West. Regarding Vygotskian terminology, Jakobson viewed markedness within the level of holistic units, while most Western theories of markedness focus on the level of elements, not connected to the whole. What results is the confusion we have seen in discussing the problems of markedness.

Functional Grammar and Markedness Related to SLA

Before beginning this discussion, we backtrack to consider a problem within the competence-performance model, namely, tacit knowledge, and later relate these findings to functional grammar and markedness. Chomsky's understanding of grammar holds an intrinsic competence of an ideal speaker-hearer representing a theory of linguistic intuition, with this intuition being defined as "tacit knowledge." For the native speaker, grammar has been internalized, which is then translated as an "internal representation of a system of rules" (Harman, 1975, pp. 166–167). The question of functionality takes on an important meaning at this point, because its exclusion is not totally intentional. As Harman (1975, p. 168) argued, "Chomsky wants a theory of performance to describe how a model functions, but he does not require that the theory specify a physical realization of the model." The nature of such a linguistic model is abstract, with Chomsky then positioning this model in direct opposition to behavoristic theories, calling it mentalistic. This understanding includes the important factor of intuition, which is directly related to inference. In order "to 'infer' the grammar from what 'data' it really has, the device [sample sentences] must already 'know' something about the theory of performance" (Harman, 1975, p. 175). At some point, transformational grammar must include environmental factors in order to have initial knowledge or information of the structure of the performance model in the first place. This aspect now includes the problem of "tacit" knowledge and what it actually is. Harman (1975) further argued:

First, Chomsky's use of the phrase "tacit competency" betrays a confusion between the two sorts of knowledge of a language. Competence is knowledge in the sense of knowing how to do something; it is ability. It is not the sort of knowledge that can properly be described as "tacit." Tacit knowledge must be knowledge that something is the case. Second, and this abets the above confusion, speakers of a language do have something that might be thought of as tacit knowledge about the language...and it is true, as Chomsky says, that for all practical purposes "there is no way to avoid the traditional assumption that a speaker-hearer's linguistic intuition is the ultimate standard that determines the accuracy of any proposed grammar, linguistic theory, or operational test"...*provided that "linguistic intuition" refers to the intuitive judgments of speakers.* But notice that this sort of intuitive or unconscious knowledge is not the knowledge of particular rules of a transformational grammar. It is, as it were, knowledge about the output of such a grammar. Chomsky's tacit competence is, however, supposed to be knowledge of the particular rules of the grammar, the rules that are explicitly represented in a performance model. Therefore, linguistic competence cannot be identified with that type of unconscious knowledge speakers actually have....Thus, Chomsky's use of the phrase "linguistic competence" embodies at least two confusions. He confuses knowing how with knowing that; and he confuses knowing that certain sentences are grammatically unacceptable, ambiguous, etc., with knowing the rules of the grammar by virtue of which sentences are unacceptable, ambiguous, etc. It follows that he has not shown the need for a notion resembling his "linguistic competence." (pp. 172–175)

The premise being made is that one of the major problems of both behaviorist empiricism and Chomskyan rationalism-intuition is the reductionist character of both. One school of thought employs the principles of inductivism, while the other school of thought uses the principles of deductivism. Since both positions lack an "abductive-analogical"[9] reasoning, which is basically "common sense–intuition," contained within a functionalist perspective, one wonders why functionalism was totally excluded from a competence-performance model, although it is now mentioned in the Minimalist Program. Of course, the traditional answer to this question is obvious, because functionalism deals with reality and not with the ideal. However, even a quasi-abstract intuitive functionalism would contribute to a dimension completely missing in transformational grammar. The question is then raised as to why functional grammar has not played a greater role in UG, and UG in second language acquisition. For example, in SLA research, a paradox has evolved with many mainstream applied linguists implementing the general UG framework taken directly from the "ideal native speaker," without a modified context linked to the real, nonnative speaker, who automatically functions in an entirely new cultural-linguistic setting. The acceptance of this logic remains puzzling, with the needs of a foreign language learner being based within a functional-developmental continuum of how to master the L2 and L3. Many dichotomies have arisen, with one mentioned here: the distinction in Krashen's applied linguistics (based on Chomsky's model) between learning and acquisition, with one of these concepts carrying much more weight than the other in terms of its valuing. Unquestionably, the answer to the most important factor is acquisition, and not learning, since by definition there is supposedly no conscious structuring involved in acquisition, such as in a classroom setting. At the same time, much of the grammatical descriptions based on UG principles are then offered at higher levels of SLA pedagogy or in graduate courses in teaching English as a second language programs for teachers of English. If UG principles are understood within the L2, with simulated acquisition via natural/innovative techniques, would it not be reasonable to establish encoding procedures for learning the principles of UG (for L2) within a new and viable framework from the very beginning stages? This approach has not been forthcoming, with the philosophical stalemate over whether L2 students have access to UG or not. What has happened is a reversal of logic: acquisition and learning have been viewed as being separate processes, obviously having separate roots, one being subconscious, the other conscious. In reality, the subconscious and conscious are not completely separate. This does not mean to imply that the genetic roots of acquisition and learning are unified, but rather that acquisition on the whole refers to L1, while learning often refers to L2. Even this analogy breaks down because a young child acquiring his L1, based only within the framework of acquisition (hence, no instructed learning such as at school), would remain limited in his own growth. Therefore, since it is reasonable to assume that L2 classroom learning alone does not lead to fluency and accuracy, and that living in a foreign culture without any instruction ultimately leads to severe fossilization in the majority of cases, why do some applied linguists view learning and acquisition as being separate, instead of bringing them together for more powerful and effective L2 strategies? Within Vygotskian terminology, the spontaneous (everyday) concepts are brought together with the scientific (academic) concepts reflecting a bottom-up/top-down, dialectical approach, where grammar is the actual mediator for internalized appropriation/mastery and meaningful growth of the individual within a socialized context.

Acquisition or spontaneous concepts, together with learning or scientific concepts, have two separate origins; however, it is the convergence of these two lines of development that poses the challenge and possible solution to many problems facing the L2 theorist/teacher. A basic paradox within SLA methodology and research is now apparent: although acquisition and learning have traditionally been viewed as being separate (despite voicing of many objections to this dichotomy), it is ironic that other dualistic concepts have not been separated for critical analysis but have for the most part been fused together, such as thought/language, comprehension/production, input/output, and syntagmatic/paradigmatic elements. Though these terms do not always represent the same phenomena, they are often placed together for the sake of discussion and research. For example, in much traditional theory on input/output, statistics show that many of the basic assumptions are nothing less than a representation of the outdated conduit model,[10] simply measuring production with almost no clarification of the internal processes involved.

When viewing these areas within a functionalist mode, one then questions the vast spectrum of research, including endless lists and categorizations of noncorresponding strategies, procedures, rules, principles, and tactics, most of which reflect as many points being made as there are authors to write them. Regarding the use of strategies as an example, Dörnyei (1995, p. 60) quoted Kellerman as stating "there is no justification for providing training in compensatory strategies in the classroom. . . . Teach the learners the language and let the strategies look after themselves." Along the same lines, Ellis (1994, p. 555) believed that "the strategies that learners elect to use reflect their general stage of L2 development."[11] What has happened within SLA is that much of the research has produced a concatenation of strings upon strings of hyperbole and verbalism, sometimes placed within an inchoate framework, with many of the existing theories not viewed from a developmental-functionalist perspective. This does not imply that the alternative would be an absolutist approach, or fewer theories produced within existing research models. What is being suggested is that a broader, more functionalist approach be adopted within the lines of the genetic-developmental continuum outlined by Vygotsky, and activated in functional grammar by A. A. Leontiev, inter alia. It is suggested that the disparate strands of theory need to be woven together into some intricate form, which is then interpreted into better theories that explain learning and acquisition skills among L2 and L3 learners. The example of markedness is offered to demonstrate the attempt to fix grammatical structures within the Cartesian system of dualism, when in reality there is no common understanding to begin with. Grammar is an emergent/emerging phenomenon, one that grows within a specific cultural context, and it is suggested that we begin to view grammar and linguistics from a multi-vocal, dialectical, and wider perspective that begins to include newer thoughts of holographic semiotics. Within a Vygotskian understanding, that would include aspects such as internalization, inner speech, and inner programming, all tied to the concrete reality of life as it is actually lived.

The rest of this book now expands into newer areas that are seldom discussed within SLA and even within the philosophy of language in the West. The next section follows on Jakobson's understanding of codes, entering a discussion of representation and perception. These ideas are linked to an understanding of Vygotskian semiotics, returning to some theories regarding the first love of Vygotsky, which was aesthetics. Many of the thoughts on image, imagination, imitation, and mimesis were taken from Vygotsky's first book, *Psychology of Art* (1965/1971). The closing comments demonstrate the future-oriented approach of Vygotsky's method. The purpose of this introduction on markedness was to establish a context for a better (although limited) understanding of linguistic codes.

The problems of form and meaning and the relationship between the two are taken up within a wider discussion related to Vygotskian language theory.

NOTES

1. Susan Gass was referring to a quote by Willis Edmondson (cited in Gass, 1988, p. 200).

2. For a discussion of Vygotskian concept formation, see Robbins, 2001, pp. 56–60. Concept formation is divided into syncretism, complexes (associative, collections, chain, and diffuse complexes), pseudoconcepts, potential concepts, and true concepts.

3. "With respect to both research design and rationale German studies on second language acquisition have frequently taken a perspective essentially different from the one pursued by American psycholinguistics. When in the early 70s various projects on L2 learning were initiated...it was generally hypothesized that L2 learners acquiring a second language in a naturalistic environment would master their task through essentially the same kind of principles that L1 learners are known to follow. Consequently, the crucial question was not whether second language acquisition is based on habit formation or constitutes a creative construction process...but rather how man's innate ability to acquire natural languages would react to different learning conditions" (Felix, 1981 p. 87).

4. See Lagopoulos (1986, p. 233).

5. See Stankiewicz (1983, p. 24).

6. For a good description of the differences of Jakobson and American linguistics, see V.V. Ivanov (1983, p. 51).

7. See Eco (1977).

8. Refer to the personal story by Dobkin (1982, p. 27).

9. "Abductive-analogical reasoning is used in a wide range of contexts during an empirical investigation:

- hypothesis from action
- pre-empirical decisions on the relevance of some facts and the irrelevance of others
- pre-empirical decisions on the theoretical relevance of some domains and the irrelevance of others
- post-empirical decisions about when to quit testing a hypothesis. Abductive-analogical reasoning also goes by the name of common sense or intuition." (Givón, 1995, p. 19)

10. For a description of Reddy's 1979 "conduit model" see Rice and Schiefelbusch (1989, p. 165).

11. Strategies devised within the framework of communicative competence have also been criticized by Cummins (cited in Oller, 1983, p. 119):

Canale (1981a) for example, distinguishes grammatical, socio-linguistic, discourse, and strategic competencies but states that their relationships with each other and with world knowledge and academic achievement is an empirical question yet to be addressed. Although this framework is extremely useful for some purposes, its applicability is limited by its static nondevelopmental nature and by the fact that the relationship between academic performance and the components of communicative competence in L1 and L2 are not considered.

CHAPTER 7

Code, Representation, and Images: Imagination, Imitation, and Mimesis

One must understand only that by language we have in mind a complex system of codes, signifying objects, attributes, actions, and relationships. On the basis of these entities, it is possible to carry on the complex functions of coding and transferring of information on the mediation of highly complex systems. A "language" lacking these characteristics is a quasi-language.
—A.R. Luria

This chapter focuses on picking up the missing strands of the discussion that are vital to understanding Vygotsky's concepts related to language theory. The topics to be discussed are offered recursively, seeking neither an overall theory nor a complete theory. It would take an entire book to do justice to a complete understanding of these strands, though it might appear to be a concatenation of concepts put together to finish thoughts not yet discussed; this, however, is not the case. The reason for waiting to discuss these areas actually represents a sense of closure, ending where Vygotsky began, within the realm of aesthetics. Many of his thoughts written in *The Psychology of Art* (1965/1971) were later modified and used in his works on psychology, and they can easily be transposed within an expanded discussion of language theory, semiotics, and second language acquisition (SLA). The purpose of this chapter is to start from the lowest level of input, namely, code. The discussion on code begins with the hope that at minimum, a focus on intention will be imputed into a completely new structuring of the classroom, one based on the success of the individual student. It is also hoped that intention setting will take place within the focus on the whole personality of the student and teacher.

The next step regards the inclusion of representation as the next highest level of internal programming for success. The discussion then turns to the role of images and imagination, something that the teacher needs to foster by creating a new atmosphere in the classroom. There is a general appeal to create more images for grammatical practice, and fewer images in terms of classroom realia. The last section deals with imitation and mimesis as the necessary stage before genuine creativity can take place in the classroom. Within the foreign language setting, the understanding of imitation and mimesis is used only as a springboard to genuine creation and meaning for each student. Placed together, the following elements form a pyramid of semiotic/ecological education: code, representation, image-imagination, imitation-mimesis, and creativity.

CODE

This section is related to Vygotskian theories of semiotics; however, code theory is not directly reflected in the psychology/philosophy of Vygotsky, although it is discussed in Russian psycholinguistics. Within contemporary American linguistics and SLA, little attention has been given to semiotics in general, or to code theory in particular. This section seeks to return to a basic, general unit of analysis, namely, code theory. Attention can be given to codes as a departure point within the genetic-developmental continuum of future theorizing about language. The understanding of code is discussed and used as a base for extending into image(s) and mimesis as they relate to language theory. At this point, code is regarded within the same general understanding of Roman Jakobson's theories of code. For example:

Jakobson…insists on a distinction put forward in the theory of information by the London school. The physicist receives from nature indices, i.e., signs, that are apprehended as being caused by nature. He translates them into a system of symbols, i.e., signs, whose content is determined by intersubjective convention….The situation for the linguist is quite different. The object of his investigation is not only the sign but also the code on the basis of which the sender emits his signs. This means that the linguist receives signs that are already determined by convention….A linguist is confronted with three data groups: the message or object language of the sender, the code of the sender, and the metalanguage or theory of the linguist. (Holenstein, 1976, pp. 59–60)

It is difficult to understand code in its totality, and it becomes even more difficult when code is understood within structuralism as binary opposition. Code as a label can be attributed to anything from culture to archetypes, from genetics to Morse code. This leads us into the field of linguistics, and although Saussure spoke of code as *la langue,* Jakobson has perhaps been given the most credit for his inclusion of code into linguistics and semiotic theory. Jakobson's approach created confusion on various levels, for example, by implying that phonological codes are devoid of meaning; however, he was aware of such problems, as stated in U. Eco (1977):

The exceptionally rich repertoire of definitely coded meaningful units (morphemes and words) is made possible through the diaphanous system of their merely differential components devoid of proper meaning (distinctive features, phonemes, and the rules of their combinability). These components are semiotic entities *sui generis*. (p. 48)

The basic matrix of Jakobson's linguistics was the understanding of language in action; therefore, it would be hard to conceive of phonemes, for example, that do not have the capability of containing or promoting meaning.[1] However, within this framework the term "code" is used differently by many scholars in various fields, often within contexts where language is not viewed as action. One of the basic features of Jakobson's overall understanding is the relationship of the part to the whole, and with that in mind, the aspect of signaling is used as a beginning step in activating the understanding of code for the purposes of this discussion. In viewing a signal, perception is involved in breaking down the components of the signal, but "not as yet *coding* or *decoding*, because the signal is not coded into the spectrum of possible meanings" (Zinkin, 1976, p. 77). A code does not exist a priori, nor does it exist outside of interpretation.[2] In going beyond the signal to the sign, the understanding of code is not placed within a static structure. It is viewed as a process, not a product. For Jakobson, Bakhtin, Peirce, and Vygotsky, the relationship between signs is the point where meaning resides, with mediation representing the focal point of meaning within a broader context. The sign with its signifier and the signified is no longer viewed as maintaining a one-to-one correspondence in a linear fashion:

What ensues is a sign model that is a dialectic of 'dia-logic' (intended as dialectic founded on dialogue) according to which the sign and semiosis coincide. Considered dialectically, the sign no longer appears as an autonomous unit endowed with a well-defined meaning, with a value of its own as determined in the relationship of mechanical opposition with the other units forming the sign system. (Petrilli, 1993, p. 106)

For Jakobson, code was the system underlying and allowing for every other message. Code is not material, but rather semiotic, requiring a collective consensus of individual speakers within a conventional understanding. Code, for Jakobson, is not monolithic; it is made up of subcodes. Since code is not static, it should be viewed as being diversified, while at the same time maintaining different functions regarding both time and space. Jakobson made an observation similar to that of Russian activity theorists by claiming that change (be it internally or externally motivated) is goal directed.[3] To view code and message together is not the same thing as Saussure's oppositional understanding of social versus individual. For example, every person has a personal code, while at the same time various messages reflect certain aspects of socialization (cf. Waugh, 1976, p. 23). Jakobson's general model lists characteristics of the "speech event," all of which represent accompanying, respective functions (figure 3).

The question remains as to whether a code is simply part of a language, a system, or both. John M. Ellis, for example, stated that "codes are only devices for disguising pieces of language so that their meaning is not immediately recognizable without removal of the disguise" (J.M. Ellis, 1993, p. 17). An example of this understanding is when a native speaker of English translates something into French or Swahili, the English is still in disguise: "[T]o function at all, a code has to latch onto something that has already done what languages do. Codes encode messages; languages do not. Codes merely transmit information; languages make information what it is" (J.M. Ellis, 1993, p. 18). The logical contradiction in this statement can be interpreted in various ways. Another approach to code is that given by Roland Barthes, who in essence did not view code as being synonymous with system. Barthes understood system as standing close to the

Figure 3.
Speech event.

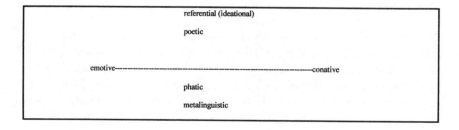

	context	
	message	
(addresser)		(encoder)
(addressee)		(decoder)
	contact	
	code	

| referential (ideational) |
| poetic |
| emotive————————————————————conative |
| phatic |
| metalinguistic |

paradigmatic axis (linguistic associative process), while code stands closer to a syntagmatic axis (the linguistic combinational process) (cf. Thomas, 1989, p. 53). Code now becomes connected with system, while system becomes connected with language. For example,

[t]he term code does not appear in de Saussure's *Course;* yet the term "system," endowed with a polemical value, is clearly a key word in it. In the first pages of the Introduction, the term system is opposed to history...one must distinguish between the *system* of the language and its *history....* Now we are closer to the notion of code since the notion of system refers to the notion of language, the term designating the internal conventions controlling any tongue. (Thomas, 1989, p. 52)

This interpretation is only one way of viewing code. Some authors such as Todorov claim that there is no ultimate code, unless it is a ready-made code transmitting ready-made messages.[4] Other authors place language within a closed system, with the understanding that users do not determine its form or meaning. For example, "adopting an intrinsic approach, structuralists concentrate on the imminent structure of the work without regard to its external meaning, hence as a code without a message, after criticism had for so long regarded it as a message without a code" (Scaglione, 1995, p. 63). Bakhtin criticized the conventional understanding of code by first offering a critique of structuralism and semiotics: " 'My attitude toward structuralism: I am against enclosure in a text.' Continuing, Bakhtin attacks semiotic theory for its reliance on a concept of textual context as a codified grammar: a code is a deliberately established, killed text" (Mandelker, 1994, p. 386). There are numerous theories of code in many areas of scholarship beyond linguistics, such as Barthes's understanding of a photographic image as being a message without a code. With various definitions in place a new process has emerged. Barthes (1985) referred to the example of photography: "[T]o shift from reality to its photograph, it is not at all necessary to break down this reality into units and to constitute these units into signs substantially different from the object they represent" (Barthes, 1985, p. 5).

There are nearly infinite examples explaining code, and some of Jakobson's thoughts are reviewed here because he understood code as being dynamic. What does this actually mean? For Jakobson it is impossible to discover final causes via code structuring, in particular within a synchronic state of balance. General tendencies can, however, be predicted; and, in order to describe this process, Jakobson used the term "recoding" (Luria also used this term, but in a context similar to A. A. Leontiev's inner programming). In opposition to Saussure, Jakobson believed that there was a general systematicity to change. The concept of recoding has been taken up by many theorists, such as George A. Miller during the 1960s, who spoke of a regrouping of input sequences into units or chunks, which allows for a multiplicator effect within memorization. Miller stated that "the input is given in a code that contains many chunks with few bits per chunk. The operator recodes the input into another code that contains fewer chunks, with more bits per chunk" (Miller, 1967, pp. 24–25). He went on to state that one way to recode is to "group the input events, apply a new name to the group, and then remember the new name rather than the original input events" (Miller, 1967, p. 25). Even at this stage, a specific understanding of code remains elusive, and it is here that Yuri Lotman offered a double understanding of the term relevant to cultural-historical semiotics/linguistics. Code for Lotman represented a part of communication that is synonymous with cultural values (cf. Shukman, 1977, p. 94). Lotman then introduced a term that was meant to serve as a mediating factor for understanding meaning, called "transcoding":

Lotman's second article (Lotman, 1965) goes some way to showing how the multi-signifying quality of the word in literature is achieved. In this article he drops the notion of context in favour of the seemingly more precise notion of transcoding (*peredodirovka*), or intersection of structural systems. Transcoding is the operation whereby meaning is created. (Shukman, 1977, p. 72)

Lotman was not totally successful in introducing this term because in the aforementioned article, Lotman used the term "transcoding" in approximately four different ways. Lotman also adopted many of his own concepts from Louis Hjelmslev, at the same time slightly changing Hjelmslev's definitions.[5] For Lotman, meaning was basically the equivalent of content, which is very difficult to understand. However, Lotman was interested in bringing the discussion back to the word, and at this juncture A. R. Luria stated: "The basic element of language is the *word*. A word can be used to refer to objects and to identify properties, actions, and relationships. Words organize things into systems. That is to say, words *codify our experience*" (Luria, 1981, p. 31).

Another aspect of code has been viewed by Russian psycholinguists as an "unconscious construction of a certain scheme on the basis of which utterance is then produced" (Průcha, 1972, p. 74). Code can be connected to L. S. Vygotsky's inner speech and A. A. Leontiev's and T. V. Akhutina's inner programming. When discussing inner speech, Vygotsky's paradigm often comes to mind, yet Zhinkin presents a different model of inner speech that is called "object-representing code" (*predmetno-izobrazitel'nyj kod*). In general, Zhinkin tried to demonstrate that the primary function of language is not only communication, but also thought. Zinkin then presented two general properties of his model:

(1) The code is unspoken, thus it is devoid of any material features of the natural language....Its elements do not form any sequence, but only diverse configurations. These are object-images independent of any form of the external language

units. (2) The code is representative (schematic), i.e., consisting of images connected by object coherence. These images in themselves cannot [be] uttered, but using them as base words any natural language can be constructed. In this respect, the language of inner speech is universal. (Průcha, 1972, p. 76)

Zhinkin established the important link of intention *(zamysl)* within his model by adding to a concept that has been used when deciding how to extrapolate Vygotsky's child development theories onto adult strategies (see Robbins, 2001, pp. 12–13). Intention is located within the inner speech code, according to Zhinkin.[6] The question arises as to whether code is fixed and subconscious, or fluid and conscious, and perhaps the truth lies somewhere between. At this point it should be mentioned that the basic understanding of inner speech is also connected to the idea of a code. Akhutina's work is important because she uses research on aphasia to develop lines of internal processing of language production for normal speech. Akhutina (Ryabova) states the following:

Along with L. S. Vygotsky and N. I. Zhinkin, we hypothesize that inner speech serves as a special code. Probably, this is a mixed code, its units are not limited to words, which in inner speech have subjective, rather than objective meanings (Vygotsky's idea), but also schematic images (N. I. Zhinkin's idea). Once we accept the hypothesis of the special code of inner speech as being consistent with the data on aphasia, we can move on to the issue of how this code is translated into the semantic units of external language, that is, to the issue of how word retrieval occurs. The results from the study of aphasia make it possible to identify two stages of word retrieval: retrieval of the word on the basis of meaning and retrieval of the full form of the word. (p. 25)

Before closing the discussion on codes, Basil Bernstein's theory needs to be briefly mentioned. Daniels (1993) claimed that Bernstein established a component missing in Vygotsky's theories, which is "a theoretical framework for the description and analysis of the changing forms of cultural transmissions" (p. 59). Instead of attempting to reframe Bernstein's argument and its various responses, some simple definitions of code were given by Bernstein (1996) that are related to pedagogic practices:

Codes never have been *defined* in terms of meanings....Codes are defined with regard to different classes or forms of relevant meanings and with regard to the forms of their appropriate realization....*But code attributes abstracted from their essential defining feature do not signify codes....* Whilst the origin of codes *historically* does not lie in the productive system but in kinship systems and religious systems, that is, in the field of symbolic control the *location* of codes lies in the class regulation of forms of social relationships *and* distribution of activities. Thus codes arise out of different modes of social solidarity, oppositionally positioned in the process of production, and differentially acquired in the process of formal education,...Code theory attempts to understand "how the distribution of power and principles of control generates, distributes, reproduces and legitimates dominant and dominated principles regulating communication within and between social groups." (pp. 159–162, 183–184)

Bernstein's theory is viewed by many as being sociopsychological, and his distinction between elaborated and restricted codes or speech styles refers to differences in cognitive functioning, which does not necessarily imply differences in competence. These differences are manifested in social relationships with mechanical and organic solidarity referring to the closeness or distance of the members within a respective relationship (cf. Doise, 1996, pp. 142–143). In viewing structural and interactional levels of analysis, the key ideas for understanding Bernstein are boundary, power support, and legitimation (cf. Daniels, 1993, p. 59). His entire model is concerned with the principles of regulation of educational transmission at any level. Bernstein writes at the macrosociological level and has been influenced by Emile Durkheim, maintaining structuralist components that some people have compared to those of Piaget (cf. Atkinson, 1985). Bernstein, however, should not be compared with Piaget or Vygotsky, because the structural differences of these theories are apparent. Bernstein's theories have to some degree been misrepresented, with many criticisms failing to understand or accommodate his macrosociological structuring. If viewed from that perspective, then Bernstein's understanding of code can surely enhance future cultural-historical semiotics/ linguistics.

The initial discussion on code and transcoding was an attempt to establish a new way of thinking at the most elemental conscious level within semiotics and the social (i.e., educational) setting. With this in mind, an overall framework is constructed in order to place aspects of code, transcoding, and representation within a discussion affecting the general second language (L2) classroom situation. This extended meaning of the word "code" is so defined:

A *code* perspective on meaning holds that all terms in the language are defined by their positional structure in the linguistic system. Thus, the meaning of *computer* is determined by all other terms it is related to (e.g., machine, calculate, technology, intelligence, brand names, science, speed, etc.), and no term is final because each one must be defined by continuously relating them to other terms in an endless process of semiosis. (D. G. Ellis, 1995, p. 533)

The shift of understanding here is that code is no longer viewed as a product, but relies on a process. In order for all members of a speech community to be able to understand mutually shared meanings, there must be an invariant code. At the same time there must be a way to break the code:

At the lowest level, the code is inviolable, but as we move up the scale we discover enhanced opportunities for freedom...until we reach the level of utterance, at which point we break free of the constraints imposed by the grammar of the code and find substantial latitude for creating novel contexts of activity (Holquist 1990:59). (Cited in Lantolf, 1993, p. 224)

The next section moves from the level of code to the next level of linguistic representation and perception. The ideas offered at this stage are theoretical but soon demonstrate a more practical approach to L2 classroom acquisition/learning.

REPRESENTATION AND PERCEPTION

In beginning this discussion on representation, five points are set forth as an initial frame of reference: (1) C. Sinha (1988), in referring to Mandler (1984), noted that representation could have a dual meaning. It can refer to signs or symbols produced by human beings, or it can refer to knowledge and "beliefs underlying sign-using and other behaviours" (p. xiii). Sinha stated that representation could be both a semiotic and a cognitive category at the same time. Also, a dual functioning is in place regarding representations where sense continuity serves to secure mental representations, yet this can change at will (cf. Sinha, 1988, pp. 62–63). (2) Within a semiotic understanding, signs (within representations) are not only used to communicate, but also to control human behavior to a large degree. As Lucid (1977) wrote: "A sign system possesses the capacity literally to mold or 'model' the world in its own image, shaping the minds of society's members to fit its structure. Signs not only passively mirror reality but also actively transform it" (p. 20). The other side of this assumption can also be invoked by viewing the individual as an active sign user. (3) Perspectives on the interpretation of representation are beyond the scope of this discussion (see Fodor, 1981). "According to this view, cognitive mechanisms extract information via an internalised system of representations called the language of thought" (Kempson, 1988, p. 5). Fodor (1981), however, noted that if

we take the computational theory of the mind as what's central to the issue, we can reconstruct the debate between rational psychologists and naturalists in a way that does justice to both their points; in particular, in a way that frees the discussion from involvement with introspectionism on the one side and behaviorism on the other. (p. 230)

The focus from a Vygotskian perspective is neither to abandon a naturalist approach, nor to get rid of behaviorism. On this point, there is complete agreement with Henry Widdowson, who is of the opinion that a "total rejection of behaviourist theory is no more reasonable than total acceptance" (Widdowson, 1990, p. 11). The perspective given here represents a rejection of the computational theory as it stands today. Much can be learned from a restricted analysis of the parallels between computers and the human brain; however, direct parallels cannot be taken literally, simply because this theory cannot account for intentionality in human beings. Intentionality is one of the core aspects of Vygotskian adult self-regulation and will never be exactly replicated in machines, or models of machines, which then attempt to replicate human behavior.[7] (4) Chomsky put forth a conception of representation in his Minimalist Program, stating that

a standard assumption is that UG specifies certain *linguistic levels,* each a symbolic system, often called representational system. Each linguistic level provides the means for presenting certain systematic information about linguistic expressions. Each linguistic expression (SD) is a sequence of representations, one at each linguistic level. (Chomsky, 1996, pp. 167–168)

The problem with this discussion is that it remains only at the intuitive level, excluding any other nonlinguistic properties of representation. (5) Some of Vygotsky's statements appear to be similar to connectionism in various respects (minus the genetic-development approach, among others).[8] A quote from Luria (cited in Vocate, 1987), mirroring many of his theories on Vygotsky, shows the affinity of both men in understanding connectionism:

The modern view regarding the possible localization of the higher mental functions is that they have a wide, dynamic representation throughout the cerebral cortex, based on constellations of territorially scattered groups of synchronously working ganglion cells, mutually exciting one another....We therefore suggest that the *material basis of the higher nervous processes is the brain as a whole,* but that *the brain is a highly differentiated system whose parts are responsible for different aspects of the unified whole.* (p. 13)

In returning to the thoughts about representation, the primary objective is to build upon the aspect of code entering the realm of thought/language processes. These processes are assumed to be primarily representational, although varying interpretations of representation are often in conflict. The major problem at this point regards the temporal and changing nature of thought and language. For example, when a student thinks about a test two days before the test, on the day of the test, during the test, and three days after the test, do these instances represent similar or different types of thought? This question leads into a discussion of propositions and to a further question of whether or not inner thoughts are actually nonlinguistic, in order for self-interpretation to take place within a representational model. This entire understanding is located within a discussion on rule learning and rule following. The problem at this stage is reminiscent of earlier discussions in linguistics, characterized by a division of either a shallow theory of thought (e.g., conscious) or a deep theory of thought (e.g., nonconscious) (cf. Moravcsik, 1990, pp. 80–84). Such a discussion tends to lose many readers at this point, because of problems relating to reductionism.[9] The traditional misunderstanding within this discussion has resulted in the confusion between mental representations and meaning structures. What is important is that

mental representation, in this sense, is no hypothetical construction but a phenomenologically based concept, which can be generalized also to pre-attentive or non-conscious mental processes. Mental representations, in this sense, can be seen as the medium of mental activity, without which no mental activity would be possible. (Lundh, 1995, p. 366)[10]

The defining criterion dealt with by most phenomenologists is the aspect of intentionality. This philosophical understanding of intentionality represents the core of Vygotskian thinking when strategizing and adapting his theories to adulthood, although Vygotsky should not be compared with European phenomenologists. It has been suggested that Vygotsky's ideas were so profound that stages of concept development, for example, can both serve as concrete thinking (via children's stages of age crises as the potential for growth) and at the same time, serve as a metaphor for adult development, which then includes the aspect of intention.[11]

REPRESENTATION-PERCEPTION-APPERCEPTION

Vygotsky often referred to Karl Bühler, a German psychologist, who wrote on language theory and semiotics from an anti-Cartesian point of view. For Bühler, signs function *in* perception and not just *over* perception as tools of mastery (cf. Innis, 1994, p. 131). Bühler demonstrated that the concept of representation makes no sense without the abstract procedures of coding, placed within an irreducible social matrix of meaning, which can include the worlds of both humans and animals. Meaning is to be found within social life, at which point it is fused with perception. Bühler believed that "social life takes place at the beginning chiefly in common perceptual—and hence, spatial...situations, making up a shared field, and that the direction of guidance or steering is also to be found in the common perceptual field" (Innis, 1985, p. 68).[12]

James Gibson's interactive model of perception is also of direct relevance to a Vygotskian model of classroom learning. Although many direct references are made between Gibson and Vygotsky, fundamental differences exist. For example, Gibson felt that perception does not need to be mediated by preparatory processes. Gibson also banned all dualisms that would have made the inclusion of the dialectic impossible; and for Gibson, meaning was not something attached or found during the act of perception. "It is simply there in the affordance" (Cutting, 1982, p. 215). Nevertheless, similarities can be found between Vygotsky and Gibson, for example,

Any goal-directed system is going to have to be engaging in interactions with the environment that are dependent upon, and modifiable by, internal indications about that environment.... We call the structure of such indications *the situation image* (clearly, a nonencoded image). It must be updated and kept current, both in terms of the passage of time and of the outcomes of interactions. This updating process is called *apperception.* Within this view, *perception* is the process of interacting with the world insofar as such interacting participates in the apperceptive updating of the situation image. (Bickhard & Richie, 1983, p. 19)[13]

Certainly the term "apperception" has different connotations for different authors. Within another framework, for example, Belyayev (1964) felt that apperception is distinct from perception,[14] "which is conditioned by the peculiarities of the actual object perceived" (p. 7). He then posited that most foreign language students perceive the phonetic, lexical, and grammatical peculiarities through the filter of their first language. Another example of perception was given by Luria (1981), writing on the thoughts of Wilhelm Wundt, who offered a description of many elementary processes, including sensations, attention, and perception:

However, he [Wundt] argued that in human mental processes there are also phenomena, which go beyond the limits of direct sensation, perception, and memory. These processes are especially evident in which [what] Wundt called apperception, i.e., active human perception arising out of the active orientation of human's will or volition. According to Wundt, these processes of active, abstract perception go beyond the limits of sensory experience. (pp. 20–21)

One of the problems in learning an L2 in a structured setting is the fact that much of the sensory data, for example, technological images, stay at the level of perception described above. Without an interactive structuring of the social environment within the L2 classroom, apperception will not take place. Yet at the same time, it is suggested that apperception is a prerequisite for L2 classroom acquisition and for the instantiation of the general genetic law of development. This understanding alone is not enough to actually change the situation in the L2 classroom. The understanding of apperception needs to be coupled with a basic approach including Vygotskian concept formation, placed within the zone of proximal development (ZPD). If the L2 student has not developed a concept relating to the new context of words, grammar, phonology, and other components of language, then that student will be learning nonmotivated concepts that are not integrated with his or her background knowledge. Leo van Lier (1996) stated it this way:

[P]erceptual effort of a certain strength must be matched or backed up by the activation of mental networks (schemata, perhaps), and this can only happen if there is a link between what is perceived and what is in the mind. Familiarity, or recognition, is an important part of this process, and this suggests that an exposure ⇒ input conversion cannot be externally driven, e.g. by a transmission-oriented teacher or curriculum, but rather, engagement with language occurs when the learner's internal knowledge system, including the language knowledge-to-date, interacts (resonates, to use an ecological metaphor from J.J. Gibson [1979]) with the environment. Under such conditions, exposure-language offers *affordances.* (p. 52)

In returning to the theories of representation, particularly those relating to language theory, Wilga Rivers (who has written about Vygotsky since 1964) made some interesting observations along the same lines as van Lier. She stated that

it is this notion of representation that is at the heart of the process of internalization of language.... What we need to know is how this mental representation is developed, what is represented, and the role of the mental representation in the individual's production of language.... For our purposes we need a broader view of mental representation than we find in current linguistic theory. (1990, pp. 53–55)

The focus on representation within an interactive, apperceptual, and affordance framework can benefit from both the inclusion of Vygotskian dialectics and the genetic-developmental approach. This approach incorporates an understanding of the shift *from whole to part to whole.* Vygotsky described this problem in notes about the perceptual speech patterns of his second daughter, Asya,[15] stating that

speech dissects perception, pushes it along the way of analysis; it does not see ears plus eyes, etc., but enumerates like this. At first there is a verbal enumeration (analytical) which was taken for the atomistic character of perception itself (from the part to the whole); now it becomes clear (Gestalt theory) that this is not the case, that perception goes from the whole to the parts. Our problem: Why does Asya, after perceiving the whole, enumerate just the parts in speech? (Vygotsky, 1983, p. 11)

The relationship of whole to part to whole within the discussion so far lacks the important aspect of reflexivity, which must be nurtured within the interactive, apperceptual, and affordance framework of the L2 classroom. For the Russian psychologist S.L. Rubinstein, as well as for G.H. Mead,[16] thought is reflexive, and it becomes apparent in a problem situation. Reflexive thought is therefore conscious and not automatic. "The process of reflexive thought enables the person to reconstruct his environment in such a way that he can act in a different fashion, using knowledge that lies inside the process itself" (Marková, 1982, p. 174).

It is suggested that reflexivity be reintroduced within a renewed understanding of image, imagination, imitation, and mimesis.

VYGOTSKIAN INTERPRETATION OF IMAGE, IMAGINATION, IMITATION, AND MIMESIS

During the 1920s in Russia and Western Europe, discussions of language included the age-old problem of asking where the correctness of names came from. Are names inherent in ultimate reality, or are they established and agreed upon via practice, and hence arbitrary? Put differently, the discussion went back to Plato trying to discern whether the name is an image (εικω) of the object grounded in a real correspondence, or an arbitrary sign (σημειον), "created by the name giver solely as an instrument (ορψανον) for the purpose of communication" (Ströker, 1982, p. 79). The problem arises as to whether meaning within the word is established externally in the cosmos and is universal and immutable, or if it is established internally, by individuals, and is therefore arbitrary and changeable. Aristotle then used his understanding of logic to establish categories (within metaphysics) where he assumed that logos was represented vicariously (cf. Ströker, 1982, p. 80). Although this is not an exact portrayal of the history of the study of language by the Greeks, it opens the discussion of signs as representations.

When jumping to modern philosophy of language, one of the first persons to be considered is Wilhelm von Humboldt, who viewed language not as a "work" of the speaker, but as an activity. Within this activity one's own worldview is brought into being, which is related to Vygotsky's understanding that thought is completed within and through the spoken (signed, or brailled) word itself. At this point, the role of image becomes important in a Vygotskian perspective. Within the history of psychology the study of the concept of imagery became a predominant factor during the nineteenth and twentieth centuries (e.g., among Binet, Titchener, and others).[17] A problem with this model, however, was the dominant trend of associationism within psychology at that time. Much of the research on imagery has retained its associationistic past, but if it is true that "an image is hypothesized to conform to the same rules of development that formulates a concept" (Rader & Tellegen, 1981, p. 39), then it is important to consider Vygotsky's understanding that mature concept formation will not be internalized if it remains only within the matrix of associationism.

Writing on the death of Vygotsky in 1934, A. N. Leontiev posited a view of consciousness based on the opposition of image and process (and not of consciousness opposed to the object world). His son, A. A. Leontyev [Leontiev] (1992), stated that

only just before his death did [A. N.] Leontyev return to the notion of the image of the world as human practice in its idealized form, the unity of individual and social experience in the form of the field of senses in which humans live, which they reflect, in which they behave and are active. It can be said that this conception of the image of the world is the result of Leontyev's rethinking, begun in the 1930s. (p. 43)

Following in A.N. Leontiev's footsteps, P. Gal'perin continued with his concept of image, which he believed was the regulator of activity. Gal'perin (cited in Davydov, Zinchenko, and Talyzina, 1983) stated that "an image is an integral reflection of reality in which the basic perceptual categories are present all at the same time.... The most important function of an image is the regulation of activity" (p. 34). In viewing the role that images held for Vygotsky, particularly within his understanding of aesthetics, the writings of E.R. Jaensch gained importance. Jaensch was of the opinion that "in most adults there is an unbridgeable gulf between sensations and images, although some adults have intermediate experiences" (Jaensch, 1930, p. 3). Without going into detail, the only aspect to be mentioned is that of afterimages, through which primitive peoples were thought to experience more images than people living in industrialized societies. The results of research experimentation on afterimages using picture stimuli go back as far as the early 1960s and suggest "that increasing urbanization, followed by more frequent contact with verbal activities, may be a possible explanation of the decrease in eidetic imagery" (G. Kaufman, 1979, p. 38). Within a Vygotskian metatheoretical-metaphorical framework the understanding of afterimage is important for the L2 classroom (or any other classroom), not only with regard to the anticipation of what image, if any, will remain after the L2 course is completed, but also with regard to the afterimage of each classroom session. This will contribute to the dialectical circuit of anticipation for the next classroom period.

In retracing the steps in the study of images within the framework of Russian theories, there are connections between some of the areas already discussed. For example: (1) one might further understand A.N. Leontiev with the following statement: "I[I]n no case is an image a code of a thing, since the relationship between a code and what is coded is completely arbitrary" (Smirnov, 1981–82, p. 10). (2) Within the work of Belyayev, the understanding of images is divided into sensory images, functional images, and motor images. Belyayev (1964) went on to state that it is possible to have four varying images of the same word:

Every word, like every other concrete object, can be perceived and imagined, and it is possible to have four different images of the same word: visual, aural, graphic, and articulational; the first two are sensory and the second two are motor. In other words, one can not only see a word when it is printed or written, and hear it when pronounced by another person, but also write or pronounce it. Moreover, one can imagine all these four verbal images. (pp. 114–117)

When strategizing about a new future L2 classroom, the goal is not to introduce more images (apart from instructing grammar), but to begin to think about presenting mediated images that can eventually be internalized by the learner. Within postmodernity, learners and teachers have grown accustomed to performing many tasks at once, often within the mutual understanding that various personal experiences take place within the simulacrum that metaphorically represents a "copy of a copy" (often where even the original is missing). In other words, images are often prefabricated (e.g., television, music, and movies) and are then presented to youth for simulation when they have never actually seen the original version. A longing for the authenticity of the original is a reason why so many people are willing to wait for hours or even days to gain entrance to a rock concert populated by tens of thousands of other people wanting to have the same experience. Oddly enough, one cannot generalize about the longing students might have to visit the target culture (i.e., the original) when studying a target language. Returning to the postmodern L2 classroom, many learners and students are often bored because the teaching methods have not kept pace with technological advancements, or the excitement of authenticity, as in the example of the rock concert. However, simply copying the images of television, or the rock concert, for example, and reproducing them in the L2 classroom usually does not come across as being authentic, often placing an automatic bind on the teacher. The question then is whether there should be motivated L2 learning that tries to keep pace with a fun-filled, exciting atmosphere, or whether there should be authentic learning, which is slower and certainly much less exciting. Jean Baudrillard has described postmodernity as a hyperreality, with a critique using the example of Disneyland.[18] Within the understanding of hyperreality is the hypersign that illustrates the problem of the traditional implementation of images in the L2 classroom. Most students and learners are simply saturated with images in the first place and do not have time to absorb, internalize, and restructure the images offered in order to change and cocreate a new individual reality. For example, Bogue (1991) continued by explaining that

[o]urs is the age of the hypersign...[a] postindustrial, information—and consumption—regulated culture of universal mediation (most obviously through the media of television, radio, film and print) in which the real has disappeared and been replaced by signs that only point to other signs and thereby produce a simulated reality effect, or hyperreal[ity]....In Baudrillard's view, the celebration of simulacra does not subvert representational norms, but simply articulates what has already taken place. (p. 5)

Within the study of images, the word "imagination" must also be discussed. In a Vygotskian account, imagination leads to both cognitive and affective understanding, with the metaphor representing a component of imagination that paradoxically provides both displacement and wholeness. With the growth of the hypersign, together with the diminished use of the metaphor on a daily basis, fantasy and creativity will at some point be weakened. Vygotsky (1965/1971) illustrated this problem by citing a riddle story:

It is interesting to note that, when applied to riddles, such a remoteness of the image from its actual meaning vouches for the riddles' poetic effect....What is it that stands in the corner and sweeps the room? Answer: the broom. Riddles like that are completely devoid of any poetic significance and effect, because they lend themselves to total literal rationalization. Shklovskii points out quite correctly that the relationship of the image to the word signified by it does not justify Potebnia's [Potebnya's] rule according to which the image is something much simpler and clearer than what is being explained; that is, since the purpose of representation is the close approximation of the image to our understanding, and since without this all graphicalness becomes meaningless, the image must be better known to us than that which it explains. (pp. 44–45)

This example demonstrates the problem many foreign language teachers experience when trying to present images of different countries by bringing in hats, food, pictures, and various realia of a different culture. Very often the attempt is simply too literal when students are already faced with a semantic saturation through similar images in their own culture and media. In many cases, L2 students are continually faced with the problem of learning words (usually through associationism), without the appropriate contextualized concept having been formed, together with teachers assuming that "the more literal the better." Tolstoy related a similar thought with a story about a "very civilized woman," who had written a novel she wanted him [Tolstoy] to read:

The novel started like this: in a poetic forest, near the water, in a poetically white garment, with poetically flowing hair, the heroine was reading poetry. The action took place in Russia, and suddenly from behind the shrubs, there appeared the hero in a hat with a plume à la William Tell (thus it was written), with two poetically white dogs accompanying him. The authoress believed all this to be extremely poetical. (Tolstoy, cited in Vygotsky, 1965/1971, p. 63)

In clarifying the concept of imagination, Vygotsky devised a law of creativity: "The creative activity of the imagination is found to depend primarily on rich and varied previous experience. The richer the person's experience, the more material his imagination has at its disposal. This is why the child has less imagination than the adult" (Vygotsky, 1990, p. 89). Vygotsky (1990) actually listed the following mechanisms of creative imagination:

1. External and internal perceptions that form the basis of our experience.
2. The complex process of reworking this material. The most important components of this process are dissociation and association of sensory impressions.

3. After the process of dissociation comes the process of alteration, to which the dissociated elements are subjected. "This process of alteration or distortion is founded on the dynamics of our internal neural excitement and coordination of images" (pp. 89–90).

4. Association, i.e., uniting the dissociated and altered elements: "this association can take diverse forms, uniting subjective images with objective science, as in geographic representation, for example" (pp. 89–90).

5. Combination of different forms into one system, constituting a complex picture (pp. 89–90).

Vygotsky criticized traditional psychologists for using images/concepts in an associationistic framework of development as their overall goal. Certainly, associationism is needed at certain levels to coordinate words, thoughts, and actions, and to afford coherence. Various psychologists of the 1920s criticized this associationist approach because it represented the highest level of explanation used to establish psychological theory. Vygotsky agreed with many of the psychologists of the mid-1920s who tried to re-create various experiments by retelling narratives or famous literary stories in order to test associationistic assumptions. Within the reconstruction of the narratives told in the experiments, learners somehow understood the situation, behavior, and personality of the protagonists, but the graphic image was not always present. Regarding L2 learning/acquisition, A. A. Leontiev warned about this problem in an experiment where phrase semanticization was enhanced by visuals, and where unnecessary and harmful effects were actually created (cf. A. A. Leontiev, 1981, p. 137). Belyayev (1964) also stated that foreign language students should be exposed not only to visuals, but also to actions and movements. Teachers should address themselves not only to visual cues, but to hearing and other sensations, including reading. Indeed, Vygotsky stated that "the process of thinking, in its higher forms, occurs without the help of graphic concepts or images" (Vygotsky, 1965/1971, p. 43). When reading about the spark of genius many great thinkers experience within a split second, the first impression is to attribute these flashes of inspiration to images; however, they may be supraimaginistic. A. A. Leontiev (1981), then, offered some guidelines when using visuals in the L2 classroom, with suggestions such as the following:

1. Visualization can be—and to a certain extent is—used to facilitate the orientation in spatial, temporal, and cause-effect relationships, expressed with the help of auxiliaries and syntactic constructions in the foreign language; 2. Visualization can be applied to the phonemic system; 3. Visualization can be used for presenting motivational and purposive aspects of a speech act; 4. Visualization can be used for the presentation of the concrete content of a communicative situation and for the introduction of a certain context; 5. Visualization can be used as an aid in the selection of a concrete lexical rendering for an utterance; 6. Visualization should be used as an aid to the phonation of whole utterances. (pp. 137–140)

Interestingly, people within postmodern society are subjected to more images than at any other point in human history. However, rarely is anything written on this topic in depth in Western linguistics, applied linguistics, or SLA. At this point, not only Vygotsky, but the entire Russian (and Ukranian) history of linguistics offers interesting perspectives for today's world, from the points of view of G. Spêt and A. A. Potebnya, to those of S. Karcevskij and L. S. Vygotsky.

Imitation and Mimesis

The word "imitation" usually conjures up picture-images of the nonauthentic, or of something artificial. Yet rarely do we sit back and realize what this term used to mean in education. Imitation has traditionally been understood as memorizing facts, for example, in order to pass down culture to later generations; or in the case of poetry for the mere joy of recitation. For example, imitation is an integral part of the harmony and joy of an orchestra playing classical music, where the performance is viewed as being authentic. Within Vygotsky's psychology/philosophy, imitation represents both the practice of internal restructuring and of gaining entrance to other worlds, in order to expand one's own consciousness. During his youth, Vygotsky and his friends established a circle to discuss topics of history, and they would often imitate famous figures by simulating discussions and arguing philosophical perspectives from their point of view. Also, Vygotsky memorized much poetry, and his daughter Gita L'vovna recalled that he would stand and recite poetry to the listener's delight. Gita L'vovna offered another example of a game Vygotsky would play, based on simple associationistic principles, not to be understood as a means of reaching mature concept formation, but rather as a simple game:

In the evenings, the family would always gather in grandmother's room...around a big table. After obligatory tea, some would remain seated by the table, while others would move to the warm stove (the flat was always cool). Then the most interesting things would begin. Someone would read aloud, and everybody else would listen. There would be debates about new plays, reciting of poems, joking. When Lev Semenovich came alone, he always took part before going to our room to work [Vygotsky used his children's room to work, not having one for himself]. In those hours, he liked to stand, his back to the masonry of the stove, his hands behind his back....He knew very many poems, loved them very much, and was always ready to recite—usually, the classics. From contemporary poetry, he would most often recite Pasternak....He could recite poems literally for hours, and everybody, having fallen silent and seated themselves comfortably, listened to him with pleasure....Right there, by the stove, Lev Semenovich would demonstrate to us his ability to remember large numbers of words. We would, working together, compile a list of 100 words...and hand it over to Lev Semenovich. He would slowly read each word, return the list, and then offer to recite it in any order. To our amazement and joy, he would, without mistake, repeat all the words on the list from beginning to end, and then repeat them in the reverse order. Then we would ask him to reproduce the 17th, 4th, 61st, 7th, and so on, word, and he without difficulty and without any mistakes, would do it. (Vygodskaia, 1995, p. 58)

Regarding contemporary education, one of the problems found within constructivism is that young children, as well as college-level students, are asked to interact with one another, collaborate in groups. Certainly this alone is an alternative for many learners when faced with a teacher-centered atmosphere, where only lecturing, note taking, and testing take place. However, within the ZPD, teacher role-modeling takes on a different meaning, as the teacher should be profoundly interested in the personality development of each and every individual learner. The classics, math, music, art, and foreign languages are then presented within a new framework, with the assumption that the teacher is an expert in her own discipline. It has been stated that much of contemporary education represents cultural values opposite to those of the 1920s, where scientific-academic concepts were learned in school and then mediated by everyday spontaneous concepts. Today, it often appears that the educational format seemingly replicates scientific concepts, actually including many spontaneous concepts once learned at home or at church. For example, while at school, pupils often learn about drugs, sex education, AIDS, how to deal with strangers, and so on, all of which represent spontaneous concepts. When scientific-academic concepts are introduced, they are often presented verbally, in the original sense of teacher-oriented learning, which often does not translate into concept development for the child, even for L2 learners in many situations. Belyayev (1964) offered an interesting approach to imitation and its role in education by stating that "reproduction is impossible without recognition, but production is impossible without reproduction" (p. 178). Because of postmodern hypersigns and hyperimages, students are saturated with images and often cannot absorb more unless internal room is made for motivated assimilation and transformation. The student needs a meaningful reason for internalizing more images when offered in the L2 classroom. Therefore, in order to become motivated there must be recognition, and at the same time reproduction must be meaningful; otherwise, the results become empty verbalism.

Rethinking what imitation might mean for the L2 classroom would be futile if not placed within the ZPD from the very beginning. Regarding the role of imitation within the ZPD needs to be viewed within a descriptive, not an explanatory, mode. As well, heuristics will be important, although imitation at the very beginning involves an algorithmic approach to memorizing. Vygotsky's understanding of the term "imitation" was similar to that of Mark Baldwin's "persistent imitation" concept:

That concept implies imitation of the (socially given) models beyond copying them (rather than merely producing an exact copy, at best). Thus, persistent imitation equals constructive experimentation with the given model, and its transformation into a novel form—both in actions directed toward the model and in the resulting internalization of understanding of the model. (Valsiner & van der Veer, 1993, p. 45)[19]

Therefore, the understanding of imitation hopefully takes on a new (or old) meaning, which is now placed within the perspective of using imitation as a bridge for internalizing given cultural information (be it poems or mathematics, for instance). However, this is only the starting point, to be continued with problem-solving exercises, role-playing, research projects, portfolios, creative journal writing, videos of self-produced activities, and plays that acknowledge the learner's cultural background. For example, students can often recite lines of their favorite music for up to six or seven minutes with astonishing accuracy. This type of imitation can, perhaps, be restructured for the classroom where the learner is in charge of motivating others, or simply demonstrating one's own interests.

In returning to Vygotsky, he clearly did not give complete answers regarding the use of imitation in the classroom, yet it is understood that imitation for him did not simply mean copying:

The concept of imitation has overtones of noncreative copying mechanisms. Although it is true that Vygotsky tried to avoid such an explanation for children's imitation by claiming that he was thinking of intellectual imitation, he did not refer to or provide a fully-fledged theory of imitation that might have solved the problem....[Vygotsky] made it very clear that he attached great value to these forms of deferred imitation both for cognitive and emotional development. (van der Veer & Valsiner, 1991, pp. 343–345)

Vygotsky carefully studied the theories of Konstantin Stanislavsky, a noted actor and director of theater productions, and the creator of the Actors Method, which was adopted by many Hollywood stars in the late 1940s and 1950s and beyond. Actors were given notes written on the side of their scripts that explained certain feelings in a particular role in a scene. In order to practice for their roles, actors would research lines in a historical context and imitate the lines or even words, using as many varying nuances as they could come up with:

In teaching this system of acting, Konstantin Stanislavsky required the actors to uncover the "subtext" of their lines in a play....Every sentence that we say in real life has some kind of subtext, a thought hidden behind it....Just as one sentence may express different thoughts, one thought may be expressed in different sentences. (Vygotsky, 1994a, p. 250)

Stanislavsky called his theory of acting the theory of emotional experience, and one of his favorite words was "grip," a concept that is used unconsciously in many L2 classroom situations:

In real life one can do without a grip, but on the stage it is needed almost every-where, continuously, every minute of this lofty creativity.... This special, concen-trated, typical summarized communication, stage communication, becomes... a grip, and demands participation of the actor's total inner and outer re-sources.... Thus, the actor's inner communication with the character he is imper-sonating merges, as it were, with his communication with other actors and is inseparable from the indirect communication with the audience. (Berkhin, 1988, pp. 11–13)

Teachers do not have to apply principles used in the theater and might not identify with such parallels in the first place. However, all L2 teachers face the problem of imitation, particularly in phonology. At the same time, the use of imitation understood by Vygotsky was pivotal in initial speech development that led to concept formation. This paradigm is radically dif-ferent for adults, which raises the problem of trying to adapt Vygotsky's philosophy to the L2 classroom. The use of Vygotsky's ideas within a new model of imitation should proceed cautiously; however, one aspect seems important, namely, disobjectivation or displacement, where students learn to step out of their own reality and envision themselves in a com-pletely new setting.

Students must be able to deal with ambiguity within these phases of learning, and the presentation of traditional fairy tales within the L2 might address this problem. However, the intentionality of the teacher will either motivate the students or turn them off. Students can learn vocabu-lary, go through slides of a fairy tale, and see a cartoon version of the fairy tale in the foreign language. They can try to rewrite the fairy tale, update it, or write their own versions. They can act it out and videotape it. They can critically analyze the fairy tale, for example, the connotations of Red Riding Hood going through her teenage years and the various implica-tions of good and bad men reflected in the story line. The German version—taking wine to a sick grandmother—can be compared to the American version. If L2 students are asked to enter this process as them-selves, surely there will be much resistance to such childish content. It is the proper understanding of displacement that allows such an approach to be effective. This approach is different from teaching everyday activi-ties in a foreign culture, for example, a visit to a train station, restaurant, bank, or post office, or even teaching literature. In addition, a problem can arise when assigning students a foreign name without any point of refer-ence for internalizing the meaning of having a foreign name. What can result in all of these exercises is the problem of students not knowing how to integrate the new identification of the target culture with their own identities. Should they just imitate the situation, which in reality would mean that they were simply playing? Strategies need to be in place where L2 students can realistically learn to identify with the target culture. To accomplish this, a first step should be to identify with the "other" in general. By introducing differences into the transcoding method, students can slowly begin to work within a dominant activity that they established themselves, moving toward cultural similarities.

One example that has been used by this author to teach German was to introduce works by Goethe.[20] Various translations were first researched in English and shared with members of a group of students, initially divided according to personal interests. By establishing similarity within the groups, students could then focus on differences. Two groups worked together temporarily to discuss the information acquired, then reported their findings to the entire class. The process of reading the same version in the German language took place within the initial group, where a sense of solidarity was established. At this point, students felt less intimidated with the foreign language, since they already knew the content in their mother tongue. The goal was to try to understand the German perspectives the students had already discussed. For example, some students wanted to focus on history, and they set up an interview with a history professor interested in Germany, Austria, or Switzerland. Some students used the Internet to find comparative information on Goethe from a German perspective, or they contacted an expert on Goethe. The next step was to try to discover the significance that Goethe has for Germans. In one experiment established by the students, an older German woman (married to an American) was asked to read a text and come to class to simply share her impressions. Never having been to college, she readily shared her anxiety at trying to interpret Goethe to college students, while the college students shared with her their fear of speaking German. A German exchange student was asked to provide his interpretation of the same text, so that another generation could provide a personal interpretation of the text from a German perspective. The last stage was to allow students time to try to interpret the text by Goethe, to see what it meant to them personally at that particular moment in their lives. The students could process the text on many levels, including visually, by watching a film. By the end of the semester, they had experienced the process of disobjectivation to the point that they could indeed reflect on their relationship with the text, be it positive or negative. Without disobjectivation, no matter what type of activity or project is presented to the students, they usually cannot identify with it immediately. Students need time to set a goal, then learn the principles of patience and hard work. They need to establish their own dominant activity for the class, and they need to have their input not only count, but be recognized as necessary for the success of the class as a whole. This is in total agreement with the approach offered by Claire Kramsch, who stated that "by teaching a foreign language we should objectivize the learner's native discourse patterns and help them adopt those of the new language" (Kramsch, 1993, p. 44).

At this point, the new or old understanding of imitation must be placed within another category, namely, mimesis. The underlying meaning of mimesis is very old and hence often forgotten in contemporary society. Originally mimesis was understood to serve the function of translating what is not seen or present (i.e., the ultimate reality, or in Kantian terminology *nouema*) into the visible, meaning the form of the representational. Therefore, the representational is ultimately perceived as being an imitation or copy of reality, while mimesis has been traditionally understood as the interface between language and reality (cf. Matthews, 1996, pp. 4–6). The L2 teacher is indeed responsible for presenting the reality of the foreign language and culture to the students, serving as a translator not only of the overall effect of the L2, but regarding the overall image of the culture(s) involved. Indeed, teachers and students, and students individually, cannot circumvent mimesis if L2 internalization is to be successful. Mimesis within this context does not carry the responsibility of the success of L2 competency, proficiency, accuracy, and fluency; rather, it serves to guide the process.

Mimesis

This section begins with Plato, who viewed signs as having two types: images and simulacra, both of which are governed by mimesis (cf. Bogue, 1991, p. 2). Plato and Aristotle differed on this concept, particularly regarding the problem of whether the original—in its archetypal form— could be copied or not, and if copying would create an automatic simulacrum, meaning a copy of a copy. Even the definition of mimesis cannot be completely offered, as it always remains within the stage of being created. A basic understanding of mimesis is key to restructuring the L2 classroom:

Mimesis is not concerned with boundaries drawn between art, science, and life. It causes accepted differentiations to lose their power to distinguish and strips definitions of their conventional meanings.... New connections, distinctions, and orders of thought come into being.... Mimetic processes are not unequivocal; they are better understood as ambivalent.... Mimesis resists a clear-cut split between subject and object.... The concept of mimesis implies a resistance to splitting the human spheres of experience, action, and symbolic production into two parts, one practical and one theoretical.... In this sense mimesis is distinct from mimicry, which implies only a physical and not a mental relation. There is a complementarity of perspectives in mimesis.... Mimesis includes both an *active* and a *cognitive* component.... Mimesis originally denoted a *physical action* and developed first in oral cultures. It has an indicative character, with attention turning repeatedly to the gestural over the history of the concept. (Gebauer & Wulf, 1992, pp. 2–5)

With this definition in place, the reader is asked to go back and rethink the examples of fairy tales (e.g., Red Riding Hood) and any simplified

Goethe text not only from the point of view of imitation, but of mimesis. How could such examples be constructed so that the student could participate and retain a meaningful afterimage of the project? Perhaps the best application of this term related to the classroom is from Paul Ricoeur (1981), who is of the opinion that "*mimesis* does not mean the duplication of reality; *mimesis* is not a copy; *mimesis* is *poiesis*, that is construction, creation" (pp. 179–180). This definition of mimesis is important because it takes the L2 classroom out of the static, technical side of a foreign language, which has to some degree become mechanistic. It is then placed within the realm of art, creativity, and aesthetics, where it actually once belonged. In fact, this aspect represents the initial starting point that Vygotsky took at the very beginning and, to some degree, at the end of his career within aesthetics. There is, however, no call to return to the past, where foreign languages were embedded within classical education.

Many of the ideas already mentioned, such as the ZPD, dialectic, transcoding, dominant activity, active versus reactive speech, images, imagination, and focus on differences and similarities, among others, all lead to the magic moment of catharsis, where frustration is transformed into meaningfulness. Varsava (1990) put it this way: "[C]atharsis becomes the emotional manifestation or…the confirmation of an *actual knowledge* of the *known mimetic object*" (p. 4).

In postmodernity there seems to be little time for "narrative" in the broadest sense of the word. Often there is a secret longing for a different time—which we have stored in our collective memory—of life as we envision it during an earlier part of the twentieth century, for example. Although one might relate to such an image, as if one were still a child, there is a longing for the narrative that has somehow been lost. The childlike image might include the narrative where grandparents relate stories from the past, or where one camps out in the backyard with a parent or grandparent telling a ghost story. At the same time, many adults also long for what Lyotard described as the larger metanarrative *(métarécits)*, most of which has been rejected in postmodernism, because it borders on an older deductive worldview. In some respects, the inclusion of journal or diary entries reflects this longing for a narrative, although when describing the L2 process, a lot of the entries seem to focus on fear, anxiety, and tension. Returning the narrative back to the L2 classroom cannot be automatic, but it can represent a meaningful step toward a new future-oriented curriculum. John Oller (1995) stated this well by claiming

as unfortunate as it may be, most language instruction is based not on the sort of formal structures that are found in narratives (or in all of ordinary experience), but on linguistic structures cut loose from nearly all of their material contextual supports. Isolated sentences, or in recent years, isolated sociocultural vignettes are commonly used. (p. 293)

In closing the discussion of images, imitation, and mimesis, one aspect should be kept in mind when relating Vygotskian theories to the L2 classroom. It should not be presumed that Vygotsky offered all of the answers to the problems of language acquisition, particularly since he wrote from the perspective of the 1920s and early 1930s. Just as Widdowson (1990) stated, "the essential point is that there are no universal solutions" (p. 25). Vygotsky viewed his theories as being "in process," never as a finished product. Although it has been suggested by many, including A. R. Luria, that Vygotsky was indeed a genius, it is not presumed that Vygotsky was a superhuman with intelligence beyond everyone else. Whether this is the case or not, thoughts should not be popularized with Vygotsky as a cult leader. In fact, Newman and Holzman (1993) addressed this very issue. "Clearly, we want to avoid the trap some Vygotskians have been accused of falling into, that of creating and/or contributing to a cult of personality around Vygotsky" (pp. 154–155). However, Vygotsky offers a unique perspective, sometimes microscopic, sometimes telescopic, all within the framework of the dialectic placed within monism. He takes on the role of a mirror within these two views (e.g., micro vs. macro), clearly focusing on the essence of human nature. J. A. Comenius (1592–1670), who lived many years before Vygotsky, wrote a cogent statement that could easily be applied to the overall tenor of the Vygotskian approach:

[T]his threefold intellectual method can be most aptly compared to the threefold artificial aid to our vision which we call the telescope, the microscope, and the mirror. Just as the telescope brings closer to our vision things far removed, so that they can be examined even in their parts, in like manner does analysis make visible even the hidden parts of anything. And just as the microscope enlarges the smallest of things and reveals even the minutest particles of indivisible units, so synthesis ever mounting from the lesser to the greater, accurately discloses the precise structure of things.... Mirrors, however are used and always have been used more frequently than telescopes and microscopes. (Comenius, cited in Jelinek, 1953, p. 136)

NOTES

1. Jakobson stated:

À l'origine du langage phonique ne se trouvent pas des associations d'élements dépourvus de sens qui présentent par la suite un sens ou sont chargés de sens. À l'origine se trouvent bien au contraire des associations de sons que reçoivent leur forme spécifiquement linguistique précisément en vue d'une fonction de signification et que ne peuvent être définies san recours à cette founction de signification.... Un phonème est défini par sa fonction de signe. Eco (1977, p. 49)

[In essence the language of phonology is not an association of nonsense elements, which subsequently present a meaning or coated meaning. On the contrary, there are associations of sounds that receive their specific linguistic form from the function of meaning; these associations cannot be defined without appeal to the function of meaning. A phoneme is defined by its function within the sign.] (trans. Mohamed Elhammoumi and D.R.)

2. At this point many parallels with C. S. Peirce can be given; however, this is not the focus here. For an excellent study of the similarities of Peirce and Vygotsky, see Petrilli (1993, pp. 103–118).

3. See Waugh (1976, p. 21).

4. See Sinha (1988, p. 31), quoting Todorov (1984, p. 56).

5. "The fundamental difference between Lotman and Hjelmslev is that Lotman does not share Hjelmslev's distinction between system and process, or between paradigm and chain, the first terms in each pair pertaining to the either-or hierarchy and the second terms pertaining to the 'both-and' hierarchy" (Hjelmslev, 1943, pp. 9, 29, 38, cited in Shukman, 1977, p. 73).

6. "With respect to a later concept of Zinkin (1967), inner speech code consists of intentions *(zamysl)*, i.e., invariant semiotic elements retained in the process of conversion of a particular expression into another equivalent expression of the natural language. On the level of intentions, differences between the meaning and sense (according to Frege) of the expression, proper to external speech, disappear" (Průcha, 1972, p. 77).

7. See William Bechtel (1988, p. 64) for a more extended discussion of computational theory and human intentionality. Certainly room will be left for the possibility of computers maintaining intentionality in the future. In new research on areas such as "vortex technology" there is talk of carbon and silicon (which both contain life-based molecule possibilities) interacting within computers, which could at some point merge into an intentional life form. However, as of this writing (2003), such discussions appear premature.

8. For information on connectionism and other models, such as the computational model, see John Dinsmore (1991).

9. See Weiskrantz (1988, p. 473).

10. "Mental representations, as defined here, are mental contents that are to a certain extent available for introspection and phenomenological description. Meaning structures, on the other hand, are hypothetical entities that are postulated in order to explain and predict human behavior, cognition, and experience" (Lundh, 1995, p. 366).

11. For an interesting discussion on Vygotsky going beyond child development, refer to Valsiner & van der Veer (2000, pp. 339–340).

12. Bühler gave his definition of representation: "Wherever there is a representation *[Stellvertretung]*, a standing in for something or someone, there are, just as in every relation, two foundations, a thing *[ein etwas]* and then something that must distinguish our way of considering it" (Bühler, quoted in Innis, 1985, p. 72).

13. "It should also be noted that there are no encoded inputs coming in from the environment to be processed in this model. There are instead interactions with the environment, which interactions yield internal outcomes, and which outcomes yield internal indications concerning possible future interactions" (Bickhard & Richie, 1983, p. 19).

14. Regarding apperception, Vygotsky stated that

[i]t is also known from experimental psychology that it is impossible under normal conditions to get absolute perceptions without associating with them meanings, understandings

and apperceptions....Perception is an integral part of visual thinking and is intimately connected with the concepts which go with it. This is why every perception is really an apperception." (Vygotsky, 1994b, 322–323)

15. In an interview with Gita L'vovna Vygodskya in Moscow (June 2, 1999), she spoke about her love for her sister. Gita L'vovna talked about how kind and gifted Asya was. She died at the age of 54 in a freak accident. Asya loved dogs very much and actually fell as a result of reaching out to a dog, breaking her leg. She died at home waiting for the ambulance to arrive.

16. Although no mention of social interaction has been provided that relates to concept formation, there is an interesting connection. G. H. Mead has been compared with Vygotsky by many scholars, beginning with Jerome Bruner. Mead contributed to ideas along the lines of action, the social element, and images. However, Mead as a social interactionist was not an experimenter, did not conceive of his theories along a genetic-developmental line, and did not have the same understanding of history as change as did Vygotsky. See Vari-Szilagyi (1991).

17. Compare with Michel Denis (1991).

18. "Disneyland is presented as imaginary in order to make us believe that the rest [i.e., the world outside Disneyland] is real, whereas in fact all of Los Angeles...surrounding it [is] no longer real, but of the order of the hyperreal and of simulation" (Norris, 1990, p. 174).

19. See Valsiner and van der Veer (2000, pp. 152–153).

20. The example of teaching German was conducted by the author at Central Missouri State University in 1997.

CHAPTER 8

Concluding Summary

This closing summary of Vygotsky analyzes the different types of logic that are being constructed as we enter a new millennium. Instead of concentrating on a revision of the scientific method, for example, a new construct is introduced. During this transition period, many people want to hold on to older values, while others want to quickly understand the new realities. One of the aspects that makes Vygotsky's approach appealing to many people worldwide is his understanding of the theories and methods of Spinoza and von Humboldt, and newer theories that can be placed within a flow-chart model.

To explain the new logic, some thoughts regarding chaos theory and the hologram are introduced to better understand this new logic. These ideas are then reconnected with Vygotsky's psychology/philosophy. Paradoxically, the underlying logic of chaos theory is not chaos, but systematicity. Many scientists and others are attempting to start to understand that level of coherence. For example Prigogine (1983) stated that

we are no longer fascinated by a rationality which depicts the universe and knowledge as something on its way to being achieved. The future is no longer given; it is no longer implied in the present. This means the end of the classical ideal of omniscience. The world of processes in which we live and which is part of us can no longer be rejected as appearances or illusions determined by our mode of observation. (p. 78)

In trying to define chaos theory, the first point of reference is nonlinear thinking, which means that one starts within a heuristic understanding of the universe. The second point of departure is the aspect of nonpredictability that changes the entire view of the Cartesian-inspired scientific method. The following excerpt synthesizes these two points of reference:

Many people believe that twentieth century science will be remembered for three main theories: quantum mechanics, relativity, and chaos. Chaos Theory is a blanketing theory that covers all aspects of science, hence it shows up everywhere in the world today: mathematics, physics, biology, finance, and even music....Chaos Theory is a developing scientific discipline which is focused on the study of nonlinear systems....Linear systems were easy to generate and simple to work with. That is because they are very predictable. (http://library.thinkquest.org/3493, August 19, 2001)

When introducing this way of thinking, it should be noted that new pieces of the puzzle are discovered every day. Therefore, one is not viewing an established product, but rather a living process, all of which is changing science—and physics in particular—as it is known today. For example, the hologram is slowly emerging within many approaches to science, with every part of the hologram representing an exact replication of the whole, and each piece used in reconstructing the whole. Dr. Karl Pribram studied the possibility that the brain's deep structure is essentially holographic, with information being distributed throughout the system. Dr. Pribram visited Moscow during the 1970s to work with A. R. Luria on neurophysiological experiments and was a guest in A. N. Leontiev's home (cf. Pribram, 1996, pp. 229–235). The hologram has been used in many areas of science and has become popular within various realms of psychology as well. Within physics, for example, Dr. David Bohm stated that primary physical laws cannot be discovered by a science that attempts to break the world into its parts without maintaining the unbroken wholeness (cf. Bohm, 1981).

Similar styles of thinking are emerging in other fields, such as perception and environmentally based studies—for example, Gibson's concepts of streaming perspective, envelope of flow, and fluid structuring. Gibson believed that to study the fluidity of perceptions, the gulf separating the perceiver from the perceived must be minimized (cf. Cutting, 1982, p. 199). Within aesthetics, Vygotsky spoke within the context of flow. Vygotsky (1965/1971), for example, quoted Lunarcharski, who stated that

it would be quite superficial to assert that art has no evolutionary law of its own. The flow of water is determined by its bed and its banks. Sometimes water stretches out in a stagnant pond. Sometimes it flows in a calm majestic current. Then it may swirl and foam along a stony bed, or drop in waterfalls, turn right or left, or even turn back. But no matter how clear it is that the course of a brook is determined by the inflexible laws imposed by outside conditions, its essence is determined by the laws of hydrodynamics, laws which we cannot derive from the outward conditions of flow without having some knowledge about the nature of water. (p. 11)

An English physician, Edward de Bono, used similar terminology and has become known for his concept of lateral thinking, or more recently, parallel thinking. De Bono (1994) presented an example of this type of theory as an alternative to Socratic dialogue, where traditionally, the best argument would win. For example, "[p]arallel thinking simply means laying down ideas alongside each other. There is no clash, no dispute, and no initial true/false judgment. There is instead a genuine exploration of the subject from which conclusions and decisions may then be derived through a design process" (p. 50). Therefore, for de Bono, the emphasis is on design rather than on analysis. One of the premises of de Bono is that every person will maintain a different understanding of the world because of individual perceptions.

With this understanding of perception in place, de Bono wrote about a new logic, called "water logic" (as opposed to "rock logic"), which he felt should have an equal footing with traditional structured approaches. De Bono (1993) gave the example of putting three rocks together (implying structures within the empiricist understanding), then asking, what do we have? Jokingly, he referred to the scientific approach in today's world by answering: three rocks is what you have. He then asked what one has when putting three "waters" together, with the answer being a more holistic water (assuming all parts are equal, and there is no contamination, etc.). With this humorous example, de Bono is not actually attempting to replace one logic with another but is trying to encourage parallel thinking. De Bono has established what he calls flowscapes, which are diagrams representing the picture of our inner world at a specific moment, establishing the flow of thinking. Flowscapes are viewed in the framework of looping, which reflects the concepts of current reflexivity and A. N. Leontiev's afferentation.

Chaos theory directly emphasizes the aspect of flow, in particular with theories such as Mandelbrot's model of the fluidity of chaos and how it achieves balance. The understanding of flow can also be found in "J. Gibson's view that awareness is a direct resonance with the flow of the world" (Hunt, 1995, p. 212). In psychology, Mihaly Csikszentmihalyi (1990) has written *Flow: The Psychology of Optimal Experience*. Vygotsky also referred to flow (1965/1971) in numerous articles, which can be found throughout his works, for example, "We must study the factors making up a work of art not in their static structure but in their dynamic flow" (pp. 219–220). Interestingly, it is necessary to be in both the flow and the zone (ZPD) for synchronicity to be a common experience in one's life. Perhaps the best example would be the comparison of Mozart (who was in the flow and the zone) and Salieri (who was only in the flow).[1]

Regarding Vygotsky and the second language (L2) classroom, for many years before and during the beginning periods of postmodernism in the United States (late 1950s, early 1960s), students usually experienced an external stability in their environment including valued job opportunities, intact families (for the most part), less environmental pollution, and a lesser degree of overpopulation. Therefore, the traditional rock logic (i.e., to be viewed metaphorically as scientific logic) was appropriate in maintaining the general status quo, with the maxim of "hard work will bring its due rewards." In postmodernity, students no longer live in a completely secure setting/environment, with the hope of a good job after college. Since school, church, and extended family have taken over many of the traditional roles of parents, it is understandable that spontaneous, everyday concepts are often embedded within the school curriculum. A total rethinking of education and the learning process is needed to find a middle point between rock logic and water logic.

Bateson (1987) encouraged a general rethinking of learning by offering two concepts to better define a problem that must be solved: "deutero-learning." "In learning a particular thing, one learns how to learn. In solving problems, each particular solving is a piece of simple learning, but in the activity of solving such problems, one learns as well how to solve problems" (Holzman & Newman, 1987, p. 112).

The other point made by Bateson (1987) concerns the concept of "metalogue":

A *metalogue* is a conversation about some problematic subject. This conversation should be such that not only do the participants discuss the problem but the structure of the conversation as a whole is also relevant to the same subject....Notably, the history of evolutionary theory is inevitably a metalogue between man and nature, in which the creation and interaction of ideas must necessarily exemplify evolutionary process. (p. 1)

This particular type of thinking—within an educational setting—then requires the genetic-developmental approach. In the future, within the L2 classroom, this will mean an exact analysis of where each student comes from and where that student is headed in terms of goal-directed development.

A translation of many of these ideas into Vygotskian terms, to be used in the L2 classroom, includes the following: (1) There will be a focus on the interrelatedness of the social framework within individual internalization processes, called the zone of fusion. (2) The term "sense" will be constantly re-created and will maintain a higher priority than the term "meaning," although sense is built upon meaning. "Sense" is used in this context as an opposition to the foundationalist understanding, which is pre-given, and it can lead to "emergent learning" or "learning activity" in V. V. Davydov's context (see Kozulin, 1986a). (3) The classroom itself will be extended within the ZPD, with the primary focus on the potential growth of each student. (4) Students will be viewed within a genetic-developmental approach, with a focus on process, not product. (5) There will be goal-oriented activities, based within a dominant activity; however, students should have the option of selecting their own dominant activity, such as projects within the framework of service learning. (6) There will be an understanding of commitment, differences, disobjectivation, and the dialectic. This approach will hopefully lead to the overcoming of the principle of maximal frustration, entering the understanding of catharsis, flow and zone, and so on. (7) The cathartic magic moment of understanding leads to an internalized transformation that can help create both self-regulation and Vygotsky's understanding of personal freedom of action (tied to Spinoza's social determinism). To repeat, this experience is understood only after having overcome the principle of maximal frustration in the overall learning process, viewing it precisely as a process and not a finalized product. Clearly, such moments of understanding come within a calm, not hectic, atmosphere. Zinchenko (2001) stated the following:

As is known from Köhler's works, insight does not occur during violent, strained action. It happens instead during some pauses, intervals, or breaks in activity and actions, which have received various names. Bakhtin (1986) referred to them as "the out-of-time gappings that are formed between two moments of real time." These breaks sometimes are also named with terms like "suspension," "breaking," "shift," "reflectional space," "gap in continual experience" (Mamardashvili 1993), and "fixed point of intensity" (Descartes). Winnicott (1971) writes about space "in between," or "resting place." Whatever it is called, this is some new space and new time constructed by a person (Ukhtomskii, 1978, called this *chronotope* from Greek *chronos* and *topos*). This is a space where the active internal is developing. (p. 143)

(8) The teacher's role will begin to be defined according to the needs of the students, not only serving as a role model, but also as an expert in his or her field. (9) The focus on traditional grammatical and everyday language use will be placed within the parallel understanding of fluidity, flow, and water logic. Grammar instruction will be offered with an accompanying awareness of the psychological component, and with the appropriate imagery for the learners. (10) Teachers and students will be aware of images and afterimages in all classwork; as well, images should not always be offered within a literal approach but should allow room for metaphor. (11) There will be a new understanding that foreign words will become motivated only when the appropriate concepts have been formulated. (12) The distinction between spontaneous and scientific concepts will be established and mediated by grammar. (13) The general genetic law of development will be respected, allowing time for external information to become appropriated, mastered, and internalized. (14) Another key component in Vygotsky's assumption is that it is easier for children to understand differences before completely understanding similarities. This aspect could represent a new approach to better understanding the positive side of diversity. Cultural problem-solving exercises could be estab-

lished, with discussions offering background information. These examples could be as simple as the following: why people in Germany will ask to join you at a table in a restaurant, or why no ice water is served with meals in Europe, or why Russians will often answer the question "How are you doing, how is everything going?" with "Normal." (15) Teachers and students will focus on the highest explanatory principle possible when committing themselves to L2 learning. Within the Vygotskian perspective, this means the whole personality of the learner (and teacher). (16) There will hopefully be a better study of code, representation, image-imagination, imitation-mimesis, and creativity.

This list can be continued or modified by any learner or teacher in order to meet the needs of the specific setting in which it is being used. The suggestions listed above are offered to help establish an entirely new format of L2 learning, teaching, and eventually research, rather than as an attempt to fit a Vygotskian method into existing structures. Much of teaching today is no longer viewed as a true art form, in spite of an element of entertainment often programmed into lessons. Today, there is still a focus on the teacher-centered classroom where students must learn what is prescribed; yet the focus here is to expand the concept of teaching to include the entire personality of each student and teacher. Vygotsky stated that

The educational process should be based on the pupil's own personal activity, and the whole art of the teacher amounts merely to guiding and regulating that activity. In the educational process, the teacher should serve as the rails along which the cars move freely and independently.... The pupil has hitherto always stood on the teacher's shoulders. He [she] examined everything through the teacher's eyes and judged everything through his [her] mind. It is time to put the pupil on his [her] own feet and force him [her] to walk and fall, to feel the pain...and to choose which way to go. The right way to go is something he [she] can learn only with his [her] own legs...and falls, and this is applicable to every aspect of education. (Vygotsky, quoted inVygodskaia & Lifanova, 1999, pp. 73–74)

The purpose of this book is to take some of the lesser-known theories of Vygotsky and to demonstrate their relevance, which can be used as a metatheory. Later, when we are well into the twenty-first century, and ideas really change, as they will, people will likely understand the future-oriented connections within the Vygotskian method. Right now, however, there is an interesting pluralism in place regarding theory building that makes the formation of a holistic theory close to impossible. With the hybrid approach of interdisciplinary studies, a focus on intersecting ideas often takes place at the expense of in-depth knowledge of one specific discipline. Today these types of theories run the risk of being labeled jargon, bandwagon theories, or reductionist theories.

With much qualitative research, there is still no measurement of growth of the individual related to society, or of society related to the individual;

in other words, there is no zone of fusion. It is hoped that each individual metanarrative will help re-create a theory of meaning for language instructors and others in education, and that such metanarratives will be placed in a wider sociohistorical/sociocultural context.

It is at this point that one can use the overall theories of Vygotsky as an anchor, while simultaneously taking the individual narrative to form a meaningful method applicable to one's own research and life. In other words, it is up to each person to establish his or her own Vygotskian method, which represents a new idea within education. This attempt will result in an interpretation of Vygotsky, while creating one's own theoretical/practical potential.

One of the main concepts within postmodernism is the simulacrum, in other words, a copy of a copy where the original is usually missing. As a result, people sometimes forget that there was an original, all of which has implications at the subconscious level regarding authenticity. Often, there is a deep longing for the original, from which all subtexts are derived. The advantages of this approach to theory building are that one or two people can no longer dictate what is good theory, film, or theater, for example, such as in foundationalism. At the same time, there is still a longing for a holistic theory.

We are possibly standing at the beginning of a post-Chomskyan era and a pre-Vygotskian era, not only within theory building, but also in living a life that reflects our personal and professional beliefs. It is clear that the "original" Vygotsky died in 1934; therefore, within the understanding of postmodern simulacra, we will only be able to interpret the original through copies of the original. The novelty of fusing theory with one's life will become more and more attractive as time goes by.

The ties we have to Vygotsky transcend his theories, all of which return to the Spinozist understanding that real personal freedom can be found only within the individual, via the assertion of will to assure personal freedom. And that freedom is related not only to the personal aspect of growth, but also to the individual who is related to the whole society, and vice versa. Perhaps de Bono's example of water logic could serve as a metaphor regarding newer forms of semiotic-ecological education. This metaphor is basically an image to foster group cohesion and creativity within the L2 classroom. Within the postmodernist tradition, as well as in other traditions, one often views individual consciousness and experiences as being private; however, within the Vygotskian method, consciousness is primarily social, placed within a "zone of fusion," which focuses on the unity of the individual and society.

Vygotsky took German philosophy and psychology as one aspect of his theoretical foundation, and at the same time he did away with the German negative sense of "totality" within that philosophy.[2] It should be emphasized that Vygotsky was a Marxist, who placed his Marxism within what can now be understood as holographic theory. He recognized that

Marx analyzes the "cell" of bourgeois society—the form of the commodity value—and shows that a mature body can be more easily studied than a cell. He discerns the structure of the whole social order and all economical formations in this cell. He says that "to the uninitiated its analysis may seem the hair-splitting of details....He who can decipher the meaning of the cell of psychology, the mechanism of one reaction, has found the key to all psychology." (Vygotsky, 1997, p. 320)

At the same time, this Marxist structure needs to be expanded and revised in light of its historical failure to promote individual free action or the freedom to establish self-regulation. The new Marxist basis will need to include areas traditionally forgotten, such as the role and development of women and children, the structuring of free time, dealing with emotional tragedies within a community of dialogue, and many other areas. Although Marxism was a fundamental aspect for Vygotsky's theories, it is claimed that it was not the ultimate level of his thinking or that it represented the highest explanatory power within his theoretical system.

It is argued, and many will disagree, that Vygotsky viewed the tenets of Spinoza as his highest principle, where monism was not understood as an all-encompassing universal principle that was stagnant. Monism was considered to be a principle that was dynamic and alive, that some called substance, nature, or God. Vygotsky overcame the dualist nature of ontology by using the dialectic (e.g., thesis plus antithesis), while focusing on the more completed aspect of synthesis. He incorporated his understanding of catharsis as the moment of sudden, internal adjustment to a new truth. Vygotsky recognized a system where the higher mental processes function differently from the lower mental functions, yet he allowed for one continuum where these processes could be developed to their highest potential. Vygotsky mixed psychology with language theory, aesthetics, semiotics, theater, poetry, education, and defectology, and he placed these ideas (many of which were borrowed from thinkers of his day) within a dynamic framework of holistic thought. Vygotsky's life was a tribute to using basic knowledge within psychology and many other fields. Just as he focused on synthesis within the academic world, overcoming dualisms that led to polarity in thinking, Vygotsky always applied similar principles to his personal life. His writings form a complete system of thought that is applicable to the social sciences and to personal values. In a letter to Natalia Grigor'evna Morozova, August 8, 1930, Vygotsky's one line sums up his life and works: "We can always be free and courageous within ourselves" (Vygodskaia & Lifanova, 1999, p. 46). N.G. Morozova's (Vygodskaia & Lifanova, 1999, p. 29) lines close these thoughts, written after Vygotsky's death:

You have left.... But your life is in me—
The memories live on.
Your noble impulses are in me,
Like the wind in a blue wave;
The departed train still hums
As if somewhere near.
Your words are in my breast
In a song still being sung.

NOTES

1. Comment made by an editor of this manuscript, Tony Shaffer at Central Missouri State University, May 2002.

2. Henri Wallon wrote the following notes about German philosophy (Voyat, 1984, p. 214): "Their [German] projects are swamped by their tendency to blow up any concept, once established, to monstrous proportions.... With an alarming facility German thinkers are wont to mold every viewpoint, every conceivable reality, into hybrid wholes. Their thinking is totalitarian and syncretic. When it comes to the relations between what is individual and what is social, their inclination, rather than analyzing the two categories, searching for their determinants, and examining the corresponding facts, is to stretch the individual's domain into realms where it has no business. The syncretization of race is a case in point" (p. 214).

References

Andrews, E. (1990). *Markedness theory.* Durham, NC: Duke University Press.

Atkinson, P. (1985). *Structure and reproduction: An introduction to the sociology of Basil Bernstein.* London: Methuen.

Babcock, B. (1980). Reflexivity: Definitions and discriminations. *Semiotica, 30 (1/2),* 1–14.

Bakhtin, M. M. (1986). *Literaturno-kriticheskie stat'I* [Articles on literary criticism]. Moscow: Khudozhestvennaia literature.

Bardovi-Harlig, K. (1987). Markedness and salience in second language acquisition. *Language Learning, 37,* 385–407.

Barthes, R. (1985). *The responsibility of forms: Critical essays on music, art, and representation.* Trans. R. Howard. New York: Hill and Wang.

Bateson, J. (1987). *Steps to an ecology of mind.* Northvale, NJ: Jason Aronson.

Bechtel, W. (1988). *Philosophy of mind: An overview of cognitive science.* Hillsdale, NJ: Lawrence Erlbaum.

Bedny, G., & Meister, D. (1997). *The Russian theory of activity: Current applications to design and learning.* Mahwah, NJ: Lawrence Erlbaum.

Belyayev, B. V. (1964). *The psychology of teaching foreign languages.* Trans. R. F. Hingley. New York: MacMillan.

Berg, E. (1970). *L. S. Vygotsky's theory of the social and historical origins of consciousness.* Unpublished doctoral dissertation. University of Wisconsin, Madison.

Berkhin, N. B. (1988). The problem of communication in K. S. Stanislavsky's works. *Soviet Psychology, 26.*

Bernstein, B. (1996). *Pedagogy, symbolic control and identity.* Exeter, UK: Taylor & Francis.

Bickhard, M. H., & Richie, D. M. (1983). *On the nature of representation: A case study of James Gibson's theory of perception.* New York: Praeger Special Studies.

Blum-Kulka, S, House, J., & Kasper, G. (Eds). (1989). *Cross-cultural pragmatics: Requests and apologies.* Norwood, NJ: Ablex.

Bogue, R. (1991). *Mimesis in contemporary theory: An interdisciplinary approach. Vol. 2: Mimesis, semiosis and power.* Philadelphia: John Benjamins.

Bohm, D. (1981). *The implicate order.* London: Routledge & Kegan Paul.

Botha, R. P. (1989). *Challenging Chomsky: The generative garden game.* London: Basil Blackwell.

Bozhovich, L. I. (1977). The concept of the cultural-historical development of the mind and its prospects. *Soviet Psychology, 16 (1),* 5–22.

Bradford, R. (1994). *Roman Jakobson.* London: Routledge.

Brown, A., & Ferrara, R. (1985). Diagnosing zones of proximal development. In J. V. Wertsch (Ed.), *Culture, communication and cognition* (pp. 273–305). Cambridge, UK: Cambridge University Press.

Brown, D. (1993). After method: Toward a principled strategies approach to language teaching. In J. E. Alatis (Ed.), *Georgetown roundtable on languages and linguistics.* Washington, DC: Georgetown University Press.

Bruner, J. (1986). *Actual minds, possible worlds.* Cambridge, MA: Harvard University Press.

Burmenskaia, G. V. (1997). The psychology of development. In E. L. Grigorenko, P. Ruzgis, & R. J. Sternberg (Eds.), *Psychology of Russia: Past, present, future* (pp. 215–251). Commack, NY: Nova Science.

Carroll, J., & Spearritt, D. (1967). A study of a model of school learning. Unpublished report, Graduate School of Education, Harvard University, Cambridge, MA. Cited in L. Cronbach & R. Snow (Eds.). (1977). *Aptitudes and instructional methods.* New York: Irvington.

Chamot, A. (1978). Grammatical problems in learning English as third language. In E. Hatch (Ed.), *Second language acquisition: A book of readings.* Rowley, MA: Newbury House.

Chaudron, C. (1988). *Second language classrooms.* Cambridge, UK: Cambridge University Press.

Chomsky, N. (1983). (Unititled chapter). In *A tribute to Roman Jakobson 1896–1982* (pp. 81–83). New York: Mouton.

Chomsky, N. (1996). *The minimalist program.* Cambridge, MA: M.I.T. Press.

Christophersen, P. (1973). *Second language learning: Myth & reality.* London: Penguin.

Cocking, R. R. (1993). *The development and meaning of psychological distance.* Hillsdale, NJ: Lawrence Erlbaum.

Cole, M. (1996). *Cultural psychology: A once and future discipline.* Cambridge, MA: Belknap Press of Harvard University Press.

Cole, M., & Scribner, S. (1974). *Culture and thought.* New York: Wiley & Sons.

Cook, V. (1992). Evidence for multicompetence. *Language Learning, 42,* 557–591.

Corder, P. (1981). *Interlanguage and error analysis.* Oxford, UK: Oxford University Press.

Crookes, G. (1993). Action research for second language teachers: Going beyond teacher research. *Applied Linguistics, 14 (2),* 130–144.

Csikszentmihalyi, M. (1990). *Flow: The psychology of optimal experience.* New York: Harper & Row.

Cutting, J. E. (1982). Two ecological perspectives: Gibson vs. Shaw and Turvey. *American Journal of Psychology, 95 (2),* 199–222.

Daniels, H. (1993). The individual and the organization. In H. Daniels (Ed.), *Charting the agenda: Educational activity after Vygotsky.* London: Routledge.

Davydov, V. V., Zinchenko, V., and Talyzina, N. F. (1983). The problem of activity in the works of A. N. Leontiev. *Soviet Psychology, 21 (4),* 31–42.

de Bono, E. (1993). *Water logic.* London: Viking Press.

de Bono, E. (1994). *Parallel thinking.* London: Viking Press.

Delacour, J. (1997). Object perception and recognition: A model for the scientific study of consciousness. *Theory & Psychology, 7,* 257–262.

Deleuze, G. (1981). *Spinoza: Practical philosophy.* Trans. R. Hurley. San Francisco: City Lights Books.

Denis, M. (1991). *Image and cognition.* Trans. M. Denis & C. Greenbaum. New York: Harvester Wheatsheaf.

Dinsmore, J. (1991). *Partitioned representation: A study in mental representation, language understanding and linguistic structure.* Dordrecht: Kluwer Academic Publishers.

Dobkin, S. (1982). Ages and days. In K. Levitin (Ed.), *One is not born a personality* (pp. 18–38). Moscow: Progress Publishers.

Doise, W. (1996). The origins of developmental social psychology: Baldwin, Cattaneo, Piaget and Vygotsky. *Swiss Journal of Psychology, 55 (2–3),* 139–149.

Dörnyei, Z. (1995). On the teachability of communication strategies. *TESOL Quarterly, 29 (1).*

Eco, U. (1977). The influence of Roman Jakobson on the development of semiotics. In D. Armstrong & C. H. van Schooneveld (Eds.), *Roman Jakobson: Echoes of his scholarship,* (pp. 39–58). Lisse, The Netherlands: Peter de Ridder Press.

El'konin, D. B. (1967). The problem of instruction and development in the works of L. S. Vygotsky. *Soviet Psychology, 5 (3),* 34–41.

El'konin, D. B. (1984). *The Collected Works of L. S. Vygotsky, Vol. 4* (in Russian; Vol. 5 in English). Moscow: Moskva Pedagogika.

Ellis, D. G. (1995). Fixing communicative meaning: A coherentist theory. *Communication Research, 22 (5),* 115–144.

Ellis, J. M. (1993). *Language, thought, and logic.* Evanston, IL: Northwestern University Press.

Ellis, R. (1985). *Understanding second language acquisition.* Oxford, UK: Oxford University Press.

Ellis, R. (1987). *Second language acquisition in context.* Englewood Cliffs, NJ: Prentice Hall International.

Ellis, R. (1994). *The study of second language acquisition.* Oxford, UK: Oxford University Press.

Ellis, R. (1995). Interpretation tasks for grammar teaching. *TESOL Quarterly, 29 (1),* 87–106.

Ervin-Tripp, S. (1974). Is second language learning like the first. *Tesol Quarterly, 8.*

Felix, S. (1981). The effect of formal instruction on second language acquisition. *Language Learning, 31 (1),* 87–112.

Felix, S., & Weigl, W. (1991). Universal grammar in the classroom: The effects of formal instruction on second language acquisition. *Second Language Research, 7 (2),* 162–181.

Florenskii, P. A. (1990). *Stolp I utverzhdenie istiny: Opyt pravoslavoi feoditsei v dve-nadtsati pis'makh* [The pillar and ground of truth: An attempt at an orthodox theodicy in twelve letters]. Moscow: Pravda. (Original work published in 1914)

Fodor, J. (1972). Some reflections of L. S. Vygotsky's Thought and Language. *Cognition, 1 (1)*, 83–93.

Fodor, J. (1981). *Representations: Philosophical essays on the foundations of cognitive science.* Cambridge, MA: M.I.T. Press.

Gair, J. W., & O'Neill, W. (1988). Kinds of markedness. In S. Flynn & W. O'Neill (Eds.), *Linguistic theory in second language acquisition.* Dordrecht: Kluwer Academic Publishers.

Gass, S. (1988). Integrating research areas: A framework of second language studies. *Applied Linguistics, 9 (2)*, 198–217.

Gebauer, G., & Wulf, G. (1992). *Mimesis: Culture, art, society.* Berkeley: University of California Press.

Gergen, K. J. (1995). Social construction and the educational process. In L. P. Steffe & J. Gale (Eds.), *Constructivism in Education.* Hillsdale, NJ: Lawrence Erlbaum Associates.

Gethin, A. (1990). *Antilinguistics.* Oxford, UK: Oxford University Press.

Givón, T. (1995). *Functionalism and grammar.* Amsterdam: John Benjamins Publishing.

Gregg, K. (1990). The variable competence model of second language acquisition and why it isn't. *Applied Linguistics, 11 (4)*, 364–383.

Gutierrez, K., Rymes, B., & Larson, J. (1995). Script, counterscript, and underlife in the classroom: James Brown versus Brown vs. Board of Education. *Harvard Educational Review, 65*, 445–471.

Harman, G. (1975). Psychological aspects of the theory of syntax. In S. Stich (Ed.), *Innate ideas.* Berkeley: University of California Press.

Harris, E. E. (1992): *Spinoza's philosophy: An outline.* NJ: Humanities Press.

Hatch, E., Shirai, Y., &. Fantuzz, C. (1990). The need for an integrated theory: Connecting modules. *TESOL Quarterly, 24 (4)*, 697–716.

Hayles, K. N. (1993). Constrained constructivism: Locating scientific inquiry in the theater of representation. In G. Levine (Ed.), *Realism and representation.* Madison: University of Wisconsin Press.

Hirschbuhler, P., & Rivero, M. (1981). Catalan restrictive relatives: Core and periphery. *Language, 57*, 591–625.

Holenstein, E. (1976). *Roman Jakobson's approach to language: Phenomenological structuralism.* Bloomington: Indiana University Press.

Holzman, L. (1997). *Schools for growth.* NJ: Lawrence Erlbaum Associates. Mahwah, New Jersey.

Holzman, L., & Newman, F. (1987). Thought and language about history. In M. Hickman (Ed.), *Social and functional approaches to language and thought.* Orlando, FL: Academic Press.

Huang, J., & Hatch, E. (1978). A Chinese child's acquisition of English. In E. Hatch (Ed.), *Second language acquisition: A book of readings.* Rowley, MA: Newbury House.

Hunt, H. T. (1995). *On the nature of consciousness.* New Haven, CT: Yale University Press.

Ignjatovic-Savic, N., Kovac-Cerovic, H., Plut, T., & Pesikan, A. (1988). Social interaction in early childhood and its developmental effects. In J. Valsiner (Ed.),

Developmental psychology in the Soviet Union (pp. 89–158). Brighton, UK: Harvester Press.

Innis, R. E. (Ed.). (1985). *Semiotics: An introductory anthology.* Bloomington: Indiana University Press.

Innis, R. E. (1994). *Consciousness and the play of signs.* Bloomington: Indiana University Press.

Ivanov, V. V. (1983). Roman Jakobson: The future. In *A tribute to Roman Jakobson 1896–1982* (pp. 47–57). New York: Mouton Publishers.

Jaensch, E. R. (1930). *Eidetic imagery.* Trans. O. Oeser. London: Kegan Paul, Trench, Trubner.

Jakobson, R., & Pomorska, K. (1983). *Dialogues.* Cambridge, MA: M.I.T. Press.

Jelinek, V. (1953). *The analytical didactic of Comenius.* Translated from Latin by V. Jelinek. Chicago: University of Chicago Press.

Jolley, N. (Ed.). (1995). *The Cambridge companion to Leibniz.* Cambridge, UK: Cambridge University Press.

Kasper. G. (1992). Pragmatic transfer. *Second Language Research, 8 (3),* 203–231.

Kaufman, D., & Brooks, J. G. (1996). Interdisciplinary collaboration in teacher education: A constructivist approach. *TESOL Quarterly, 30 (2).*

Kaufman, G. (1979). *Visual imagery and its relation to problem solving.* Bergen, Norway: Universitetsforlaget.

Kellerman, E. (1995). Crosslinguistic influence: Transfer to nowhere? *Annual Review of Applied Linguistics, 15,* 125–150.

Kempson, R. (Ed.). (1988). *Mental representations: The interface between language and reality.* Cambridge, UK: Cambridge University Press.

Kennedy, G. (1973). Conditions for language learning. In J. Oller & J. C. Richards (Eds.), *Focus on the learner: Pragmatic perspectives for the language teacher.* Rowley, MA: Newbury House Publishers.

Klein, W. (1990). A theory of language acquisition is not so easy. *Studies in Second Language Acquisition 12,* 219–231.

Kozulin, A. (1986a). *Psychology in utopia: Toward a social history of Soviet psychology.* Cambridge, MA: M.I.T. Press.

Kozulin, A. (1986b). The concept of activity in Soviet psychology. *American Psychologist, 41 (3),* 264–274.

Kozulin, A. (1990). *Vygotsky's psychology: A biography of ideas.* New York: Harvester-Wheatsheaf.

Kozulin, A. (Ed.). (1994). *Thought and Language.* Cambridge, MA: M.I.T. Press.

Kozulin, A. (1996). The concept of activity in Soviet psychology: Vygotsky, his disciples and critics. In H. Daniels (Ed.), *An introduction to Vygotsky* (pp. 99–122). London: Routledge.

Kozulin, A., & Presseisen, B. (1995). Mediated learning experience and psychological tools: Vygotsky's and Feuerstein's perspectives in a study of student learning. *Educational Psychologist, 30 (2),* 67–75.

Kramsch, C. (1993). *Context and culture in language teaching.* Oxford, UK: Oxford University Press.

Kramsch, C. (1995). The applied linguist and the foreign language teacher: Can they talk to each other? In G. Cook & B. Seidlhoffer (Eds.), *Principles and practice in applied linguistics: Studies in honour of H. G. Widdowson* (pp. 43–56). Oxford, UK: Oxford University Press.

164   References

Lagopoulos, A. (1986). Semiotics and history: A Marxist approach. *Semiotica, 59* (3–4), 215–244.

Lantolf, J. P. (1993). Cultural theory and the second-language classroom: The lesson of strategic interaction. In J. E. Alatis (Ed.), *Georgetown university round table on languages and linguistics* (pp. 220–233). Washington, DC: Georgetown University Press.

Lantolf, J. P., & Pavlenko, A. (1995). Sociocultural theory and second language acquisition. *Annual Review of Applied Linguistics, 15,* 108–124.

Larsen-Freeman, D. (1976a). Teacher speech as input to the ESL learner. University of California. *Working Papers in TESOL, 10,* 45–49.

Larsen-Freeman, D. (1991). Second language acquisition research: Staking out the territory. *TESOL Quarterly, 25 (2),* 315–350.

Lee, B. (1985). Origins of Vygotsky's semiotic analysis. In J. V. Wertsch (Ed.), *Culture, communication, and cognition* (pp. 66–93). Cambridge, UK: Cambridge University Press.

Leont'ev, A. A. (1973) Some problems in learning Russian as a foreign language (essays on psycholinguistics). Special issue of *Soviet Psychology, 11 (4),* 1–103.

Leont'ev, A. A. (1981). Sign and activity. In J. V. Wertsch (Ed.), *The concept of activity* (pp. 241–255) Armonk, NY: M. E. Sharpe.

Leont'ev, A. A. (1984). The productive career of Aleksei Nikolaevich Leont'ev. *Soviet Psychology, 23 (1),* 6–56.

Leont'ev, A. A. (1998). Recent writings of A. A. Leont'ev. *Journal of Russian and Eastern Psychology, 36,* 9–88.

Leont'ev, A. N. (1974–75). The problem of activity in psychology. *Soviet Psychology, 12 (2),* 4–33.

Leontiev, A. A. (1975). The heuristic principle in perception, emergence, and assimilation of speech. In *Foundations of Language Development, Vol. 1.* New York: UNESCO.

Leontiev, A. A. (1981). Psychology and the language learning process. C. V. James (Ed.). New York: Pergamon Press.

Leontiev, A. A. (1990). *L. S. Vygotsky* (in Russian). Moscow: Prosveschenie Publishers.

Leontiev, A. A. (1992). Personality-culture-language: Acquisition of language: Acquisition of Culture. In *AfinLA Yearbook.* Finland: Jyväskylä.

Leontiev, A. A. (1995). Ecce Homo. *Journal of Russian & East European Psychology.* July/August 41–45.

Leontiev, A. A. (1996). *Lev Semyonovich Vygotsky as the first psycholinguist* (in Russian). Moscow: n. p.

Leontiev, A. N. (1983). *A. N. Leontiev. Selected Works, Vol. 2* (in Russian). Moscow: n. p.

Leontiev, A. N. (1994). *A. N. Leontiev: The philosophy of psychology* (in Russian). Moscow: Publishing House of Moscow University.

Leontiev, A. N. (2003). Letter to L.S. Vygotsky. *Psychological Journal, 24 (1),* 14–28.

Leont'yev, A. A. (1968–69). Inner speech and the processes of grammatical generation of utterances. *Soviet Psychology, 7 (1),* 11–16.

Leontyev, A. A. (1992). Ecce Homo: Methodological problems of the activity-theoretical approach. *Multidisciplinary Newsletter for Activity Theory, 11 (12),* 41–45.

Lerch, C. (2001). The "unfossilization" of mathematical concepts by adult college students in elementary algebra and developmental mathematics courses. In E. Kravtsova & V. Spiridonov, *Works of the L. S. Vygotsky Institute of Psychology* (pp. 73–88). Moscow: Russian State University for the Humanities.

Liceras, J. M. (1986). *Linguistic theory and second language acquisition.* Tübingen, Germany: Gunter Narr Verlag.

Lidz, C. (2000). Theme and some variations on the concepts of mediated learning experience and dynamic assessment. In A. Kozulin & Y. Rand (Eds.), Experience of mediated learning. Amsterdam: Pergamon.

Lincoln, Y. S. (1996). The making of a constructivist. In E. G. Guba (Ed.), *The paradigm dialog.* London: Sage.

Lodder, C. (1983). *Russian constructivism.* New Haven: Yale University Press.

Lucid, D. P. (Ed.). (1977). Introduction. In D. Lucid (Ed.), *Soviet semiotics.* Baltimore: Johns Hopkins University Press.

Lundh, L. G. (1995). Meaning structures and mental representations. *Scandinavian Journal of Psychology, 36,* 363–385.

Luria, A. R. (1928). Psychology in Russia. *Journal of Genetic Psychology, 35,* 347–349.

Luria, A. R. (1981). *Language and cognition.* New York: John Wiley & Sons.

MacIntyre, P. D., & Gardner, R. C. (1991). Methods and results in the study of anxiety and language learning: A review of the literature. *Language Learning, 41 (1),* 359–382.

MacWhinney, B. (1978). The acquisition of morphophonology. Monographs of the Society for Research, Serial No. 174. *Child Development, 43 (1–2).*

Maier, M., & Jacob, P. (1966). The effect of variations in self-instruction programs on instructional outcomes. *Psychological Reports, 18,* 539–546.

Mandelker, A. (1994). Semiotizing the sphere: Organicist theory in Lotman, Bakhtin, and Vernadsky, *PMLA, 109 (3),* 385–396.

Marková, A. K. (1978). Periods in language development. In J. V. Wertsch (Ed.), *Recent trends in Soviet psycholinguistics* (pp. 188–205), New York: M.E. Sharpe.

Marková, I. (1982). *Paradigms, thought, and language.* New York: John Wiley & Sons.

Martin, B., & Ringham, F. (2000). *Dictionary of semiotics.* London, New York: Cassell.

Matejka, L. (Ed.). (1980b). *Sound, sign and meaning: Quinquagenary of the Prague Linguistic Circle.* Ann Arbor: University of Michigan.

Matthews, G. L. (1996). *Euripides and mimesis: Helen, Orestes, and Iphigenia at Aulis.* Ph.D. dissertation, University of California, Berkeley.

McLaughlin, B. (1988). *Theories of second-language learning.* London: Edward Arnold.

Mercer, J. R., & Ysseldylke, J. (1977). Designing diagnostic-intervention programs. In T. Oakland (Ed.), *Psychological and educational assessment of minority children.* New York: Brunner/Mazel.

Miedema, S., Gert, J., & Biesta, J. (1994). Constructivism and pragmatism: How to solve the problematic relation between methodology and epistemology in the debate about replication. In R. van der Veer, M. LJzendoorn, & J. Valsinser (Eds.), *Reconstructing the mind: Replicability in research on human development.* Norwood, NJ: Ablex Publishers.

Miller, G.A. (1967). The magical number seven, plus or minus two. In D.C. Hildum (Ed.), *Language and thought* (pp. 3–32). Princeton, NJ: D. van Nostrand.

Minick, N. (1987). The development of Vygotsky's thought: An introduction. In R. Rieber (Ed.), *The collected works of L.S. Vygotsky. Vol. 3: Problems of the theory and history of psychology* (pp. 17–36). New York: Plenum Press.

Moll, L.C. (Ed.). (1992). *Vygotsky and education: Instructional implications and applications of sociohistorical psychology.* Cambridge, UK: Cambridge University Press.

Moravcsik, J.M. (1990). *Thought and language.* London: Routledge.

Newman, D., Griffin, P., & Cole, M. (1989). *The construction zone: Working for cognitive change in school.* Cambridge, MA: Cambridge University Press.

Newman, F., & Holzman, L. (1993). *Lev Vygotsky: Revolutionary Scientist.* London: Routledge.

Newman, F., & Holzman, L. (1996). *Unscientific psychology: A cultural performatory approach to understanding human life.* Westport, CT: Praeger Publishers.

Newman, F., & Holzman, L. (1997). *The end of knowing.* London: Routledge.

Norris, C. (1990). *What's wrong with postmodernism.* Baltimore: Johns Hopkins University Press.

Odlin, T. (1989). *Language transfer: Cross-linguistic influence in language learning.* Cambridge, UK: Cambridge University Press.

Oller, J. (1973). Some psycholinguistic controversies. In J. Oller & J.C. Richards (Eds.), *Focus on the learner: Pragmatic perspectives for the language teacher.* Rowley, MA: Newbury House Publishers.

Oller, J. (Ed.). (1983). *Issues in language testing research.* Rowley, MA: Newbury House.

Oller, J. (1995). Adding abstract to formal and content schemata: results of recent work in Peircian semiotics. *Applied Linguistics, 16 (3).*

Pavesi, M. (1987). Variability and systematicity in the acquisition of spatial prepositions. In R. Ellis (Ed.), *Second language acquisition in context* (pp. 73–82). Englewood Cliffs, NJ: Prentice Hall International.

Payne, T.R. (1968). *S.L. Rubinštejn and the philosophical foundations of Soviet psychology.* Dordrecht, Holland: D. Reidel.

Petrilli, S. (1993). Dialogism and interpretation in the study of signs. *Semiotica, 97 (1–2),* 103–118.

Pienemann, M. (1984). Psychological constraints on the teachability of languages. *SSLA, 6 (2).*

Pierce, B.N. (1995). Social identity, investment, and language learning. *TESOL Quarterly, 29 (1),* 9–32.

Prahbu, N.S. (1987). *Second language pedagogy.* Oxford, UK: Oxford University Press.

Pribram, K.H. (1996). Of Russians and Russia. In V.A. Koltsova (Ed.), *Post-Soviet perspectives on Russian psychology.* Westport, CT: Greenwood Press.

Prigogine, I. (1983). Probing into time. In M. Balaban (Ed.), *Biological foundations and human nature.* New York: Academic Press.

Průcha, J. (1972). *Soviet psycholinguistics.* The Hague: Mouton.

Rader, C.M., & Tellegen, A. (1981). A comparison of synesthetes and nonsynesthetes. In E. Klinger (Ed.), *Imagery. Vol. 2. Concepts, results, and applications.* New York: Plenum Press.

Rauch, I. (1980). Distinguishing semiotics from linguistics and the position of language in both. In R.W. Bailey (Ed.), *The sign: Semiotics around the world* (pp. 328–334). Ann Arbor, MI: Michigan Slavic Publications.

Reed, E.S. (1996). *The necessity of experience.* New Haven, CT: Yale University Press.

Rice, M.L., & Schiefelbusch, R.L. (1989). *The teachability of language.* Baltimore: Paul H. Brookes Publishing.

Ricoeur, P. (1981). *Hermeneutics and the human sciences.* Trans. and edited by J.B. Thompson. Cambridge, UK: Cambridge University Press.

Rintell, E. (1979). Getting your speech act together: The pragmatic ability of second language learners. *Working Papers in Bilingualism, 17,* 97–106.

Rissom, I. (1985). Der Begriff des Zeichens in den Arbeiten Lev Semenovic Vygotskijs (The concept of sign in the works of Lev Semonovich Vygotsky). Göppingen, Germany: Kümmerle Verlag.

Rivers, W. (1983). *Communicating naturally in a second language.* Cambridge, UK: Cambridge University Press.

Rivers, W. (1990). Mental representations and language in action. In J.E. Alatis (Ed.), *Georgetown university roundtable on languages and linguistics.* Washington, DC: Georgetown University Press.

Robbins, D. (1999). Prologue. In R. Rieber (Ed.), *The Collected Works of L.S. Vygotsky. Vol. 6. Scientific legacy* (pp. v–xii), New York: Kluwer Academic/Plenum Publishers.

Robbins, D. (2001). *Vygotsky's psychology-philosophy: A metaphor for language theory and learning.* New York: Kluwer Academic/Plenum Publishers.

Rubin, J. (1975). What the "good language learner" can teach us. *TESOL Quarterly, 9 (1),* 41–51.

Ruder, K.F., & Finch, A. (1987). Toward a cognitive-based model of language production. In H.W. Dechert & M. Raupach (Eds.), *Psycholinguistic models of production* (pp. 109–138). Norwood, NJ: Ablex.

Rutherford, W.E. (1982). Markedness in second language acquisition. *Language Learning, 32 (1),* 85–108.

Ryabova, T.V. (Akhutina, 2003). Mechanism of speech production based on the study of aphasia. *Journal of Russian and East European Psychology, 41 (3).*

Santos, T. (1987). Markedness theory and error evaluation: An experimental study. *Applied Linguistics, 8 (3),* 207–219.

Saussure, F. de. (1959). Course in general linguistics. In C. Bally & A. Secherhaye (Eds.), New York: Philosophical Library.

Saville-Troike, M. (1988). Private speech: Evidence for second language learning strategies during the silent period. *Child Language, 15,* 567–590.

Scaglione, A. (1995). Linguistics and other semiotic arts. *Word, 46 (1),* 55–76.

Scribner, S. (1997). Vygotsky's uses of history. In E. Tobach (Ed.), *Mind and social practice: Selected writings of Sylvia Scribner* (pp. 241–265). Cambridge, UK: Cambridge University Press.

Seliger, H. (1977). Does practice make perfect? A study of interaction patterns and L2 competence. *Language Learning, 27,* 263–275.

Sharwood-Smith, M. (1994). *Second language learning: Theoretical foundations*. London: Longman.

Shukman, A. (1977). *Literature and semiotics: A study of the writings of Yu. M. Lotman*. Amsterdam: North-Holland Publishing.

Siewierska, A. (1991). *Functional grammar*. London: Routledge.

Sinha, C. (1988). *Language and representation*. New York: Harvester.

Skehan, P. (1989). *Individual differences in second-language learning*. London: Edward Arnold.

Slama-Cazacu, T. (1983). Theoretical prerequisites for a contemporary applied linguistics. In B. Bain (Ed.), *The sociogenesis of language and human conduct* (pp. 257–271). New York: Plenum Press.

Smirnov, S. D. (1981–82). The world of images and the image of the world. *Soviet Psychology, 20 (2)*, 3–27.

Smith, L. M. (1990). Ethics, field studies, and the paradigm crisis. In E. G. Guba (Ed.), *The paradigm dialog*. London: Sage Publications.

Snow, C. (1986). Conversations with children. In P. Fletcher & M. Garman (Eds.), *Language acquisition* (Second Edition). Cambridge, UK: Cambridge University Press.

Sokolik, M. E. (1990). Learning without rules: PDP and a resolution of the adult language learning paradox. *TESOL Quarterly, 24 (4)*.

Sokolov, A. N. (1972). *Inner speech and thought*. New York: Plenum Press.

Stankiewicz, E. (1983). Roman Jakobson: Teacher and scholar. In *Tribute to Roman Jakobson 1896–1982* (pp. 17–26). Berlin: Walter de Gruyter & Co.

Stein, D. (1989). Markedness and linguistic change. In O. M. Tomić (Ed.), *Markedness in synchrony and diachorony* (pp. 67–86). Berlin, NY: Mouton de Bruyter.

Ströker, E. (1982). Introduction. In R. E. Innis (Ed.), *Karl Bühler: Semiotic foundations of language theory*. New York: Plenum Press.

Thomas, J. J. (1983). System vs. code: A semiologist's etymology. In S. Ungar & B. R. McGraw (Eds.). *Signs in culture: Roland Barthes today* (pp. 49–62). Iowa City: University of Iowa Press.

Todorov, T. (1984). *Mikhail Bakhtin: The dialogical principle*. Manchester, UK: Manchester University Press.

Tomasello, M., & Herron, C. (1988). Down the garden path: Inducing and correcting overgeneralization errors in the foreign language classroom. *Applied Psycholinguistics, 9*, 237–246.

Valsiner, J. (1996). Development, methodology, and recurrence of unsolved problems: on the modernity of "old" ideas. *Swiss Journal of Psychology, 55 (2/3)*, 119–125.

Valsiner, J., & van der Veer, R. (1993). The encoding of distance: The concept of zone of proximal development and its interpretations. In R. R. Cocking (Ed.), *The development and meaning of psychological distance*, (pp. 35–62). Hillsdale, NJ: Lawrence Erlbaum.

Valsiner, J., & van der Veer, R. (2000). *The social mind: Construction of the idea*. Cambridge, UK: Cambridge University Press.

van der Veer, R., & Valsiner, J. (1991). *Understanding Vygotsky: A quest for synthesis*. Oxford, UK: Blackwell.

van der Veer, R., & Valsiner, J. (1994). *The Vygotsky Reader*. Oxford, UK: Basil Blackwell.

van der Veer, R., & van IJzendoorn, M. H. (1985). Vygotsky's theory of the higher psychological processes: Some criticisms. *Human Development, 28,* 1–9.

van Lier, L. (1996). *Interaction in the language curriculum: Awareness, autonomy & authenticity.* London: Longman.

Vari-Szilagyi, I. (1991). G. H. Mead and L. S. Vygotsky on action. *Studies in Soviet Thought, 42 (2),* 93–122.

Varsava, J. A. (1990). *Contingent meanings:* Postmodern *fiction, mimesis, and the reader.* Tallahassee: Florida State University Press.

Vocate, D. (1987). *The theory of A. R. Luria.* Hillsdale, NJ: Lawrence Erlbaum.

Vološinov, V. N. (1973). *Marxism and the philosophy of language.* Cambridge, MA: Harvard University Press.

Voyat, G. (1984). The World of Henri Wallon. Northvale, NJ: Jason Aronson Pub.

Vygodskaia, G. (1995). Remembering Father. *Educational Psychologist, 30* (2), 57–59.

Vygodskaia, G. L., & Lifanova, T. M. (1999). Lev Semenovich Vygotsky (Part 1). *Journal of Russian & East European Psychology, 37 (2),* 3–90.

Vygotsky, L. S. (1971). *The psychology of art.* Cambridge, MA: M.I.T. Press. (Written in 1925; published in Russian in 1965)

Vygotsky, L. S. (1978). *Mind in society.* M. Cole, V. John-Steiner, S. Scribner, and E. Souberman (Eds.). Cambridge, MA: Harvard University Press.

Vygotsky, L. S. (1981). The genesis of higher mental functions. In J. V. Wertsch (Ed.), *The concept of activity in Soviet psychology* (pp. 144–188). Armonk, NY: M.E. Sharpe.

Vygotsky, L. S. (1983). From the Notebooks of L. S. Vygotsky. *Soviet Psychology, 21 (3),* 3–17.

Vygotsky, L. S. (1987). In R. Rieber & J. Wollock (Eds.), *The collected works of L. S. Vygotsky. Vol. 3: Problems of the theory and history of psychology.* New York: Plenum.

Vygotsky, L. S. (1989). Concrete human psychology. *Soviet Psychology, 27 (2),* pp. 53–77. (Original work published 1929)

Vygotsky, L. S. (1990). Imagination and creativity in childhood. *Soviet Psychology. 28 (1),* 84–96.

Vygotsky, L. S. (1994a). In Alex Kozulin (Ed.), *Thought and language.* Cambridge, MA: M.I.T. Press.

Vygotsky, L. S. (1994b). Thought in schizophrenia. In R. van der Veer & J. Valsiner (Eds.), *The Vygotsky reader* (313–326). Oxford, UK: Basil Blackwell.

Vygotsky, L. S. (1996). In A. A. Leontiev (Ed.). *Vygotsky (Anthology of humanistic pedagogy)* (in Russian). Moscow: n. p.

Vygotsky, L. S. (1997). In R. W. Rieber & J. Wollock (Eds.), *The collected works of L. S. Vygotsky. Vol. 3. Problems of the theory and history of psychology.* New York: Plenum.

Vygotsky, L. S. (1998). R. W. Rieber (Ed.), *The collected works of L. S. Vygotsky. Vol. 5. Child psychology.* New York: Plenum.

Wardekker, W. L. (1996). Critical and Vygotskian theories of education: A comparison. www.glas.apc.org/~vega/vygodsky/wardekkr.html

Waugh, L. (1976). *Roman Jakobson's science of language.* Lisse, The Netherlands: Peter de Ridder.

Weiskrantz, L. (Ed.). *Thought without language.* Oxford, UK: Clarendon.

Wells, G. (1999). *Dialogic inquire: Toward a sociocultural practice and theory of education.* New York: Cambridge University Press.

Wertsch, J. V. (1981a). *The concept of activity in Soviet psychology.* Armonk, NY: M. E. Sharpe.

Wertsch, J. V. (1981b). The concept of activity in Soviet psychology: An introduction. In J. V. Wertsch (Ed.), *The concept of activity in Soviet psychology.* Armonk, NY: M. E. Sharpe.

Wertsch, J. V. (1984). The zone of proximal development: Some conceptual issues. In B. Rogoff & J. V. Wertsch (Eds.), *Children's learning in the zone of proximal development* (pp. 7–18). San Francisco: Jossey-Bass.

Wertsch, J. V. (1985a). *Vygotsky and the social formation of mind.* Cambridge, MA: Harvard University Press.

Wertsch, J. V. (1985b). *Culture, communication, and cognition: Vygotskian perspectives.* Cambridge, UK: Cambridge University Press.

Wertsch, J. V. (1988). L. S. Vygotsky's "new" theory of mind. *The American Scholar,* 81–89.

Wertsch, J. V. (1992). The voice of rationality in a sociocultural approach to mind. In L. Moll (Ed.), *Vygotsky and education: Instructional implications and applications of sociohistorical psychology* (pp. 111–126). Cambridge, UK: Cambridge University Press.

Wertsch, J. V., & Bivens, J. A. (1993). The social origins of individual mental functioning: Alternatives and perspectives. In R. R. Cocking (Ed.), *The development and meaning of psychological distance* (pp. 203–218). Hillsdale, NJ: Lawrence Erlbaum.

Wertsch, J. V., & Tulviste, P. (1992). L. S. Vygotsky and contemporary developmental psychology. *Developmental Psychology, 28 (4),* 548–557.

Widdowson, H. G. (1990). *Aspects of language teaching.* Oxford, UK: Oxford University Press.

Yaroshevsky, M. (1989). *Lev Vygotsky.* Moscow: Progress Publishers.

Zimmerman, M. (1969). Is linguistic rationalism a rational linguistics? In S. Hook (Ed.), *Language and philosophy: A symposium* (pp. 198–207). New York: New York University Press.

Zinchenko, V. P. (2001). External and internal: Another comment on the issue. In S. Chaiklin (Ed.), *The theory and practice of cultural-historical psychology* (pp. 135–147). Aarhus, Denmark: Aarhus University Press.

Zhinkin, N. I. (1967). Thought and speech. In J. Průcha (Ed.), *Soviet studies in language and language behavior.* Amsterdam: North-Holland Publishing.

Index

Activity theory, 3, 5, 17, 19, 25, 40, 74, 79; act, 76–78; European international, 1; goal of, 76–77; international, 74; motive of, 76–77; and need, 76–77; operation of, 76–77; Russian, 1, 3, 12, 32, 62, 67, 71, 73–78, 84; Russian activity theorists, 124

Aesthetics, 117, 121, 135, 145, 150; aesthetic aspects, 45

Akhutina, T. V., 126–27

Aphasia, 108–9, 127

Apperception, 132, 133, 148

Applied linguistics, 1, 7, 11, 70, 95, 113–14, 139; and Accessibility Hierarchy, 113; anxiety, 65–66, 72 n. 7, 85, 89; applied linguistic theory, 4; contrastive hypothesis theory, 103; error analysis, 64; error correction, 64–65; communicative competence, 58, 61, 82, 118; competence and performance, 68, 114; functionalism, 104–5; functionalist approach, 117; functional grammar, 75, 84, 114–18; grammar, 60, 64, 69, 83, 90, 114, 116–17, 132, 135; illocutionary force, 103; input–output, 95–99, 116; intake, 96; intralingual errors, 63; interference, 102; Natural Order Hypothesis, 113; pragmalinguistic transfer, 103; proficiency, 58, 82, 8, 89, 96; state or situation anxiety, 66; sociolinguistics, 11; sociolinguistic models, 68; transfer, 99–104; transfer analysis, 100; transfer errors, 63, 65; universal grammar, 60, 68, 109–11, 115–16, 130; Variable Competence Model, 68

Appropriation, 32, 33, 52 n. 5, 79, 116; mixed appropriation, 33

Ashpiz, Solomon, 37

Assessment, 49

Asymmetrical, 4–5, 42, 100, 106; asymmetrically defined binary opposition, 106; nonlinear, 4, 99, 149–50

Bakhtin, Mikhail, 16, 125

Barthes, Roland, 88, 124–25

Basov, L. S., 24, 25, 153

Bateson, Gregory, 152

Baudrillard, Jean, 135. *See also* Postmodernism

Behaviorism, 3, 10, 25, 27, 6, 73, 129; approach, 85; empiricism, 115; paradigm, 101; and empiricist tradition, 27; theories, 63, 114; trends, 101

Bekhterev, V., 25

About the Author

DOROTHY ROBBINS is Professor of German at Central Missouri State University.

gift

R